Praise for *Beyond the North Wind*

"Like the runes he explores, Christopher McIntosh's use of language contains 'capsules of magical power.' His shamanistic journey to Hyperborea leads the reader through myths, place names, folktales, star lore, and intriguing and outlandish archaeological traces. He shows how in another dimension Hyperborea never went away, how it is still a root of primal forces, giving individuals in politics and the arts a sense of energy and power—for good or for ill."

—**Mark Booth**, author of *The Secret History of the World*

"Unique among scholars, Christopher McIntosh knows Iceland and the leaders of its Pagan revival: Russia, with its new wave of art and literature; and the popular genres of folk music, fiction, and film. All this is backed by a profound knowledge of Western esoteric traditions. In his new book *Beyond the North Wind*, he not only chronicles the rise of the Northern egregore but also contributes his own loyalty and learning to it. He argues persuasively for the reality of Hyperborea as a prehistoric circumpolar culture, and for the perennial value of its legacy."

—**Joscelyn Godwin**, author of *ARKTOS*

"In *Beyond the North Wind*, Christopher McIntosh takes us on a journey to explore all the profound cultural history and nuances of Hyperborea in the European heritage, expertly guiding us to understand the Northern Mysteries of Paganism in new and deeper ways. Numerous important historical figures and traditions and all manner of ancient ideas are here, presented in an engaging way. If you're interested in finding your spiritual North, read this book!"

—**Arthur Versluis**, author of *Entering the Mysteries*

"*Beyond the North Wind* is a masterful example of academic detective work, leading to the astounding conclusion that our Arctic northlands were once home to a lost prehistoric civilization. Highly recommended."

—**Herbie Brennan**, author of *The Atlantis Enigma*

"Among many other things, Christopher McIntosh's book deals with the fascinating topic of Hyperborea, the legendary northern homeland. This mysterious land has captured the imagination of many esotericists, artists, and explorers, especially those in Russia. Based on a variety of documentary sources and beautifully written, *Beyond the North Wind* makes compelling reading."

—**Alexander Andreyev**, author of *The Myth of the Masters*

"*Beyond the North Wind* is important and deserves celebration for the profound, but, until now, hidden truth it contains suggesting a Nordic origin of civilization, backed up by solid research in archaeology. Both esoteric scholars and educated Heathens will find it of inestimable value. The book contains a wealth of information from Russia, not seen before in the West, to my knowledge, as well as an extensive appendix listing gods and other beings from Norse mythology. Fascinating and pleasant to read."

—**Freya Aswynn**, author of *Northern Mysteries* and *Magick and Leaves of Yggdrasil*

"I commend this work highly both to fellow scholars and to anyone seriously interested in the highly charged meaning of the word "Nordic." McIntosh's genial text is consistently illuminating, easy to read and digest, scholarly but by no means dry or obscure. He wants to communicate his knowledge and interest, clearly and fairly, and succeeds wonderfully in a work representing the achievements of a lifetime of open-hearted study and valid experience."

—**Tobias Churton**, author of *Occult Paris*

"The North is back with a vengeance. So says Christopher McIntosh in his latest book, *Beyond the North Wind*. In a mixture of scholarly research, historical evidence, archaeological findings and speculative musings, the author invites the reader on an adventure of exploration to find the truth about a 'mysterious, advanced, prehistoric culture in the North.' I would definitely recommend this book."

—**Ingrid Kincaid**, author of *The Runes Revealed*

"This is an amazing and deeply original book; a work of immense erudition written in an elegant, approachable, and luminously intelligible style. Its quiet wit tempers its awe-inspiring and sometimes terrifying perspectives. I have been educated and delighted by this book."

—**Frederick Turner**, Founders Professor of Arts and Humanities, University of Texas at Dallas

BEYOND THE NORTH WIND

The Fall and Rise of the Mystic North

CHRISTOPHER McINTOSH

Foreword by Hilmar Örn Hilmarsson

WEISER BOOKS

This edition first published in 2019 by Weiser Books, an imprint of

Red Wheel/Weiser, LLC
With offices at:
65 Parker Street, Suite 7
Newburyport, MA 01950
www.redwheelweiser.com

ISBN: 978-1-57863-640-2
Library of Congress Cataloging-in-Publication Data available
upon request.

Cover design by Kathryn Sky-Peck
Interior by Debby Dutton
Typeset in Minion and Warnock

PRINTED IN THE UNITED STATES OF AMERICA
IBI

10 9 8 7 6 5 4 3 2

For Donate

I have reached these lands but newly
From an ultimate dim Thule—
From a wild weird clime that lieth, sublime,
Out of SPACE—Out of TIME.

—EDGAR ALLAN POE, DREAM-LAND

Some Characterizations of "North"

At once alluring and elusive, unabashedly imaginary and tempered by realism . . . an elemental force . . . a place of early fading light, of rain, twilight, melancholy and loneliness . . . a place of purification and escape from the limitations of civilization . . . a hard place, a place of uplands, adverse weather, remoteness . . . a place of quiet, a land of long snows . . . a place of darkness and dearth . . . a place of austere felicity, where virtuous people live behind the north wind and are happy . . . a place of isolation, absence, stillness, remoteness, and the absence of alternatives . . . a shifting idea, always out of reach, always leading to a further north, to an elsewhere . . . a place of prodigies, icebergs, volcanoes, and the magnetic mountain; a place of treasures . . . a place of geographical and cultural isolation, simultaneously lush and hard . . . a place of contrast between nature and urban civilization . . . a place that is dark, cold and timeless . . . a place where you can be truthful to yourself . . .

—QUOTATIONS ASSEMBLED BY DR. MARJORIE ROTH
FROM VARIOUS SOURCES TO ACCOMPANY HER LECTURE
"FIRE AND ICE, SEA AND SKY: NORTHERN MUSIC AS A
MIRROR OF NATURE," DELIVERED AT THE NEW YORK OPEN
CENTER CONFERENCE "MYSTERIES OF THE NORTH IN
ICELAND," AUGUST 2016.

CONTENTS

FOREWORD

*Good sense is needed
by him who travels far.*

—HÁVAMÁL/SAYINGS OF THE HIGH ONE,
FROM THE POETIC EDDA

The author of this book has indeed traveled far, and reading it I often thought about how our respective journeys through life have intersected with each other in ways that suggest the intention of the Norns of fate.

My initial encounter with the writings of Christopher McIntosh (personal contact was to come later) was during my first visit to London in late March 1979 when I had to sneak out of Paris where I was living with my girlfriend, as my three months' visa had not been renewed. I was told by friends that a weekend return trip to the UK through a cheap student travel agency would solve my problem, which it did. I was armed with two addresses: the Atlantis Bookshop in Museum Street and Watkins Books in Cecil Court. The Atlantis was nearly everything I had dreamed of, but Watkins was closed.

My previous months in Paris had been disappointing. I had arrived with "light luggage," which meant two pairs of trousers, two Icelandic sweaters, underwear, socks, and my old army bag containing my favorite books: Gore Vidal's *Kalki* and *Julian*, Crowley's

Magick, *777*, *Confessions*, and *Moonchild*, an Ephemeris and Table of Houses, and a book tailored for the destination: *Eliphas Lévi and the French Occult Revival* by Christopher McIntosh, which I and my artist friend Alfreð Flóki had devoured with great interest. Flóki had given me a list of places and graves to visit and the Eliphas Lévi book was an inspiration and a companion on those journeys.

Occult Paris was not what I had dreamed of. I scoured antiquarian bookshops and only found one Eliphas Lévi and one Stanislas de Guaita first editions and they were really really expensive. I thought I would be surrounded by mystics and adepts in the Librairie de la Table d'Emeraude, but the only redeeming feature there was the occasional presence of Robert Amadou and his heavily painted wife Catherine (whom I always thought of as Cleopatra), who oozed alchemy, and they both looked like they had stepped out of a novel by J. K. Huysmans, which they probably had.

Later that year my girlfriend and I moved back to Iceland via London in an epic journey of sorts (we were supposed to stay at the Hansel and Gretel Hotel, which was hopelessly overbooked and this may be the subliminal reason for my near total disdain of Jacob Grimm and all his works), but again the Atlantis Bookshop was inspiring and I struck up a friendship which has lasted thirty-nine years and stretches over three generations. And in nearby Coptic Street I found my first Crowley collectible: *The Mother's Tragedy* (highlights: "The Whore in Heaven" and "The Lesbian Hell" . . .).

Watkins bookshop was open, and I bought a copy of *The Rosy Cross Unveiled* by my new favorite author Christopher McIntosh. The earnest young man in the bookshop warned me against my unhealthy interest in Aleister Crowley and directed me to books by the Truly Enlightened Master Gurdjieff and told me in hushed tones that "The Work" really worked. I could not argue with that as I had used *Beelzebub's Tales to His Grandson* as a sleeping draught for quite some time.

And now fast-forward to my third London visit. I had saved up a considerable amount of money to buy books and had spent over a year ordering catalogues and mapping out the antiquarian bookshops in London with the help of my friends: the lawyer and bookseller Bragi Kristjónsson and the Scottish poet and translator David McDuff.

My first stop was the Atlantis (as it has been ever since), the second was the nearby bookshop of Arthur Page (Peace be Unto Him), and the third was Bertram Rota, booksellers of distinction, est. 1923. I wandered around that hallowed ground but could not find anything of interest, and the staff were clearly not interested in me. I bought *King Jesus* by Robert Graves and took some catalogues with me and went to a nearby café. Among the catalogues was one which I had taken by mistake issued by Orpheus Books, and there I found a few must-have items. There was an address in Tufnell Park and a telephone number. I went to the nearest pay phone and tried to get in touch. The line was busy. I checked the nearest Tube station and saw that the Northern Line would take me directly to Tufnell Park, and on a whim I decided to go there. I phoned again from the Tufnell Park station and the line was still engaged. After orienting myself, I decided to walk to the address.

I thought I would find a small bookshop, but this was a family house. I looked at the name on the door, C. A. McIntosh, and summoned up enough courage to ring the bell. A moment later the door was opened by a tall young man, and I was nearly certain that I was at the wrong address. I blurted out that I had been interested in books that I had seen were for sale, but that this might be an awful misunderstanding. The young man surprisingly invited me inside and said that he had a small mail order business where he sold books that were in his field of interest.

We went into a back room, and I saw familiar titles in the bookshelves. One shelf had a few copies of *The Astrologers and Their*

Creed, Eliphas Lévi and the French Occult Revival, and *The Rosy Cross Unveiled.* A bolt of lightning struck and I said: "My name is Hilmar Örn Hilmarsson, and I come from Iceland and I admire your work." To paraphrase Rick Blaine in the movie *Casablanca,* this was the beginning of a beautiful friendship.

> *Know, if you have a friend*
> *whom you fully trust,*
> *and from whom you would good derive,*
> *you should blend your mind with his,*
> *and gifts exchange,*
> *and go to see him often.*

—Hávamál/Sayings of the High One

In retrospect I am surprised how many meetings we had in the ensuing months and years and how they have affected our lives ever since. Christopher became a sort of *axis mundi,* connected to all the worlds, and through him I encountered weird and wonderful practitioners of the various Occult Arts—scholars, writers, booksellers, and the most inspiring and special people I have had the pleasure to meet in this lifetime: Gerald Joseph Yorke and his wife Angela, who enriched my life immeasurably.

The Norns were busy weaving their web, and my best laid plans were subverted and had unexpected results. With hindsight it is obvious that both Christopher and I were moving away from the Qabalistic Tree of Life to the Ash of Yggdrasil. This can be gleaned from our separate works from 1982.

In my case nearly everything from that time became "Nordic." The album design made by me and Sigríður Vala Haraldsdóttir for the Þeyr LP *Mjötviður Mær / Great Measuring Tree* had the opening verses of *Völuspá (Sayings of the Seeress)* written in runes around a stylized photographic version of Leonardo da Vinci's Vitruvian Man.

The English title of the album was *As Above*, but now it is obvious that I had realized I had been barking up the wrong tree. That album design would have unexpected consequences which are totally in tune with what happened later in our lives (our Dutch friendly neighborhood witch, Ellie, transformed into Freya Aswynn after the poster of the album design triggered an Odinic revelation).

Christopher came to Iceland on his way to the United States, and I introduced him to the Icelandic Saga Steads that had a mystical and magical connection. Our trip to the Commonwealth farm at Stöng was historic as our car got stuck in the middle of a river and we had to take turns in pushing and steering the car to safety. In our retellings of this story it has taken on a mythological significance which was there from the beginning. We had traveled to Stöng as it was an important place in the theories of Icelandic scholar Einar Pálsson, who speculated that there was a deeper and more esoteric strand to the *Eddas* and sagas.

During that visit the gods of Thule and the Mythical North became central in our discussion and we moved toward the Pole so to speak. We joked about this in our correspondence, inventing impressive titles for each other (my favorite being the "The Xophic Grand Wizard of Thule"). Prior to that visit our mutual love of the German language and literature had been peripheral to our friendship, but from then on it became a shared enthusiasm.

I know an Ash standing
Yggdrasill hight,
a lofty tree, laved
with limpid water:
thence come the dews
into the dales that fall
ever stands it green
over Urð´s fountain.

Thence come maidens,
much knowing,
three from the hall,
which under that tree stands;
Urð hight the one,
the second Verðandi,
—on a tablet they graved—
Skuld the third.
Laws they established,
life allotted
to the sons of men;
destinies pronounced.

—Völuspá/Sayings of the Seeress

One of Christopher's many strengths is his linguistic ability. All his writings rely on primary sources, be they in French, German, or Russian. No other English writer could have written his groundbreaking book about Eliphas Lévi. And were it not for Christopher's fluent German he could not have produced his studies on the Rosicrucians, his translation of the Rosicrucian *Fama Fraternitatis* together with his wife Dr. Donate Pahnke McIntosh, and his monumental and still unsurpassed biography of King Ludwig II of Bavaria. In 1982 I took those qualities for granted, but later I realized how unique he was.

The next few years changed many things. I was increasingly involved in the workings of Ásatrúarfélagið, the Icelandic Pagan Association, and trying to expand upon an essay on the magical use of the runes that I had written with the encouragement of Gerald J. Yorke, while at the same time pursuing a strange musical career where I tried to stay in the background as an ideologue, producer, and art designer. I spent weeks and months in the Icelandic National Library and the University Library going through books on runes and Norse mythology. My book mojo was working as I came across and bought two wonderfully eccentric libraries of books on "Germanic Studies" written by various folkish authors, most of whom went by the title "Herr Doktor." One of those libraries came from geologist, writer, philosopher, and errant genius Herr Doktor Helgi Pjeturs, and it has been a lasting pleasure to read Helgi's copious and mostly angry annotations to texts written by cranks such as Albrecht and Herman Wirth (in effect lamenting that they were not cranky enough . . .). "The Devil met his Grandmother" as the Icelandic saying goes . . .

In late 1984 and early 1985 Christopher and I shared a flat in London's Notting Hill district, and there I met his friend Nicholas Goodrick-Clarke who had a lasting influence on us both. Nick had written a doctoral thesis which later became the seminal book *The Occult Roots of Nazism.*

Nick filled in the missing gaps of my library when he showed me his collection of folkish esoterica which convinced me that some of the most revered and now mythologized "translations" of the Eddas were total crap. Christopher and Nick were the academics, but I was the blameless artist and relied on them to set the record straight.

In the coming years our ways sometimes parted, but the Norns kept their watch. I have lost track of so many friends and acquaintances that I met prior to the cell/mobile phone/Internet revolution, but it was a given that Christopher and I would meet at opportune moments in odd and surprising locations.

In 1994 I was sitting in Café Krasnapolsky in Copenhagen with a group of artists thinking about Christopher when I saw him pass by. I ran after him and since then we have always kept in touch. I have consulted him and he has consulted me, and ever since we have been together at the most important times of each other's lives.

In this book Christopher comes up with amazing and original insights, backed by his erudition, linguistic skills, esoteric knowledge, and magical understanding that nearly all scholars lack. Here he works the same wonder as he did with Eliphas Lévi and King

Ludwig II. The subjects are eccentric, larger than life, and outrageous judged by normal standards, yet they have had a great impact on our world and modern thought. You can see their influence in films, books, art, and philosophy. The excluded has become mainstream. Christopher shows us again how an idea takes on a life of its own and becomes a transforming force.

He takes us on a spellbinding journey through time, starting with Plato, Pindar, and Pliny the Elder and exploring many facets of the Northern mystique, including its fascinating repercussions in Russia, to which he devotes two chapters, including much material that is entirely new and has never appeared before in any book. A further chapter is devoted to the remarkable way in which the theme of the North has been taken up in literature, film, comics, computer games, pop music, and other aspects of modern mass culture. The concluding chapter is a clear and balanced summing up of the evidence for and against the existence of a primal Hyperborean civilization. Christopher tackles the subject both with nerve and respect, and I am sure that the ideas explored here will resonate and inspire for years to come.

I think back to our times with our mentor Gerald J. Yorke and the time when we tried to heat up the apartment in Notting Hill during that special winter 1984–1985:

Fire is best
among the sons of men,
and the sight of the sun,
if his wholeness
a man can have,
with a life free from blame.

—*Hávamál/Sayings of the High One*
Hilmar Örn Hilmarsson
Allsherjargoði of the Ásatrúarfélagið, Iceland
(High Priest of the Icelandic Ásatrú Association)

PREFACE AND ACKNOWLEDGMENTS

The idea for this book emerged out of a lecture on "The Legacy of Nordic and Teutonic Mythology" that I delivered in August 2016 at a conference in Iceland on the "Mysteries of the North," organized by the New York Open Center as one of its series of "Esoteric Quests." The venue itself was a departure for the Open Center, which had previously held these events mainly on the continent of Europe and around the Mediterranean, and the choice of Iceland was something of an experiment. The location was on the coast of the Snaefells Peninsula, a rugged, volcanic, mountainous area in the west of the country, alive with ancient lore and legend. A mountain looming up close to our hotel was sacred to Barður, a variation of Odin—his description in one of the sagas corresponds closely to J. R. R. Tolkien's description of Gandalf in *The Lord of the Rings*. The conference program was commensurately rich, the topics of the lectures including Nordic mythology, poetry, shamanism, the runes, and much else. One of the highlights was a stunning performance of Icelandic music by a group led by Hilmar Örn Hilmarsson, composer and Allsherjargoði (high priest) of the Pagan religion Ásatrú in Iceland (and author of the foreword to this book).

Most of the conference participants had not had much exposure to the Nordic mysteries, but in the feedback session at the end they spoke with great emotion about the intense effect of the whole experience, to the point where two of them were actually close to tears. On the bus back to Reykjavik one of the lecturers, Scott Olsen, a professor of philosophy and comparative religion from Florida, suggested that I expand my lecture into a book. This work grew out of that suggestion, although the result goes way beyond the scope of the lecture.

At the outset I should explain that, when I talk about north and south merely as compass points it will be with a lowercased term, but when I use them in a sense that is not merely geographical, but has wider and deeper connotations, they will be capitalized.

Where would we locate the boundaries of the North with a capital N? These have varied with time and changing perspectives, so it would be a mistake to attempt to map the territory too precisely, but clearly the northern extremity is the North Pole itself. Below the Pole is the Arctic region, and a glance at the map shows that the largest landmass hugging the Arctic Circle is Russian territory, stretching over a vast area from the Finnish border to the Bering Strait. Furthermore, it is in Russia that the northern reawakening is happening in a particularly vigorous form—a fact that the public outside Russia is largely unaware of. To most non-Russians, lacking a knowledge of the Russian language and affected by decades of russophobia, that country is a closed book, "a riddle wrapped in a mystery inside an enigma," as Winston Churchill put it. The two chapters of this book dealing with Russia will, I hope, begin to unwrap at least part of the riddle by showing how the so-called Hyperborean movement (from *Hyperborea* the Greek word meaning the "Land beyond the North Wind") is part of the current striving of the Russians to rediscover their national soul in the wake of the collapse of communism.

These developments in Russia, while forming a key part of this book, can only be understood in the context of the wider revival of the northern spirit. Following the introduction, chapter 2 explores the mystique of the North from ancient Greek times and examines the evidence for a prehistoric northern homeland. The book goes on to discuss the influence of the Nordic legacy in different places and spheres of culture. Aspects covered include the Nordic religion and worldview, the importance of shamanism in the Nordic tradition, the runes, the Vikings, the survival of the northern gods and their revival in Iceland in the twentieth century. Following the chapters on Russia there is a chapter focusing on manifestations of the northern spirit in modern culture and the media. The last chapter offers some concluding reflections.

It must be recognized that the northern discourse is sometimes associated with xenophobic sentiments and politically extremist movements—"dragons," as I call them, following the convention of the old mapmakers to depict little fire-breathing monsters when indicating dangerous territory. I have attempted to address this issue frankly, although the dragons often turn out to be more like the paper variety familiar from Chinese New Year processions. To mix metaphors, I try not to confuse the baby with the bathwater.

In concluding this preface, I must express my thanks to several people: to my wife Dr. Donate McIntosh for her valuable input, boundless support, help, and encouragement along the way; to my old friend Hilmar Örn Hilmarsson for writing the foreword and for his valuable advice, insights, and corrections; to Scott Olsen for prompting me to write the book; to Ralph White, director of the New York Open Center, who caused the seminal conference in Iceland to happen; to Anita Stasilane of the University of Latvia, Riga, for her comments and advice; to the Russian scholar Alexander Andreyev for giving me the benefit of his unrivaled knowledge of some fascinating and myth-laden aspects of Russian history; to Halvard Hårklau for allowing me to include his remarkable discoveries about the runes; to Pavel Zarifullin for checking part of the text; to Stephen Flowers and Alexander Dugin for the same reason; to Pavel Tulaev for sharing his knowledge and for putting me in touch with the artist

Alexander Uglanov, whom I thank for allowing me to include one of his works; to Michael Kerber, president of the publishers Red Wheel/ Weiser, for taking the book on and for his helpful suggestions during the planning phase; to my editor, Judika Illes, for her careful and sympathetic handling of the book, and to all the supportive staff at Red Wheel/Weiser. Finally, thanks are due to the publishers, copyright holders, and authors of the books from which I have quoted, as well as to the artists, photographers, and copyright holders of the illustrations that I have included.

BEYOND THE NORTH WIND

CHAPTER 1

INTRODUCTION

The North is not just a compass point but a state of mind. It has a geographical location and at the same time it exists wherever its call is felt. Certain words and names evoke it: Hyperborea, "the land beyond the north wind," as the ancient Greeks called it; Thule, the northern promised land; Asgard, home of the Nordic gods. The writer C. S. Lewis was one of those who felt the call. In his autobiography, he describes how, as a boy, he was reading a translation of a Swedish elegiac poem called *Tegner's Drapa* and came across the lines:

> I heard a voice that cried
> Balder the beautiful
> Is dead, is dead—

"I knew nothing about Balder," he writes, "but instantly I was uplifted into huge regions of northern sky, I desired with almost sickening intensity something never to be described (except that it is cold, spacious, severe, pale, and remote) and then . . . found myself at the very same moment already falling out of that desire and wishing I were back in it."[1]

Lewis's fascination with the North was shared by his friend J. R. R. Tolkien, a fellow member of the Inklings circle in Oxford in the 1930s and '40s—the name is partly a play on the title of the Old

Norse *Ynglinga Saga*. Tolkien brilliantly created his own version of the Nordic epic in his trilogy *The Lord of the Rings*, with its numerous borrowings from Old Norse literature and mythology.[2] And, significantly, Tolkien locates his evil empire in the south.

The subsequent phenomenal success of *The Lord of the Rings* is one symptom of a remarkable upsurge of enthusiasm for things northern, which has become a feature of the present age, although its roots go back several centuries. It is difficult to say precisely when this modern revival began, but certainly it was not in evidence when I was growing up in the 1950s and '60s. Throughout my education, if we learned anything about mythology it was the classical gods and goddesses of Greece and Rome who were dominant. I, along with most of my school contemporaries, could easily have said who Zeus and Apollo and Aphrodite were, but we would have been hard pressed to say anything about, say, Tyr, Odin, Thor, or Freya (despite the fact that we invoked their names every time we said the words Tuesday, Wednesday, Thursday, and Friday), let alone Balder.

If we thought about the Nordic deities at all, we considered them as belonging to a primitive and barbaric world. Similarly, we knew quite a lot about the Romans, and we could quote, say, Julius Caesar's "Veni, vidi, vici" (I came, I saw, I conquered), but about the Druids or the Vikings we had only the vaguest notions, and they were largely distorted. Essentially, we were taught that European civilization spread from south to north and that northern Europe was first civilized by the Romans and further civilized by the Christianization process in the early Middle Ages. So the whole early culture of northern Europe tended to be marginalized. Culturally and spiritually, the northern part of the compass was semi-invisible.

Now all that has changed dramatically. The North is back with a vengeance. It is everywhere you look—in culture, high and low, in academia, in religion, and in politics. Take its influence in the cinema, where in recent years the Beowulf story has been the subject of two films and a British television series. Two other movies have appeared about the god Thor, based on how he is depicted in Marvel Comics, and there are many further examples in film. The North is also writ large in the domain of global popular music, as for example in the case of the Icelandic group Sigur Rós, which has attracted a worldwide following with its subtle, hypnotic tones and falsetto singing. Innumerable other bands have picked up the Nordic theme in recent years, from the German group Faun, with its rather gentle, folk-music style, to heavy metal groups like Forefather (UK), Helrunar (Germany), Pagan Blood (France), and Tyr (Faroe Islands).

The digital realm offers an enormous sphere for Nordic themes. There are numerous video games with names like God of Thunder, Heimdall, Rune, and Valhalla, in which you can take on the role of Thor or some other Nordic god or hero in a great cosmic struggle involving perilous journeys and fights with all manner of malevolent beings. And then there is the Internet, which reveals a whole other dimension to the Nordic revival, namely the growing number of people who follow the Nordic way as a belief system—a phenomenon that is part of a wider and steadily growing Pagan movement. One can see this in the number of websites belonging to the various Pagan groups that identify themselves as Heathen, Odinist, or Asatru (a term meaning "faithfulness to the Aesir," one of the two main groups of Nordic deities). In a number of countries, Nordic Paganism is now officially recognized as a religion—most notably in Iceland which led the way in the 1970s with the official establishment of *Ásatrú* as a religious community. Neo-Paganism also encompasses a revival of the Celtic gods and goddesses as well as a neo-Druid movement, a neo-witchcraft movement, and similar phenomena. I shall touch on these insofar as they relate to the general theme of the North.

We have also seen an increase in the number of books published about the North. An interesting case in point is the work of the Italian researcher Felice Vinci, author of a book called *The Baltic*

Origins of Homer's Epic Tales, in which he argues that the setting of Homer's *Iliad* and *Odyssey* was not the eastern Mediterranean but the Baltic, the North Sea, and the North Atlantic. The increasing fascination exerted by northern mythology and the mystique of the North is further attested by works such as Joscelyn Godwin's *Arktos*, Heather O'Donoghue's *From Asgard to Valhalla*, Kevin Crossly-Holland's *The Norse Myths*, and Andrew Wawn's learned and witty study *The Vikings and the Victorians*, as well as by numerous novels on Nordic themes. Books on the runes and runic divination are also abundant.

The northern mystique is particularly strong in Russia, and this opens up a vast and intriguing territory, which is explored in detail in chapters 12 and 13. It is a territory that has its alarming aspects, as it can overlap with xenophobia and political extremism. "Here be dragons"—or in Russia's case "here be bears." The Russian bear can be a fierce animal, and we would do well to understand what stirs him.

The interesting questions that now arise are: Why is all this happening? How can we account for this phenomenon of the Nordic revival? Let us return to C. S. Lewis's boyhood vision after reading the lines:

Balder the beautiful

Is dead, is dead—

What is striking here is how Lewis notes that he "knew nothing about Balder" and yet, *merely by hearing the word*, he was instantly lifted into "huge regions of northern sky" and had a sense of something "cold, spacious, severe, pale, and remote." If this account is accurate, it means that a word can convey something powerful to a person, even if he or she is completely unaware of its meaning or connotations. That is to say the word acts as a link to some source of energy outside the hearer.

Here we enter a subject area where many historians fear to tread, but which has long fascinated me, namely the way in which historical events can be driven by intangible things like words, myths, symbols, thought forms, and what the psychologist Carl Gustav Jung called archetypes. Jung wrote a famous essay on Wotan/Odin,[3] which has often been held against him as an apology for National Socialism, but the central argument of the essay is worth considering: He posits that a deity is like a riverbed, dug over many centuries in the collective mind of a people. When the river dries up, the bed remains, and when the water begins to flow again, the river returns to its old course. Similarly, Jung argues, a god can remain dormant and inactive for a period, like the dried-up riverbed, until some spring is reopened and the god comes to life again.

Jung's argument, however, does not explain what precisely links the individual mind to the collective archetype. Here, I believe, it may be useful to introduce the concept of the egregore. Professor Joscelyn Godwin, in his book *The Golden Thread*, writes as follows about this notion:

> There is an occult concept of the "egregore," a term derived from the Greek word for "watcher." It is used for an immaterial entity that "watches" or presides over some earthly affair or collectivity. The important point is that an egregore is augmented by human belief, ritual and especially by sacrifice. If it is sufficiently nourished by such energies, the egregore can take on a life of its own and appear to be an independent, personal divinity, with a limited power on behalf of its devotees and an unlimited appetite for further devotion.[4]

Thus any collectivity—from a football crowd to a religious or political movement—possesses an egregore which is larger and more powerful than the sum of the individuals in the collectivity. This would be no surprise to anyone who has studied mass psychology or the morphic resonance theory of Rupert Sheldrake, which says that each member of a species "inherits a collective memory from past members of the species, and also contributes to the collective memory, affecting other members of the species in the future"[5]—e.g., monkeys on one side of the world figure out how to crack open a coconut, and others on the other side of the world follow suit.

I suggest that there is a northern egregore which has been built up over the centuries. At certain times it has been eclipsed or has gone out of favor, as in the aftermath of National Socialism, but it has now returned in full force and is manifesting itself in the ways that I have outlined. The question then arises whether the egregore is based on actual historical experience. Was there a real Hyperborean civilization, the memory of which has been transmitted down over the centuries? I have not yet found conclusive evidence for it, but what I have found are many mysterious things indicating that something *like* Hyperborea might have existed, that is to say a prehistoric civilization that left its traces on the world and then vanished—a missing link in the early history of humankind.

Something similar is the theme of Graham Hancock's thought-provoking book *Fingerprints of the Gods*.[6] Hancock produces a range of evidence for such a civilization, which foresaw a coming cataclysm and created great monuments in order to enshrine its knowledge for the survivors. Hancock places this civilization on a landmass which, he says, now lies under the Antarctic ice—like a kind of southern Atlantis—whereas I focus on the opposite pole of the earth. Nevertheless, I found much in Hancock's book that might support the Hyperborean thesis. I also appreciate the way he questions the widespread dogma that the whole history of humankind is one of continuous progress from the world of the cavemen to that of space travel and the Internet, a dogma which can blind us to the possible existence of earlier civilizations that were actually superior to those that followed.

Whether such a civilization existed in the far North is still an open question, but there is no denying that the idea of it has long exerted a powerful mystique. In this book I shall explore that mystique, and inevitably I shall be drawn into some speculation about what might or might not lie behind it.

NOTES

1. C. S. Lewis, *Surprised by Joy* (London: Geoffrey Bles, 1955), 22–23. Quoted in Raynor C. Johnson, *Watcher on the Hills* (London: Hodder & Stoughton, 1959), 40.
2. As Heather O'Donoghue writes: "He re-uses Norse names, or elements of them, throughout *The Lord of the Rings*—the list of dwarf names in the poem Völuspá, for example, is a very productive source for him, and the name Gandalf, Tolkien's immensely wise and knowledgeable wizard, can be found there in Old Norse, Gandálfr." Heather O'Donoghue, *From Asgard to Valhalla* (London: I. B. Tauris, 2007).
3. First published as "Wotan," *Neue Schweizer Rundschau* (Zürich, March 1936). Trans. by Barbara Hannah in *Essays on Contemporary Events* (London, 1947), 1–16. Available on the website http://www.philosopher.eu/others-writings /essay-on-wotan-w-nietzsche-c-g-jung/.
4. Joscelyn Godwin, *The Golden Thread* (Wheaton, Illinois: Quest Books, 2007), 50.
5 Quoted from Sheldrake's website: http://www.sheldrake.org/research /morphic-resonance.
6. London: Heinemann, 1995.

CHAPTER 2

THE SEARCH FOR THE LAND BEYOND THE NORTH WIND

The mystique of the North is encapsulated in a name: Thule, a word that conjures up an icy, fog-wreathed northern land, mysterious, penumbral, lying far away across perilous seas. Our conception of Thule has been handed down from a remarkable Greek mariner called Pytheas, who sailed in the early fourth century BCE from the Greek colony of Massalia, present-day Marseilles. Using highly advanced measuring techniques to calculate factors such as latitude and distance, he and his crew sailed out of the Mediterranean, then went via Britain into the North Atlantic, and eventually reached a land of ice and fog he called Thule, which may have been Iceland. The Romans later called it Ultima Thule. Sadly, Pytheas's original account of the voyage was lost, but it was transmitted at second or third hand by later chroniclers such as Strabo, Diodorus Siculus, and Pliny the Elder.

Over time the notion of Thule merged with an older Greek motif, namely that of Hyperborea, meaning the land beyond Boreas, the north wind. One of those who wrote about it was the Greek poet Pindar (c. 518-442 BCE), who described the Hyperboreans as having an ideal way of life:

Neither by ship nor on foot could you find the marvel-
ous road to the meeting-place of the Hyperboreans . . . In
the festivities of those people and in their praises Apollo

rejoices most . . . The Muse is not absent from their customs; all around swirl the dances of girls, the lyre's loud chords and the cries of flutes. They wreathe their hair with golden laurel branches and revel joyfully. No sickness or ruinous old age is mixed into that sacred race; without toil or battles they live without fear of strict Nemesis.[1]

The Hyperborean theme also captured the imagination of the Romans. Pliny the Elder in his *Natural History* (of about 77 CE) writes as follows:

Then come the Ripaean mountains and the region called Ptephorus . . . it is a part of the world that lies under the condemnation of nature and is plunged in dense darkness, and occupied only by the work of frost and the chilly lurking-places of the north wind. Behind these mountains and beyond the north wind there dwells (if we can believe it) a happy race of people called the Hyperboreans, who live to extreme old age and are famous for legendary marvels. Here are believed to be the hinges on which the firmament turns and the extreme limits of the revolutions of the stars, with six months daylight and a single day of the sun in retirement, not as the ignorant have said, from the spring equinox till autumn: for these people the sun rises once in the year, at midsummer, and sets once, at midwinter. It is a genial region, with a delightful climate and exempt from every harmful blast. The homes of the natives are the woods and the groves; they worship the gods severally and in congregations; all discord and all sorrow is unknown. Death comes to them only when, owing to satiety of life, after holding a banquet and anointing their old age with luxury, they leap from a certain rock into the sea: this mode of burial is the most blissful.[2]

Over subsequent centuries the theme of Hyperborea could be intermittently heard, like a faint leitmotif within the culture of the west. Among the numerous writers who referred to it were the Greek theologian Clement of Alexandria (second century), the philosopher Porphyry (fourth century), the monk and scientist Roger Bacon (thirteenth century), and the alchemist and physician Paracelsus (sixteenth century). During the great age of exploration in the sixteenth century the Flemish cartographer Gerardus Mercator (1512–1594) produced a map of the north polar region (Fig. 1), based on a description which he said he had copied from an earlier author

1. Map of the North Pole by the 16th-century cartographer Gerardus Mercator.

he does not name. In Mercator's depiction, the polar region is a vast land divided by four rivers which flow inward from the surrounding ocean and disappear into an enormous whirlpool. In the midst of the whirlpool, exactly at the Pole, is an island of magnetic rock. This is an interesting reversal of the biblical description of Eden, where four rivers flow *outward* from the center. Today Mercator's map of the North Pole remains iconic for aficionados of the Hyperborean theory.

Parallel to the story of Hyperborea/Thule and sometimes overlapping with it is the legend of Atlantis, the lost continent described by Plato in two of his works, *Timaeus* and *Critias*. In the former, he writes of Atlantis:

> There was an island situated in front of the straits which are by you called the Pillars of Heracles; the island was larger than Libya and Asia put together . . . Now in this island of Atlantis there was a great and wonderful empire which had rule over the whole island and several others, and over parts of the continent . . . But afterwards there occurred violent earthquakes and floods; and in a single day and night of misfortune . . . the island of Atlantis . . . disappeared in the depths of the sea.[3]

In *Critias* there is a much more detailed account of Atlantis. We are told that it was "greater in extent than Libya and Asia," a fertile land with abundant wildlife including elephants, named after Atlas, son of Poseidon (hence the names Atlantis and Atlantic), and had a large empire. The speaker, Critias, gives a description of its inhabitants, their way of life, and their system of government.[4]

The descriptions of Atlantis and Hyperborea have much in common, including the story of a natural catastrophe that caused them both to sink beneath the ocean. By shifting the location of Atlantis from a position "in front of . . . the Pillars of Heracles" to the far north, one could combine the two places. This is essentially what the Swede Olaus Rudbeck did in the seventeenth century in his book *Atlantica or Manheim*,[5] in which he identified Atlantis with Sweden.

Another Swede who celebrated the mystique of the North was Johannes Bureus (1568–1652), a royal archivist who became tutor and confidant of King Gustav Adolph.[6] Bureus believed that there had been an ancient northern civilization, possessing a precious Hyperborean tradition of wisdom, a kind of Nordic Kabbalah, which was encoded in the runes and had at some time in the past been transmitted southward and influenced all the main esoteric traditions of Europe. He also believed that Christianity had been foreshadowed in the Nordic pantheon. So, for example, the Trinity was presaged by the three Nordic deities Odin, Thor, and Freya.[7]

Bureus created a symbol that he called the Adulruna, a kind of runic monogram or matrix with many different symbolic levels from which all the runes could be derived.[8] He tied all this in with the Rosicrucian vision of a new age, which he enthusiastically adopted when the Rosicrucian manifestos were published.[9] Inspired by the first Rosicrucian manifesto, *Fama Fraternitatis*, he wrote a work entitled *F. R. C. FaMa e sCanzia reDUX*,[10] pointing to the dawning of the new age and drawing attention to portents like the appearance of the new stars in the constellations of Serpentarius and Cygnus, as the Rosicrucian *Fama* had done. Bureus also believed in a prophecy current at the time foreshadowing the advent of a great leader called the Lion of Midnight, whom he identified with King Gustav Adolph. He was convinced that Sweden under Gustav Adolph would lead a revival of the Hyperborean civilization.[11]

The French polymath Jean-Sylvain Bailly (1736–1793) also located Atlantis in the north and in effect identified it with Hyperborea, although he rarely referred to the latter. Bailly maintained that "enlightenment came from the north, contrary to the received preconception that the world was enlightened from south to north."[12] In support of his thesis he provided some thought-provoking arguments drawn from mythology. He referred for example to the Roman god Janus, who was said to hold the number 300 in his right hand and 65 in his left. Bailly argued that the two numbers must represent the days of the year. The 300 days in the right hand, he said, represent the light days and the 65 in the left signify those when the sun is absent for the peoples of the North. From this he concluded that Janus was a northern god, transported to the south through migration.[13] He also alluded to a passage in the *Edda* referring to an agreement between the father of the Nordic gods Odin and his wife Frigg,[14] by which Odin was free to absent himself from the marital bed for 65 days in the year, provided that he fulfilled his marital duty during the remaining 300. Again, Bailly interprets the 65 days of absence as referring to the period of the Arctic night.[15]

A century later the idea of an ancient northern homeland was taken up by the Rev. Dr. William F. Warren, president of Boston University, in a book published in 1885 called *Paradise Found: The Cradle of the Human Race at the North Pole*. As the title implies, Warren saw the northern polar region as the source of the human species, the original Eden destroyed in the great flood. Writing from the perspective of his Wesleyan background, Warren rejected the Darwinian notion of humans having evolved from the apes and believed in a contrary process of degeneration from the noble and exalted people of the polar Eden. Although writing with a strong religious agenda, Warren argues his case eloquently, drawing on theology, mythology, ancient literature, geography, astronomy, climatology, and much else. While Warren's work has generally not been taken seriously by mainstream science, it is now coming into its own again. It has, as we shall see, been published in Russian and is eagerly read by Russian Hyperborean enthusiasts.

A few years later the torch of Hyperboreanism was taken up by the Indian writer Bâl Gangâdhar Tilak (1856–1920), a leading nationalist imprisoned for a time by the British authorities for his part in the struggle for independence. In his book *The Arctic Home in the Vedas*, Tilak argues the case for an ancient Arctic civilization and supports this by drawing on many quotations from the ancient scriptures of the Vedas. For example, they mention a "realm of the gods" where the sun rises and sets once a year, as it does at the North Pole. And there are references to a "dawn of many days," describing the half-light lasting for about thirty days before the end of the Arctic night.[16] First published in 1903 and long consigned to obscurity, the book is now coming back into its own, especially in Russia, as we shall see.

Another person who challenged the received notion of a south-north transmission of civilization was the German scholar Ernst Krause (1839–1903). In three weighty tomes, he brought together a mass of linguistic, archaeological, and mythological evidence in support of the north-to-south model.[17] In all three works Krause deals with, among other things, the world of the ancient Greek poet Homer and his treatment of the theme of the Trojan War and its aftermath in his *Iliad* and *Odyssey*, written possibly around the ninth century BCE, although the date is uncertain. Before reading Krause, I had often wondered why mazes and labyrinths are often called Troy towns or in Germany *Trojaburgen*. I had never been convinced by the explanation that the walls of Troy were laid out like a labyrinth to confuse invaders. And it seemed odd that these labyrinths were not named after the most famous labyrinth of mythology: the one said to have been constructed by Daedalus on Crete, which harbored the dreaded Minotaur and from which Theseus escaped with the aid of Ariadne's thread after killing the Minotaur and releasing its other intended victims.

The myth goes on to relate that, having accomplished his goal, Theseus and his companions set off to return home to Athens, but on the way they stopped on the island of Delos, where Theseus made a sacrifice to Apollo and he and his friends celebrated with a labyrinthine dance called the *geranos*, from the Greek word for "crane," in which the dancers imitate this bird's movements. The "crane dance" became popular in the Hellenic world and is still danced today in certain places. But the questions arise: Was it simply a reenactment of the dance of Theseus and his friends? Or did it have deeper layers of meaning and perhaps an earlier origin?

Krause argues that the story of Ulysses's attack on Troy to rescue Queen Helen is simply one version of an ancient nature myth concerned with the return of spring. Thus, Helen is the spring goddess who is rescued from the underworld (Troy).[18] And the dance through the labyrinth (the underworld) is a symbolic enactment of this vernal event. And what of the name Troy itself? According to Krause it is another moniker for winter. "In southern Slavic folklore there still exists today a nocturnal and hibernal demon named Trojano."[19] This would explain why the name Troy crops up in different forms in various parts of Europe, e.g., Troyes in France and Dhronecken (originally Troneck) in Germany. It seems that the city of Troy was therefore named after an ancient word for "labyrinth" and not vice versa. This is supported by the great British classical scholar W. F. Jackson Knight in his book *Cumaean Gates*, where he writes: "The safest thing to do is to suppose that Homer's Troy and all the other Troys were called after the word used for mazes and labyrinths. Troy was called Troy because it had some quality of a maze."[20]

But which came first: the labyrinth or the dance? The German art historian Hermann Kern puts forward the intriguing theory that the ancient labyrinths were patterns to guide the dancers.[21] A labyrinth could either be laid out on the ground for the dancers to weave their way through or depicted on a smaller scale, on an object such as a stone tablet, to function as a transportable guide. But this still leaves open the question of what the dance was for. Ancient labyrinths often have seven spirals, and the number seven has a special significance

2. Labyrinth of the classic Cretan design on the island of Gotland, Sweden.

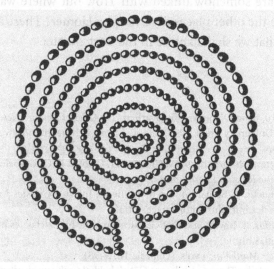

3. Stone labyrinth in Finland.

as the number of stars in the Great Bear. So there appears to be a connection between the Great Bear and the spiral dance through the labyrinth, which we shall come to in chapter 3.

The labyrinth can also symbolize a downward journey into the underworld. As Mircea Eliade points out in his classic study of shamanism, "the cave and the labyrinth continue to have a function of the first importance in the rites of . . . archaic cultures . . .; both, indeed, are concrete symbols of passage into another world, of a descent into the underworld."[22] Thus, in that case the underworld would represent not winter, as in the story of Helen, but the world of the dead and demons through which the shamanic initiate must pass.

Labyrinths of similar pattern—often variations of the classic Cretan model—are found over a large part of the world, including Scandinavia (Figs. 2–3), Siberia, India, Indonesia, and the Native American territories in the United States, and it is tempting to see this as another vestige of the Hyperborean culture. Much depends on where the tradition of the labyrinth originated. We have seen that labyrinths are somehow linked with Troy. But where was Troy and where were the other places described by Homer? These are relevant questions that we shall explore in the next chapter.

NOTES

1. Pythian 10, from Diane Arnson Svarlien, *The Odes of Pindar* (New Haven, CT: Yale University Press, 1991). Quoted from website: http://www.perseus .tufts.edu.
2. Pliny, *Natural History*, Book IV, Chapter 11. Quoted in Otto Boele, *The North in Romantic Russian Literature*, 42.
3. Plato, *Timaeus*, tr. Benjamin Jowett, online via Internet Classics Archive: http://classics.mit.edu/Plato/timaeus.html.
4. Plato, *Critias*, tr. Jowett, Internet Classics Archive: http://classics.mit.edu /Plato/critias.html.
5. *Atland eller Manheim*, 4 vols. (Uppsala 1675–98).
6. See the study by Thomas Karlsson, *Götisk kabbala och runisk alkemi: Johannes Bureus och den götiska esoterismen* (*Gothic Kabbalah and Runic Alchemy:*

Johannes Bureus and Gothic Esotericism) (Stockholm: University of Stockholm, 2009).

7. Karlsson, *Götisk kabbala*, 121.
8. Karlsson, *Götisk kabbala*, 140–41.
9. The three so-called Rosicrucian manifestos were published in Germany in 1614, 1615, and 1616, setting in motion a movement of spiritual and intellectual reform characterized by an esoteric form of Christianity.
10. Stockholm (1616).
11. Karlsson, 247–50.
12. Bailly (1781), 95.
13. Bailly (1781), 99.
14. According to some sources Odin's wife is Frigg, according to others Freya.
15. Bailly (1781), 326.
16. B. G. Tilak (1903), 69.
17. Ernst Krause (1891, 1893a, 1893b).
18. Krause (1891), 449–69.
19. Krause (1893b), x.
20. W. F. Jackson Knight, *Cumaean Gates* (Oxford: Basil Blackwell, 1936), quoted in Janet Bord, *Mazes and Labyrinths of the World* (London: Latimer, 1976), 13.
21. Hermann Kern, *Labyrinthe* (Munich: Prestel-Verlag, 1982).
22. Eliade, 51.

CHAPTER 3

MIDNIGHT LAND, NORTHERN LIGHT

Count Vasiliy Kapnist (1758–1823), a Russian man of letters, who wrote biting satires and campaigned for the abolition of serfdom, was also a passionate believer in Hyperborea. In his book *A Short Survey on the Hyperboreans* (1815), Kapnist claimed that the events portrayed in ancient Greek mythology and epic literature took place not in the Mediterranean but in the far North. He pictured the classical deities and heroes inhabiting the shores of the Arctic Ocean. Most interestingly, he located the adventures of Ulysses, as described by Homer in the *Iliad* and *Odyssey*, not in and around the eastern Mediterranean and Aegean but also far to the north. Thus, when Homer spoke of "the land plunged in darkness," he did not mean the west, as scholars have mistakenly thought, but rather the North, the "midnight land," as it is sometimes called. Although partly of Greek ancestry himself, Kapnist was anxious to show that not only Greece but also all southern cultures "have become illuminated by the northern light."[1]

In the twentieth century the list of advocates of the "northern light" theory included Herman Wirth (1885–1981), a Dutch-German musicologist, folklorist, and ethnologist and author of a work entitled *Ascent of Humankind* (*Der Aufgang der Menschheit*),[2] one of those mammoth, polymath works like Oswald Spengler's *Decline of the West*, and like Spengler's book it was published in the bleak aftermath of World War I. Probably Wirth hoped that his book would bring some glimmer of the northern light into the midst of a devastated Europe. For a while he placed high hopes in Nazism and got involved in the Ahnenerbe (Ancestral Heritage) organization of the SS, but after a time he became persona non grata with the Nazi establishment and narrowly escaped being placed in a concentration camp. At the time, his book was largely dismissed by mainstream researchers, and today in the English-speaking world very few people have even heard of him. But in Russia he now has an enthusiastic following, as we shall see in a later chapter.

In arguing for an ancient northern homeland, Wirth produces an extraordinarily wide range of evidence, from human physiology to climatology and from archaeology to linguistics, drawing on the work of recognized scientists of the time. His argument rests partly on the notion that the North Pole has wandered over time owing to a sliding of the earth's crust. To give one small example of his evidence, he reports that, on Grinnell Land in the far north of Canada, prehistoric remains of a variety of trees have been found, including yew, elm, lime, birch, poplar, and hazel. This indicates, he argues, that the area must at one time have been comparable in climate to the northern parts of the temperate zone, as such trees would require an average annual temperature of +8 degrees Centigrade, as opposed to the present −20 degrees. He then goes on to compare the different circumpolar peoples in terms of blood groups, burial practices, myths, symbols, language, and technology and claims that it all points to there having been two cultures in the North, which he calls the Arctic-Nordic and the Atlantic-Nordic. The former comprised the migrants who came via the land bridge that once connected Russia with Alaska and became the Inuit and other indigenous people of America. At some point these two cultures apparently met, interacted and interbred, which is why, according to Wirth, there are fair-haired and fair-skinned Inuit, and why the Guanches, the original inhabitants of the Canary Islands, were also fair-haired and fair-skinned. (In Wirth's scenario, they were part of a far-reaching Hyperborean diaspora.)

Wirth jeopardized his reputation by endorsing and publishing an edition of the *Oera Linda Book*,[3] a mysterious manuscript that came to light in the Dutch province of Friesland in 1867. It was dated 1256, but was evidently a nineteenth-century copy. A number of experts pronounced it a forgery, but it has remained controversial to this day. Purporting to be a chronicle of the Frisian people recorded over several millennia and preserved by the Over de Linden family, it was written in a form of Old Frisian in a rune-like script, for which a key was included.

The manuscript came to the attention of the Dutch folklorist Jan Gerhardus Ottema, who published a Dutch translation in 1872. This was followed by an English translation by William Sandbach, published in 1876, and later by Wirth's German translation in 1933. At the time of writing a new English translation is being prepared by the Dutch researcher Jan Ott. The book begins with a creation story in which the supreme deity Wr-alda made the earth, out of which arose three progenitrices: Lyda, Finda, and Freya, the last named being the mother of the Frisians. Their home was a paradisiacal place called Adland or Atland where a matriarchal order reigned, every settlement having its own "virgin" as the highest authority. This golden age came to an end when the land was ravaged by earthquakes and volcanic eruptions before finally sinking into the ocean. In other words, we have here another version of the Atlantis legend.

The location of Atlantis has been a Holy Grail for many a seeker. One of them in the twentieth century was the German pastor and amateur archaeologist Jürgen Spanuth (1907–1998), who identified Basileia, the main island of Atlantis as described by Plato, with a vanished island in the North Sea close to Heligoland.[4] This area, he argues, was the original home of the northern sea people who, according to Plato and other ancient sources, invaded Greece and Asia Minor but were turned back by the Egyptians. He dates these events to around 1200 BCE.

The long list of places with which Atlantis has been identified includes Troy, but this brings us to the question of where Troy was located. The German archaeologist Heinrich Schliemann thought he had settled the matter when he excavated an ancient city at Hissarlik in Turkey in the 1870s and identified it as Homer's Troy. Today most experts accept this identification, but in recent decades a number of people have come forward to challenge it. One of them is the Dutchman Iman Jacob Wilkens, who in 1990 published *Where Troy Once Stood*, in which he located Troy in eastern England near Cambridge. Even more startling is the route he plotted for Ulysses's voyages, which involved crossing the Atlantic to the Caribbean and back.

The Italian researcher Felice Vinci has also taken up the question of the location of the events related by Homer. He presents his case in a book called *The Baltic Origins of Homer's Epic Tales*[5] and in an article entitled "The Nordic Origins of the Iliad and Odyssey" in the *Athens Journal of Mediterranean Studies*.[6] Vinci's ultimate conclusion is that there was a big migration from Scandinavia in prehistoric times, the migrants eventually settled in what is now Greece and became the Mycenaeans, and they brought with them their epic narratives and reassigned them to the Mediterranean region.

Vinci's argument, conveniently summarized in his journal article,[7] rests on a careful comparison of the world described in Homer's texts with that of the Baltic and North Atlantic in about the second millennium BCE. For example, the climatic conditions described by Homer are a far cry from those of the sunny eastern Mediterranean. The *Iliad* describes violent storms, fog, and snow, but rarely mentions the sun. Homer's characters wear thick cloaks, sometimes lined with fur, similar to those found in northern Bronze

Age tombs. Their diet does not include the olives, figs, and other staples of the Mediterranean, but rather large quantities of meat, as with the Vikings. They drink from beakers of metal or, in the case of poor people, wood, but not from pottery vessels, as would have been usual in the ancient Greek world. There is also abundant support for Vinci's theory from mythology. For example, the story of the abduction of Helen to Troy has a parallel in a Norse myth about how Snion, son of the Danish king, abducts the beautiful queen of Sweden and precipitates a war as related by the medieval chronicler Saxo Grammaticus in his *Gesta Danorum.*

Many names from Norse mythology are paralleled in Mediterranean mythology and topography. Aegir and Ran, the giant husband and wife who rule the seas in Nordic legend, correspond in Greek mythology to Aegaeon, the god of sea storms, after whom the Aegean Sea is named, and his sister Rhea. Another sea god named Briaros is, according to some versions, the son of Aegaeon, and in others a different version of the same god. At any rate, the name appears to be cognate with a Nordic mythological being called Brímir,[8] also associated with the sea, who is said to have given his name to my neighboring port of Bremen in north Germany.

The most powerful evidence adduced by Vinci is geographical. Homer's description of the lands visited by Ulysses does not correspond to any places in the Mediterranean, whereas they fit perfectly when shifted to the north. Calypso's island was already identified by the Greek author Plutarch (c. 44–120 CE) as lying in the North Atlantic, and Vinci identifies it as Nolsoy in the Faroe Islands. The Peloponnese, described as a plain in both the *Iliad* and the *Odyssey*, is, of course, mountainous, while Ulysses's own island of Ithaca fits exactly the Baltic island of Lyø.

What of Troy itself? Vinci writes that "100 km west of Helsinki there is a village, Toija, whose characteristics correspond exactly to those Homer passes down to us: a hilly ground dominating the valley with the two rivers, a plain stretching to the coast and a mountain-ous area . . ."⁹ Equally striking is the passage in the *Odyssey* referring to a people called the Ciconians or, in Greek, Kíkones, who attacked Ulysses and his men shortly after the Trojan campaign had ended. Vinci has discovered that, at the corresponding spot, about fifty kilo-meters inland from the coast of Finland is a town called Kíikoinen.¹⁰

Then there is the figure of Ulysses himself, whom Vinci links with the Nordic god Ull, a warrior, hunter, and, like Ulysses, a skilled archer. Vinci also discusses a highly important aspect of Ulysses, namely his shamanic characteristics. He draws attention to a passage in the *Odyssey* that describes how Ulysses constructed his bedroom around an olive trunk: "I built my bedroom around it with thick stones / till I finished it, then I suitably covered it above properly / and built sturdy doors" (*Odyssey* 23, 192–94).¹¹ Mircea Eliade states that a central pillar in a dwelling is a common feature in communi-ties where shamanism is practiced and represents the axis of the world. He writes: "This pole is sacred; it is regarded almost as a god. At its foot stands a small stone altar, on which offerings are placed."¹² We shall return more than once to the subject of shamanism.

Comparing the work of Wilkens and Vinci, the Norwegian researcher Morten Alexander Joramo decided that neither had dis-covered the full truth, although both were right on certain points. He therefore carried out his own investigation, which gave rise to his book *The Homer Code*,¹³ in which he came up with a new chart of Ulysses's journeys, involving sites around the Baltic, the Norwegian coast, and the Lofoten Islands. Comparing names, Joramo finds some interesting correspondences. For example, the Achaeans (Greeks) are also referred to by Homer as Danaans, and Joramo draws the conclusion that they were Danes. Of key importance for Joramo is the Finnish capital Helsinki, which before 1050 CE was simply called Hel. "Hel was the very heart of the ancient Norse fertil-ity culture, and only there did the stories from old never stop being told. They are still being told there today . . . For all of those in the second millennium BC who left the north for Greece to start a new life there, it became natural to call themselves Hellenes, and their new country Hellas."[14] Joramo goes even further and suggests that the North Pole was formerly located in a group of islands close to Helsinki—presumably because of a shift in the earth's crust.

> Frey and Freya, the first people, were born in Hel at the
> time when it was the North Pole. . . . Hel is positioned at
> the coast, and just outside the mainland there used to be
> seven islands, before two of them were fused together. They
> were called the Sun Islands. On the Island of Oden, the
> main island of the seven, the arch Valhalla was once erected.
> There, on that spot, which was called Midgard, there is still
> supposed to be a round little hole on the exact point where
> the North Pole once was. Today that point is off limits
> in a room in the basement of a house in the Sveaborg or
> Suomenlinna fortress.[15]

Joramo, like Vinci, believes that an advanced people lived in the north in ancient times and were forced to migrate to other parts of the world because of climatic changes. This would mean, he says, that "contrary to all accepted dogma on the matter, important roots of our Western Civilization could be in the north and not in the Mediterranean."[16]

Let us for a moment consider one of the arts that might have been transmitted to the Hellenic world from the North, namely the art of poetry. As we know from the *Edda* and the sagas, the figure of the bard played an enormously important role in Nordic society, and to become one involved acquiring complicated skills. One had to master several different poetic meters and know which one to use for a particular subject matter. One had to know how to chant the different meters. One also had to master elaborate metaphors called kennings. This is when, for example, you describe sunlight as the sword of the gods or a warrior as the feeder of the ravens, referring to the ravens scavenging among the corpses after a battle. And sometimes you would replace one word of the kenning with another kenning, creating elaborate layers of metaphor. All this had to be painstakingly acquired, so to be a bard carried great prestige. This is reflected in the fact that Odin, the father of the Nordic pantheon, is also the god of poetry. Poets had a similar prestige in Homeric Greece, and many of the same kennings appear in both traditions. For example we find in Homer the term "sea horses" (*Odyssey* IV: 780), meaning ships, identical to the Norse *vágmarr* ("horse of the waves"). And Vinci suggests, intriguingly, that the famous "wooden horse" is probably actually a kenning indicating a ship.[17]

By now we have seen that there is a considerable—if circumstantial—body of evidence to suggest that: (a) in the distant past there was a people enjoying an advanced culture living in the far North; (b) they were forced to migrate to other parts of the world because of climatic changes that made their homeland uninhabitable; (c) they have left their mark on the languages, customs, myths, and literature of the regions into which they migrated.

For mainstream experts in geography and prehistory, this notion has long been confined to a cupboard reserved for crackpot theories, but occasionally it has been taken out of the cupboard and examined more objectively. One person who took it seriously was J. G. Bennett, better known for his role in promoting the Gurdjieff movement in Britain. In 1963 in his journal *Systematics* he published an article entitled "The Hyperborean origin of the Indo-European culture,"[18] a sober and detailed investigation drawing on evidence from the latest research in geophysics and climatology as well as from linguistics, archaeology, and ancient writings. Before summarizing it, let me review a few things about the Indo-Europeans.

We know from linguistic and archaeological evidence that such a people existed,[19] but there are different theories about the location of their original home. Candidates include the Danube valley, the Caucasus and Central Asia. According to the generally accepted time-scale, by about 4000 BCE the Indo-Europeans were a unified people with a unified language that we can call proto-Indo-European. From about 2500 BCE, they dispersed throughout Europe and eastward to India, taking with them their language, which in turn gave rise to the multiplicity of languages derived from it, including Sanskrit and most European languages.

Turning to Bennett's article, a major plank of his argument rests on linguistic evidence. There are very basic differences, he points out, between the various language families in the world. The Indo-European group is characterized by a particular kind of complexity. Take a language like Russian with its intricate grammar—nouns with three genders and six different cases; word endings that change according to gender, number, and case; complex verb conjugations; etc.—and one can form an idea of what proto-Indo-European must have been like. To create such a language was a monumental achieve-ment and, Bennett argues, must have a required a concerted effort over a long period of time by a community settled in an area shielded from outside interference and under circumstances that permitted a degree of leisure and freedom from the pressures of the struggle for survival. Moreover, it must have been created by minds of enormous intelligence and subtlety, "an independent caste of priest-scholars who elaborated both language and ritual and who were poets of no mean order," in the words of the British classical linguist Leonard Palmer.[20]

Where could such an achievement have been accomplished? Bennett argues for the Arctic Circle region. He takes seriously Tilak's evidence from the Vedas for an Arctic homeland of the Indo-Europeans, but says that Tilak was far out in dating it to 40,000 BCE, which is far too early and would explain why Tilak has had little impact in the world of mainstream learning. Bennett quotes subsequent research by the climatologists Maurice Ewing and William Donn[21] who have shown that a more recent date is possible. The north polar ocean, they point out, is like a partially landlocked basin, surrounded by Scandinavia, Russia, North America, Greenland, and a North Atlantic submarine ridge. Owing to a complex interaction of different factors—ocean currents, the melting and reforming of the ice, and water flowing in and out of the basin—the temperature in the lands bordering the Arctic has fluctuated considerably over time.

At certain periods, Ewing and Donn argue, the coastal areas of the Arctic would have been temperate owing to a combination of the Gulf Stream flowing in from the southwest and the ocean absorbing heat from the sun. At the same time, these areas would have been cut off to the south by a belt of glaciers, which at other times would have melted sufficiently to allow access to the coast. On the basis of this theory Bennett proposes the following scenario. About 15,000 years ago the glacial barrier opened sufficiently to allow human beings to colonize the coastal areas of the Arctic. The glaciers then reformed, trapping the settlers in the Arctic for many millennia and providing exactly the conditions that were necessary for the development of the proto-Indo-European language. Subsequently, about 10,000 years ago, the Ice Age began to subside and the glacial barrier reopened, allowing the settlers to leave the Arctic and spread out to the south, west, and east.

By comparison, Vinci proposes a much later scenario, in which the thawing of the ice from around 8000–10,000 BCE was what enabled settlers to *enter* the north rather than exit from it. This temperate phase, according to Vinci, came to an end in about 2000 BCE, when the Ice Age returned, and this, he says, was what precipitated the exodus of the northern tribes who eventually settled in Greece around 1600 BCE.[22] These two scenarios may not be incompatible if·

in fact we are talking about two different phases of settlement in the north. I shall return to this possibility later.

The period of the late Stone Age and early Bronze Age (i.e., circa 5500–1500 BCE) produced remarkable achievements in the north of Europe: sophisticated metalwork and pottery and astonishing feats of building like Stonehenge in England, the Callanish Stones in the Hebrides, Skara Brae in Orkney, and the gigantic tomb of Bredarör near Kivik in Sweden. Remains like these are a profound challenge to those who hold to the paradigm of south-to-north development. For example, the distinguished British archaeologist Stuart Piggott, confronted with the miracle of Stonehenge, made the following observation: "In Britain . . . the final monument of Stonehenge, with its architectural competence and sophistication, is best explained in terms of the momentary introduction of superior skills from an area of higher culture, which in the circumstances can hardly be other than Mycenae."[23] Thus Piggott, great archaeologist though he was, could only explain Stonehenge in terms of an influence flowing from the south to the north, when all that we have seen contradicts this notion.

Let us now imagine that we are among a party of ancient seafarers in a ship somewhere in the North Atlantic. It is a clear night in March, and we are looking up at the sky, which would appear as shown in Fig. 4. Overhead and to the north we would see the two constellations of the Great Bear and the Little Bear (sometimes called the Big Dipper and Little Dipper). In Latin, the names are Ursa Major and Ursa Minor. The latter contains the polar star, Polaris, which has been used since time immemorial as direction-finder. Note that the Great Bear has seven stars and that the Latin word for north is *septentrio*, which is cognate with *septem* (seven), as is the Russian word for north, *sevyer*. Clearly, therefore, the north, the two constellations, the number seven, and the figure of the bear are all connected and have some special mystique attached to them. Let us see what this tells us.

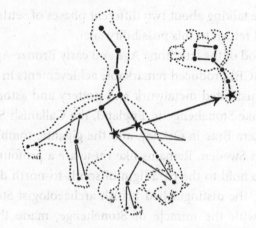

4. Constellations of the Great Bear (Big Dipper) and Little Bear (Little Dipper). The polestar is indicated by the arrow.

The names of the two constellations are curious, as neither obviously resembles a bear. So why are they so named? The word for bear in Greek is *arctos*, hence the word *Arctic*. But why the bear? Part of the answer is that the bear is found over a large part of northern Europe as a symbol of the warrior caste. In Celtic, the word for bear is *artos*, a slight variation of the Greek, hence the name of King Arthur or Artus, the warrior king. And in the Germanic world, there is the tradition of the berserker, from the old Norse word *berserkr*, meaning a bear's garment. Thus, a berserker was a warrior who took on the strength and ferocity of a bear. And it is surely no coincidence that the bear is Russia's national symbol.

However, the bear is not only a symbol of martial strength and courage. It also frequently appears in shamanism, which is found throughout the world, but especially in Siberia, Central Asia, and the far northern parts of Europe and North America. Here we have arrived at one of the key arguments of this book, namely that shamanism was central to the northern culture that we are speaking about. The shaman is a healer and magician who is able to travel in trance to the underworld or to the world of the gods and demons, and the bear is one of the totem animals or the animal spirits that guide and protect the shaman on his or her trance journeys.

The totem animal of the Celtic goddess Artio is a bear, as her name suggests. The bear is also the totem animal of the Greek goddess Artemis, whose name is also cognate with *arctos*. Artemis is the twin sister of Apollo. Both Artemis and Apollo have names that in Greek consist of seven letters, and Apollo has a lyre of seven strings and was born on the seventh day of the month. Furthermore, Apollo was said to have come from Hyperborea and to return there for three months every year.

I suggest that the name Apollo is actually a variant of the name of the Nordic god Balder (also spelt Baldur or Baldr) who, like Apollo, is a god of light. The British scholar and expert on the ancient Greek pantheon, the late W. C. K. Guthrie, links Apollo with shamanism. He points out that Apollo's devotees went in for shape-shifting, astral traveling, oracular trances, and the like—techniques typical of the shamans, the medicine men of Siberia. And Siberia is where Guthrie locates Hyperborea and identifies it as the place where Apollo's career as a god began. From there, Guthrie maintains, his cult spread southwestward, via Asia Minor, into the Hellenic world.[24]

There are also indications that the cult of the Great Bear as an element of shamanism spread eastward and southeastward into Asia, where it is found in Taoism and in Buddhism. According to the Taoism expert Eva Wong, Taoism can be traced back to a tribe of hunter-gatherers practicing a shamanic religion, who settled on the Yellow River in northern China some 5,000 years ago. One of the legendary chiefs of this tribe was Yü, who shape-shifted between man and bear, walked with a bearlike shuffle, and journeyed frequently to the stars and their spirits by means of a dance called the Pace of Yü, which has been handed down through generations of Taoists ever since. The pattern of the dance moves in a spiral toward the center, symbolizing the journey to the polestar and the Great Bear.[25] This reminds us of the labyrinth dances mentioned earlier.

In Chinese Taoist yoga, the Great Bear and the polestar are sources of healing energy that can be drawn down into the human body. This energy is absorbed from the polestar through the pineal gland and from the Great Bear through the thalamus and hypothalamus glands.[26] The Great Bear also plays a role in Hindu tradition, where the seven stars of the constellation are referred to as the seven Rishis or Wise Ones. Are these perhaps further variations of a Hyperborean shamanic tradition?

Shamanism is one of the themes that the British researcher Geoffrey Ashe writes about in his book *The Ancient Wisdom*.[27] He sees the mathematician Pythagoras, a devotee of Apollo, as one of the transmitters of Hyperborean wisdom. "He founded a mystical community which admitted women—shamanistic rather than Hellenic behavior—and he is credited in legend . . . with taming a bear. . . . Pythagoras is said to have been instructed himself by a Hyperborean guru called Abaris . . . Pythagoras was the first Greek to form the conception of a Cosmos[28]—a conception of order, interrelation, measure . . ."[29] When we remember that Pythagoras is credited with inventing the basis of trigonometry, without which modern civilization would not work, then we begin to see the profound implications that emerge if we accept the transmission of a shamanic wisdom from the North.

Ashe identifies the ultimate source of Hyperborean wisdom not in the Arctic but in the Altai, a mountainous region in southern Siberia at the borders with Kazakhstan, Mongolia, and China. He equates it with Shambhala, the fabled hidden kingdom that has captured the imaginations of many, including the Russian artist Nikolai Roerich who twice set out across Central Asia in search of it. Ashe suggests that Mount Belukha, the highest peak in the Altai range, might be the original model for Mount Meru, the mountain at the center of the world, as described in the Hindu epic, the *Mahabharata*, and which has its counterparts in many traditions.[30]

The notion of a northern promised land also features in the writings of René Guénon (1886–1951), founder of the Traditionalist school of religious thought, which also includes figures such as Ananda Coomaraswamy (1877–1947), Frithjof Schuon (1907–1998), and to some extent Julius Evola (1898–1974). The Traditionalists teach that all "true" religions stem from a single primordial tradition or perennial philosophy largely lost sight of in modernity, which the Traditionalists see as a degenerate aberration in the history of the world. Concomitant with this belief is the notion that the tradition originated from a primal geographical center and over time other centers came into being which were reflections of the original one, the "supreme country." Here is a relevant passage from Guénon's book of *The Lord the World*:

> Many other traditions accord with all that has been dis-
> cussed about the "supreme country". There is notably
> another name for it. . . . This name is *Tula*, which the Greeks
> called *Thule*. . . . The name has, however, been given to
> many different regions, so that even today it is still to be
> found as far afield as Russia and Central America. No doubt
> each of these regions constituted the seat of a spiritual
> power in some era more or less long past, and which was an
> emanation of the power of the primordial *Tula*.

He goes on to say the Mexican Tula was originated by the Toltecs, who came from Aztlan, which was evidently Atlantis. However, he says, the Atlantean Tula has to be distinguished from the Hyperborean Tula. The latter, he says, "represents the first and supreme center for the entire current *Manvantara* [period of over 300 million years in the Hindu cycles of ages] and is the archetypal 'sacred isle', situated . . . in a literally polar location. All the other 'sacred isles', although everywhere bearing names of equivalent meaning, are still only images of the original."[31]

The Italian conservative thinker Julius Evola, with his own brand of traditionalism, perceived a fundamental antagonism between North and South, which he describes as follows in his book *Revolt against the Modern World* (*Rivolta contro il mondo moderno*):

> Thus also in the esoteric domain, the antithesis of North and South is reflected in two types: the Hero and the Saint, the King and the Priest [. . .]. In every historical epoch since the decline of the Boreal races, one can recognize the action of two antagonistic tendencies, repeating in one form or another the fundamental polarity of North and South. In every later civilization we have to recognize the dynamic product of the meeting or collision of these tendencies [. . .].[32]

So far we have encountered several different and sometimes contradictory depictions of the mysterious northern land. In some accounts it is identical to Atlantis and described as an island that disappeared into the ocean. Sometimes it is in the Atlantic by the Strait of Gibraltar, sometimes in the North Atlantic, sometimes in the Baltic, sometimes in the Altai mountain range of Siberia, sometimes on the north coast of Russia. Sometimes it is described as cold and inhospitable, sometimes as temperate and fertile.

As we have seen, the time frames assigned to the northern civilization also vary widely between, for example, Tilak (c. 40,000 BCE), Bennett (c. 13,000–10,000 BCE), and Vinci (c. 10,000–2000 BCE). The earlier scenarios make it unlikely that the Hyperboreans were Indo-Europeans, as the findings of archaeology and philology point to the Indo-Europeans not having dispersed until about 2500 BCE.

Where they dispersed from is a matter of dispute, but the general consensus is that their original homeland was somewhere between the Caucasus and Central Asia, not the northern polar region. So let us keep in mind the possibility that the earlier inhabitants of Hyperborea were not Indo-European but left their mark on Indo-European culture.

NOTES

1. Boele, 41–43.
2. Wirth (1928).
3. Wirth (1933).
4. See Spanuth's book *Das enträtselte Atlantis* (*Atlantis Demystified*) (Stuttgart: Union Deutsche Verlagsgesellschaft, 1953).
5. English version, Rochester, Vermont: Inner Traditions, 2005.
6. Issue of April 2017, 163–85.
7. Vinci (2017), 163–69.
8. Vinci (2005), 272.
9. Vinci (2017), 172.
10. Vinci (2005), 48.
11. Vinci (2005), 96–97.
12. Eliade (1989), 261.
13. Lofoten: Norse Odyssey, second edition 2014.
14. Morten Joramo, *The Homer Code*. Kindle positions 530–34.
15. Joramo, *The Homer Code*. Kindle positions 2113–18.
16. Ibid. Kindle positions 1984–86.
17. Vinci (2017), 176.
18. *Systematics*, Vol. 1, No. 3, December 1963.
19. For a good, concise introduction to the subject, see Jean Haudry, *The Indo-Europeans* (Lyon: Institut d'Études Indo-Européens, 1994).
20. Inaugural lecture by L. R. Palmer, "Achaeans and Indo-Europeans" (Oxford: Clarendon Press, 1955).
21. Ewing and Donn (1956 and 1958).
22. Vinci (2005), 172.
23. Quoted by Vinci (2005), 173.
24. Guthrie (1935 and 1950), summarized by Geoffrey Ashe, 110.
25. Eva Wong, *Taoism: An Essential Guide* (Boston MA: Shambhala Publications, 1997), 11–13.

26. See Mantak and Maneewan Chia, *Awaken Healing Light of the Tao* (Huntington, NY: Healing Tao Books, 1993).
27. London: Macmillan, 1977.
28. Meaning literally "beautiful order."
29. Ashe, 176.
30. Ashe, 173.
31. René Guénon, *The Lord of the World* (Ripon, UK: Coombe Springs Press, 1983), 56.
32. Quoted by Joscelyn Godwin in *Arktos*, 60.

CHAPTER 4

CHILDREN OF THE POLESTAR: EVIDENCE FOR MIGRATION FROM THE NORTH

Let us look for a moment at the actual circumpolar region and its geography (Fig. 5). If you were to travel clockwise through the lands bordering the Arctic Circle, starting in the North Atlantic, you would pass close to Iceland, through Greenland, across Canada to Alaska, over the Bering Strait, through a massive swath of Russian territory to Finland, and then through Sweden and Norway and back to the starting point in the Atlantic.

Over the centuries these regions have drawn many expeditions. Apart from the voyage of Pytheas, already mentioned in chapter 2, these include the Englishman Martin Frobisher in search of the North-West Passage in the 1570s, the Dutchman Willem Barentsz's discovery of Spitzbergen in 1596, the Russian Admiral Chichagov's expeditions in search of the North-East Passage in the 1760s (more on this in chapter 12), the British Arctic expedition in 1849 of Sir John Franklin, which perished in the ice off northern Canada, the American Robert Peary's (disputed) reaching of the North Pole in 1909, and the first airplane flight over the Pole (also disputed) by Richard E. Byrd and Floyd Bennett in 1926. Subsequently there has been a steady succession of feats and records of exploration involving the Arctic and the North Pole: first submarine to pass under the Arctic ice, first confirmed overland conquest of the Pole (by snowmobile), first person to reach the Pole on foot, first to sail alone

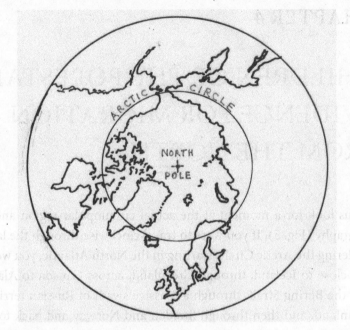

5. Map of the northern circumpolar region.

through the North-West Passage, first team to reach the magnetic North Pole in a car. And today those tourists who prefer to travel through the icy passages of the north in greater comfort can do so in a floating luxury hotel.

What about the inhabitants of these regions? Living within the area bordering the Arctic Circle there are just over thirteen million people,[1] of whom roughly 10 percent are indigenous.[2] The latter include the Inuit of Greenland, Canada, and Alaska, various First Nations people of North America, the Buryat and Samoyedic people of Siberia, the Sami of Russia and Scandinavia, and a number of others.

Now the interesting question arises: what similarities, if any, exist between these indigenous circumpolar people and the northern

Europeans that might throw light on the Hyperborean theory? First, there is the fact that all of these peoples have shamanic traditions—shamanism being a religious phenomenon found in many parts of the world and particularly strongly in the far northern areas of North America, Europe, and Asia.[3] It centers around the figure of the shaman, who is at once magician, healer, miracle worker, visionary, and priest. Essential to the shaman's role is the ability to travel in trance between the world of the gods, the everyday world of humans, and the underworld of spirits and demons. In the case of the Germanic peoples, a long time has passed since shamanism was a living and integral part of their society, but the evidence for it is clearly there in the mythology and in the Eddic poems and the sagas. A prime example is the story of Odin's self-sacrifice on the World Tree, which we shall come back to shortly.

Looking at the symbols and motifs that occur in Nordic shamanism as well as in that of the circumpolar indigenous peoples, we find that, predictably, the polestar features strongly in both. Mircea Eliade writes:

> In the middle of the sky shines the Pole Star, holding the celestial tent like a stake. The Samoyed call it the "Sky Nail".
> ... The same image and terminology are found among the Lapps, the Finns and the Estonians ... As we should expect, this cosmology has found an exact replica in the micro-cosm inhabited by mankind. The Axis of the world has been concretely represented, either by the pillars that support the house, or in the form of isolated stakes called "World Pillars." For the Eskimo, for example, the Pillar of the Sky is identical with the pole at the center of their dwellings.[4]

A similar symbology is found in the Irminsul, the sacred tree of the Saxons, cut down by Charlemagne in 772.

Something else that may be significant with regard to the Hyperborean theory is the ubiquitous presence of ancient stone labyrinths. These are found all over the world, but in particularly dense concentration in Scandinavia, especially around the Baltic coast of Sweden and Finland. They are also found on the Arctic coast and islands of Russia, and in North America but not in the Arctic territories, rather farther south, among the indigenous tribes such as the Hopi in Arizona. There are many variations of the labyrinth, but one that mysteriously crops up all over the world is the classic Cretan model. We have already seen in chapter 2 how this pattern is found in places widely separated from each other. As already mentioned in chapter 2, labyrinths have a symbolic role in shamanism, and possibly we have here a shamanic feature transmitted far and wide by the Hyperborean culture.

So could there have been a gradual Hyperborean diaspora, spreading out from the Arctic, mingling with and influencing the peoples and cultures of other regions? Let us imagine that this diaspora happened and see where it leads us.

An obvious place to start would be the Stone Age archaeological sites of Europe, of which there are many thousands—originally tens of thousands—ranging from the aforementioned labyrinths to giant megalithic monuments like Stonehenge. These remains, most of which date from what is commonly called the Neolithic or New Stone Age (roughly 4500–2000 BCE), have always presented a puzzle for archaeologists. In the case of a site such as Stonehenge, the sheer force needed to build it is almost unimaginable. According to one calculation it would have taken the whole population of Britain at that time, working for seven years, to raise the main circle and the central trilithons.[5] Furthermore many of these megaliths reveal immensely sophisticated mathematical and astronomical knowledge. So how were these monuments constructed? And who created them?

Over the centuries, antiquarians and archaeologists have puzzled over these remains and speculated about the nature of the people who built them. The more these monuments were studied by archaeologists, the more they had to raise their estimation of our Stone Age forebears in terms of technical knowledge and skills. In the 1960s and '70s, some particularly startling ideas about the megalith builders were presented by Alexander Thom, a retired Scottish engineering professor with a passion for archaeology. In his books *Megalithic Sites in Britain* (1967) and *Megalithic Lunar Observatories* (1970), as well as in numerous articles, Thom presented the megalithic sites as astronomical observatories, whose proportions were based on a unit that he called the megalithic yard, measuring just over 2.72 feet. If this unit was used all over Europe in Neolithic times, this would clearly have big implications for our understanding of the peoples of that period, since they must have had some shared standard of measure and highly accurate measuring techniques. This again would support the notion of an exodus from some original homeland, during which the fixed measure of the megalithic yard was carried by the people of the diaspora and consistently maintained in their disparate settlements.

Thom's theories were sensational in their impact and highly controversial, especially his theory of the megalithic yard. Archaeologists were sharply divided as to whether such a measurement existed, but subsequent investigation has yielded much evidence in its favor. Take, for example, the prehistoric site known as the Knap of Howar on the small island of Papa Westray in the Orkneys off the northeast coast of Scotland.[6] The site, consisting of two houses side by side connected by a passageway, has been dated to around 3700–3500 BCE. The British researcher Nicholas Cope who, together with Keith Critchlow, has made a detailed study of the Knap of Howar, interprets the two structures as representing a mother and child, joined by an umbilical cord, which he argues is borne out by the fact that the smaller structure fits exactly into the interior space of the larger one. He found that the proportions of the site all made sense when he used the megalithic yard as a measurement. Furthermore, he found that the golden section and the Fibonacci numbers are everywhere present in the dimensions of the buildings.[7] Thus, what appears at first sight to be two modest stone structures turns out to have deep levels of symbolic meaning and to have been built by people with sophisticated mathematical knowledge and the ability to measure with great accuracy.

Another Orkney site, Skara Brae, dating from around 3100 BCE, has yielded a remarkable find in the form of a series of petrospheres, stone balls measuring about 2.75 inches or 7 centimeters in diameter, with between 3 and 160 protruding bulges, the surface often etched with elaborate patterns. Many more such spheres have been found all over Scotland, with a particularly large concentration near the coast of Aberdeenshire. Some of them are now kept in the Ashmolean Museum, Oxford, where five of them were examined by the sacred geometry expert Keith Critchlow, who observed: "Of the five, three were carved of granite or a similar very hard stone, one apparently of sandstone and the fifth, the most complex, of an unrecognizable stone."[8]

The remarkable thing about these spheres, as Critchlow has pointed out, is that they embody the Platonic solids—that is to say, the five solid geometrical shapes that Plato believed to be the essential building blocks of the universe, as described in his dialogue in *Timaeus*. The five solids and their corresponding elements are: tetrahedron, four-sided (fire); cube, six-sided (earth); octahedron, eight-sided (air); icosahedron, twenty-sided (water); and dodecahedron, twelve-sided (ether or the quintessence of all the others). Plato describes the four solids corresponding to the elements, but deliberately avoids describing or naming the dodecahedron, as it was considered by the ancient Greeks to have special properties that should be known only to the initiated. Probably this had to do with the fact that the dodecahedron incorporates the golden section, the basic proportion running through the whole universe. Plato lived around 427–347 BCE, but the Scottish petrospheres are estimated to be from between 3200 and 1500 BCE, thus predating Plato by at least a millennium. These objects, Critchlow writes, are "clearly indicative of a degree of mathematical ability so far denied to Neolithic man by any archaeologist or mathematical historian." He adds: "Here we have the hardest stone found in Scotland being chosen to create beautiful mathematical symmetries for no apparent utilitarian use!"[9] One of the many mysteries about these spheres is how they could have been shaped and decorated so precisely using stone tools. Did the people of that culture perhaps already have the use of metal?

Further mysteries surround the numerous megalithic stone circles found in many parts of Europe. A good example is provided by the Callanish Stones, a complex of megalithic sites spread over a large area near the west coast of Lewis in the Outer Hebrides (Fig. 6). The main site is a ring of thirteen stones with a larger central stone. A cruciform pattern is formed by a long avenue and three shorter rows of stones radiating out from the circle. Construction of the complex is thought to have begun around 3000 BCE, making it older than Stonehenge, and it is estimated to have remained in use as some kind of ritual center for about 2,000 years. Alexander Thom and others have concluded that the site was a lunar observatory, designed to mark certain key positions in the moon's complex cyclical movements. The moon's orbit, as seen from the earth, moves up and down over two different cycles, and the Neolithic people evidently attached special importance to the times when it was at its highest and lowest positions. At one of these "lunar standstills" the moon, seen from a certain position in the Callanish Stones, seems to skim low, gently caressing a range of hills to the south. Moreover, with a little imagination, one can see the outline of the hills as resembling

6. The Callanish Stones, Lewis, Outer Hebrides.

the recumbent form of a female body. There is here both powerful symbology and high technical skill, a combination that can be found at thousands of other megalithic sites.

Even older than any of the above-mentioned sites—in fact the oldest known site of its kind in the world—is the solar observatory at Goseck in Saxony-Anhalt, Germany, discovered in 1991 and estimated to date from nearly 7,000 years ago. The original site consisted of a circular ditch and embankment, enclosing two concentric rings of wooden palisades, which have now been reconstructed. There are three entrances—to the north, southeast, and southwest. The latter two marked, respectively, the position of the sunrise and sunset at a certain time of year. Archaeologists believe that the observatory was used to determine the right times for sowing and reaping, and that the enclosure was also used for rituals.[10] The northern opening

BEYOND THE NORTH WIND

suggests that the North had a particular significance for the people who worshipped there.

Until recently archaeologists tended to explain the existence of these sites and the skills of the people who built them in terms of the "diffusionist" theory that all the essential technical attributes of civilization spread from the Near East to Europe. The problem with this explanation is that the above-mentioned sites and many others predate the civilizations of the Middle East. So we appear to be dealing with a mysterious, advanced prehistoric culture of the North.

From what we can see of the traces they have left behind, we can deduce quite a lot about the people of this culture. They appear to have practiced shamanism, judging from cave art showing human figures in animal costumes. They had a knowledge of astronomy, as indicated by the solar and lunar observatories that they built. They were good mathematicians, as witnessed in the petrospheres found in Scotland. Their buildings and artifacts show that they must have had accurate measuring instruments and standards of measurement (e.g., Thom's megalithic yard) as well as tools for cutting and shaping stone, wood, and other materials very precisely. We can guess that they were expert boatbuilders if we assume that they passed on their boatbuilding techniques to the Vikings, as I shall suggest in chapter 7. And they arguably had a sophisticated tradition of poetry, which I shall return to later.

All of this adds up to a level of civilization far above that which we associate with the Stone Age. So is that term perhaps a misnomer? We should bear in mind that the three-age system (stone, bronze, iron) was invented in the nineteenth century by the Danish antiquarian Christian Jürgensen Thomsen and is not sacrosanct, and in any case it varies from one region and group of people to another. In 2015, Danish archaeologists excavating in Greenland found evidence that prehistoric Inuit made tools and weapons from iron contained in meteorites. According to the Danish researchers, one meteorite fell in Greenland in about 8000 BCE and broke into several pieces weighing up to over thirty tons each. The pieces are now housed in the American Museum of Natural History in New York City, where they were deposited in the nineteenth century. The Danish archaeologists discovered that over many centuries the Inuit repeatedly chipped iron fragments off these boulders using basalt stones as hammers. They then used the iron to forge knives and harpoon blades. Admittedly the Danish experts dated this activity to a period from around 800 CE, but human settlement in Greenland dates from about 2500 BCE.[12] So it is surely conceivable that the Inuit discovered this technique much earlier. And if that were the case, then it is also conceivable that it was discovered by other prehistoric cultures, such as the one that I have just described.

On the other hand, if this mysterious people possessed no metal, it makes their achievements all the more remarkable. Who were these people? Were they perhaps the original Hyperboreans, who lived in the North before the Indo-Europeans, but left their mark on Indo-European culture as well as on other parts of the world through a diaspora and then disappeared as an identifiable entity?

We can imagine their legacy in terms of a metaphor that appears in Oswald Spengler's *Decline of the West*. Spengler writes about a phenomenon in geology where mineral crystals become trapped in a layer of rock. Over time, water trickles down through cracks in the rock and washes the crystals out, leaving their hollow forms behind. Then molten volcanic rock flows into these forms and cools down, taking on the alien form of the vanished crystals.[13] One could say that the new rock is shaped by the ghost of the crystals. Similarly it is conceivable that many of the symbols, myths, customs, and techniques that have been handed down to us bear the ghostly imprint of the Hyperboreans.

NOTES

1. Mark Nuttall, *Encyclopedia of the Arctic*, 473–75.
2. Website: http://www.arcticcentre.org/EN/communications/arcticregion/Arctic-Indigenous-Peoples.
3. See Eliade (1989).
4. Eliade, 261.
5. Critchlow (2007), 26.
6. See the detailed study on the site by Nicholas Cope and Keith Critchlow, *The Knap of Howar and the Origins of Geometry*, 2016.
7. The golden section or golden mean is the proportion 1:1.618. The Fibonacci series is a numerical sequence in which each number is the sum of the previous two. By proceeding through the series, dividing each number by the previous number, one approaches progressively closer to the golden mean.
8. Critchlow (2007), 177.
9. Critchlow (2007), 179.
10. https://en.wikipedia.org/wiki/Goseck_circle
11. See article in the Mail Online, January 14, 2015: http://www.dailymail.co.uk/sciencetech/article-2909898/Before-iron-Greenland-METEORITE-Age-Prehistoric-Eskimos-mined-giant-space-rocks-make-tools-weapons.html.
12. Ibid.
13. Oswald Spengler, *Der Untergang des Abendlandes*, Vol. 2 (Munich: C. H. Beck, 1922), 227.

CHAPTER 5

THE NORDIC WORLD AND ITS LEGACY

If there was once a Hyperborean culture in the North with a shamanic ethos, then it is likely to have included the common shamanic practice of using psychedelic drugs to induce altered states of consciousness. And indeed, we find that most, if not all, of the circumpolar shamanic traditions involve the use of narcotic plants such as fly agaric or *Amanita muscaria*, the mushroom with the distinctive red cap and white spots. Long ago human beings discovered that one way to imbibe the psychoactive component of the amanita was to drink the urine of a person or animal that had eaten the mushroom. This used to be a common practice among the Inuit[1] and apparently still is among the Sami of northern Europe, who feed the mushroom to reindeer then collect and drink their urine.[2] Today the favored scientific term for such psychoactive substances, when used for spiritual purposes, is entheogens (from the Greek, meaning "generating the divine within").

As the Nordic peoples also had a shamanic tradition, as we have seen, it is not surprising that we find disguised references to entheogens in the Nordic literature and mythology, as has been pointed out by the American scholar of religion Scott Olsen, who writes:

> Odin drinks from the well of Mimir, the Well of Memory, consumes the sacred mead (esoterically the psychotropic

Amanita Muscaria mushroom), and hangs inverted for nine days on the Yggdrasil tree entering into non-ordinary states of consciousness. Enduring this intense ordeal in an expanded and timeless (nonlocal) state of consciousness, he discovers the secret of the runes, the mathematical patterns of Nature. While riding on the magical eight-legged Sleipnir he descends on the winter solstice to seed the Amanita Muscaria. This same plant is none other than the Hindu Soma that transports the sage across the final divide. Its description in the Rig Veda leaves no doubt that the Soma is Amanita Muscaria.[3]

There are further details that confirm Odin's character as a sha-man. In order to obtain second sight, he sacrificed an eye by throw-ing it into the well or fountain of Mímir, one of the three fountains at the foot of Yggdrasil. He is accompanied by two wolves and two ravens, typical of the animals that function as shamanic totems or accompany shamans on their trance journeys, and he rides a horse called Sleipnir which has eight legs, another shamanic motif. Furthermore he could change his shape and perform weather magic, as the *Ynglinga Saga* tells us: "Odin could transform his shape: his body would lie as if dead, or asleep; but then he would be in the shape of a fish, or worm, or bird, or beast, and be off in a twinkling to distant lands upon his own or other people's business. With words alone he could quench fire, still the ocean in tempest, and turn the wind to any quarter he pleased."[4]

Olsen takes the Nordic connection with shamanism further and sees the symbol of the hammer of Thor (Fig. 7) as a representation of an amanita mushroom. Often the hammer is shown with a series of small dots, which he believes represent the white dots on the mushroom.[5]

7. Hammer of Thor pendant, based on an original found in a Viking grave in Sweden.

As Olsen points out, the shaman's trance can be a way of accessing higher knowledge and obtaining profound philosophical or scientific insights. He compares shamanism with the system of higher magic in the ancient world known as theurgy. According to one of its practitioners, Iamblichus (c. 245–325 CE), "the objective of the theurgist was to use ritual actions to resonantly identify with aspects of the Divine Source which was accomplished through recognition of the numinous cues, tokens or 'signatures' of the Divine present in our world, progressively ascending to the non-material 'ratios and proportions' that ultimately lead the soul back to the Divine Source."[6]

As a more modern example, Olsen mentions the Indian mathematician Srinivasa Ramanujan (1887–1920), who "confounded his colleagues by producing amazing continued fractions" through connecting with his family goddess Namagiri. "When the resonant connection was successful, he had visionary dreams of drops of blood that symbolized her male consort, the Lion-Man Narashima. Visions of scrolls then appeared with complex mathematical equations unfolding before him."[7]

Such visionary flights of illumination among the northern shamans could account for the appearance of Platonic solids in Neolithic Scotland, as mentioned in the previous chapter, and the complex mathematics of the megalithic sites, including the frequent use of the golden section. This kind of illumination might also be what Odin achieved through his ordeal on Yggdrasil when he discovered the secret of the runes, which, as we shall see in next chapter, have profoundly subtle mathematical dimensions.

Yggdrasil itself is also a shamanic symbol. It is so named because Yggr is one of Odin's names, and *drasill* means "steed" or "gallows." Yggdrasil encompasses nine worlds: the world of human beings, the world of the gods and goddesses, the world of the giants, the worlds of the light elves and the dark elves, the worlds of fire and water, the world of the dead, and the nether world of darkness and fog. The motif of the tree plays a role in many mythologies, often symbolizing the central axis of the world, the *axis mundi*, which connects different levels or realms. While in Yggdrasil there are nine worlds, more often in shamanic tradition there are basically three: the world of the gods, the everyday world we live in, and the underworld of the dead. Sometimes the tree is purely a symbol; sometimes it's an actual tree.

We find counterparts of Yggdrasil in many cultures. Sometimes it is symbolized by a tent pole, as with the Siberian shaman and the Native American medicine man. We find it also as the bodhi tree under which the Buddha obtained enlightenment. We find something similar in the Jewish Kabbalistic Tree of Life, and there is the interesting example in Chinese mythology of the Kien Mu tree, which grows at the center of the world and has nine branches reaching out to nine heavens and nine roots reaching out to nine springs where the dead have their abode. So it is very similar to Yggdrasil and possibly an example of the transmission of the northern tradition far beyond its original home.

There are various beings that dwell in Yggdrasil. There is a squirrel, Ratatosk, who carries messages up and down the tree. There is a cock, symbol of watchfulness and protection, who is perched at the top of the tree to keep a lookout for danger, the so-called Cock of the North (Fig. 8). This may possibly be the origin of the custom of putting a weather vane in the form of a cock on top of a church steeple.

Then at the base of the tree are three fountains or springs. One is the already mentioned fountain of Mímir, the god of wisdom. Then there is Hvergelmir, a swirling, bubbling spring which is the source of all the rivers of the world. And there is the fountain of Urd, which is associated with the three Norns or goddesses of fate: Urd, Verdandi, and Skuld, who correspond to past, present, and future.

8. The Yggdrasil or World Tree, copied by the author from a design on a runestone at Ockelbo, Sweden.

The names of the first two Norns are related to a word that occurs in various Germanic languages meaning "to be" or "to become." The Old English is *weorþan* (pronounced *weorthan*) and the modern German equivalent is *werden*. Thus, Urd is the past tense (in modern German *wurde*), i.e., that which became and therefore contains the future. Verdandi is the present participle (modern German *werdend*), that which is becoming. Skuld (cognate with the modern English word *shall*) represents the future. Since the past is the determining factor in fate, the name of the first Norn is also, in some languages, the word for fate itself (e.g., Icelandic *urðr*), and the fountain is named after her.

Urd and Verdandi are also cognate with a root word meaning "to spin" or, in a variant, "to weave." In Latin there is the related word *vertere*, meaning "to turn," and the Old High German word *wirtel* means "a spindle." This is in keeping with the notion that fate is a fabric that is spun and woven. Urd spins the thread, Verdandi weaves it into cloth, and Skuld cuts the thread when life's destiny has run its course.

The same root can also be found in the Old English word *wyrd* and the related modern English word *weird*, as in the English folklore tradition of the three Weird Sisters. In an article on this subject Nigel Pennick writes: "In medieval England William of Waddington (thirteenth century), Robert Mannyng of Brunne (ca. 1330), Geoffrey Chaucer (1385), and Bishop Reginald Pecock (ca. 1450) all acknowledged the Three Weirds as the sisters who shape human destiny at birth."[8] Most famously they appear as the three witches in Shakespeare's play *Macbeth*.

The fountain of Urd is also the place where unborn souls wait to be fetched by a stork, which places the soul in the womb of its future mother. This is the origin of the tradition that the stork brings babies into the world. In many places in Europe the story is told as the stork fetching babies from the local fountain or lake, which is obviously derived from the fountain of Urd. So the stork is a form of psychopomp, a being who either guides the soul into the world or to heaven at death or who guides the soul of the shaman during a trance journey. In the Old Norse language, the stork is called the Adebar or Odebar, meaning the bringer of the Od, an all-pervading life force, similar to the Taoist concept of chi or the Hindu *prana*. Od is also cognate with the Norse word *odr*, meaning "breath," from which comes the German word for breath, *Atem*. So the stork brings life energy into the world. In other parts of the world various other animals—and especially birds—have this function. In Hungary, for example, it is the swan that brings children into the world.

Another animal that features in Nordic mythology is the Midgard Serpent, a terrifying creature that lives in the ocean that encircles the world. The *Edda* and a number of other poetic sources describe how the god Thor goes out in a fishing boat, lures the serpent with an ox-head bait, and almost succeeds in killing it. Possibly this legend is based on actual sightings of mysterious sea creatures that have been reported from time to time in northern latitudes. In his book *Mythical Monsters*, Charles Gould states his conviction that the Midgard serpent "is only a corruption of accounts of the sea-serpent handed down from times when a supernatural existence was attributed to it," adding that "we have in the Sagas probably the earliest references to it."[9] Gould quotes a number of eyewitness descriptions of such monsters, such as the following one, written by the missionary and later bishop Hans Egede in his *Full and Particular Relation of my Voyage to Greenland, as a Missionary*, in the year 1734: "On the 6th of July 1734, . . . off the south coast of Greenland, a sea-monster appeared to us, whose head, when raised, was on a level with our main-top. Its snout was long and sharp, and it blew almost like a whale; it had large broad paws; its body was covered with scales

... and when it dived, its tail, which was raised in the air, appeared to be a whole ship's length from its body."[10] Gould includes a depiction of one of these creatures attacking a vessel, as printed in *Historia de gentibus septentrionalibus* (*History of the Northern Peoples*, 1555) by the Swedish ecclesiastic and cartographer Olaus Magnus. There is a strong similarity between that image of the serpent and modern representations of the beast, such as the one on the cover of the board game Yggdrasil (Fig. 9).

As the Nordic tradition spread into different regions, it became mixed with the local mythological traditions of those regions. Certain deities were emphasized more in some regions than others, and the tradition survived to different degrees, depending on how rigorously it was suppressed during the Christianization process. Let us look at some of the other ways in which the heritage of the Nordic tradition has survived and influenced European culture. One of the most obvious is that, in a number of European languages, certain days of the week are named after Nordic gods and goddesses. In English Tuesday after Tyr, Wednesday after Woden or Odin, Thursday after Thor, and Friday after Freya.

Then we have the Nordic alphabet, the runes, which we know were not just an alphabet, but also used for divination and magic. During Christianization they became increasingly taboo, but nevertheless survived in certain places well into the Middle Ages, and there are even many Christian monuments with runic inscriptions in Scandinavia and Britain, such as the Tunwinni Cross in Northumberland in England. And the mystique of the runes has lived on. An example is the story *Casting the Runes*, by the English writer M. R. James, written around 1900. The runes will be dealt with more fully in the next chapter.

The Nordic influence also survives in place-names all over northern Europe. Just to give a few examples in Britain: from Woden, the English form of Odin, we get names like Weedon and Wednesbury.

9. Cover created by Pierô Lalune for the board game Yggdrasil, produced by Z-Man Games, showing Thor fighting the Midgard Serpent.

And one of Odin's many names is Grim, meaning the "masked one," and from that we get the town of Grimsby and names like Grimsditch or Grim's Dyke. From the Nordic god Tir we have Tuesley, Tysemere, and Tysoe. And there are also many places named after Thor, the thunder god, such as Thunderfield, Thundridge, and Thorley. Places named after the goddess Hel or Holle include Holland as well as many locales in Germany such as Holbeck, Holbach, and Holberg.

The Snorri *Edda* tells us that Thor had two sons by a giantess called Jarnsaxa, whose names were Móði and Magni. We are told very little about them, but the names are probably cognate with the English words *might* and *main*—as in the expression "to do something with all one's might and main"—which again are related to two old Norse words *mott* and *megin*. In fact these are two variations of the same word, and if we go back to the original Indo-European root, we find the word *megh*, meaning something like "to be able" or "to have the power to do something." This is another example of how Nordic motifs are embedded in the English language.

Then there is the area of folk customs. Take, for example, the tradition of the Easter rabbit and Easter eggs. The origin of these lies again in Nordic mythology. The winter goddess Skadi travels on skis and has a hare as her animal—not a rabbit but a hare (the hare is generally larger than the rabbit and has longer ears). There is a Stone Age rock carving of her in Norway, showing her as a hare on skis (Fig. 10). In England one talks about the Easter Bunny, but in Germany they call it the Easter Hare. If the hare is the symbol of Skadi, what about the egg? The spring equinox is when the hens begin to lay again after their winter break, so eggs are associated with the spring goddess Eostre (or Ostara), from whom we get the name Easter. So rabbits or hares and eggs together symbolize the moment when the winter goddess hands over the season to the spring goddess. Another custom derived from the pre-Christian cult of Ostara still widely practiced in Germany at the spring equinox is the tradition of the

10. Prehistoric rock carving from Sweden thought to depict the goddess Skadi on skis.

Osterfeuer (Easter Fire), involving much drinking and merrymaking around an enormous bonfire.

In chapter 2, I spoke about labyrinths and the tradition of dances performed in a labyrinthine pattern. If, as I suspect, these dances have been handed down over many thousands of years, they could be a vestige of the Hyperborean culture. It's easy to imagine when watching one of the traditional dances of the Faroe Islands. Typically the dancers join hands in a long chain and move in a spiral, repeating the pattern of one step to the right, two to the left, while singing a song with a heavy, repetitive rhythm. Similar dances are found throughout Europe and Asia in many different variations. Another example is the farandole dance of Provence and Catalonia, which is said to be derived from the crane dance of Theseus on Delos. Possibly the crane dance in turn is derived from a Hyperborean source. The abundance of ancient labyrinths of the Cretan pattern in Scandinavia would seem to support that possibility.

Then there are customs involving the hammer as the symbol of Thor. In the *Edda* there is a story of how Thor's hammer was stolen by a giant, and he retrieved it by disguising himself as the giant's bride and having the hammer placed in his lap during the wedding feast.

Consequently, it used be the custom at wedding feasts in Scandinavia to place a hammer in the lap of the bride. And, at least in Sweden, this custom is now being revived. Ancient images in rock show the hammer being used as an instrument for solemnizing a ritual. Figure 11, for example, shows a very tall figure, holding up a hammer with which he appears to be blessing someone or something. The hammer has also evidently been a symbol of authority since the Stone Age, and there are numerous rock art images of figures with hammers. Today we possibly have an echo of this tradition in the gavel wielded by a judge or chairperson to bring a meeting to order.

Another way in which Nordic traditions have been preserved is through folktales and fairy stories. Let us consider that old favorite for children's pantomimes, *Jack and the Beanstalk*, which some folklorists believe to be derived from an ancient tale called *The Boy Who Stole the Ogre's Treasure*. The story goes that young Jack lives in a humble cottage with his widowed mother and a dairy cow, which is their only source of income. When the cow stops giving milk, Jack's mother sends him to the market to sell the cow. There he meets a man who buys the cow from him for a bag of magic beans. When

11. **Swedish rock image depicting an ithyphallic, hammer-wielding figure.**

he returns home, his mother is furious, throws the beans on to the ground, and sends Jack to bed without any supper. In the morning Jack wakes up to find that a giant beanstalk has grown outside his window overnight. He climbs the beanstalk and reaches a land high in the sky, where he comes to a castle and enters it. The owner of the castle, who is a giant, returns home, smells the presence of Jack, and growls out the rhyme:

Fee, fi, fo, fum,
I smell the blood of an Englishman,
Be he living or be he dead,
I'll grind his bones to make my bread.

While the giant is sleeping, Jack steals a bag of gold coins and returns twice more to steal a goose that lays golden eggs and a magic harp that plays itself. The giant wakes up and pursues Jack down the beanstalk, but Jack cuts through the beanstalk with an axe, and the giant falls to his death.

Pondering the giant's rhyme, it struck me that the first line sounds like a spell with the rune Fé, the first in the Futhark, used, among other things, when one wants to find something. In this case it is repeated in combination with different vowels—a feature of certain magical spells. The beanstalk is arguably another version of the shaman's pole, doubling as the World Tree, the *axis mundi*. Jack is then the shaman who ascends the tree into the world of the giants—Jötunheim in the *Edda*—the realm of the primal forces of the universe, where he has to undergo an initiation involving confronting a giant who threatens to "grind his bones." In shamanism bones are of great symbolic importance. Eliade tells us that "among the Yakut, the Buryat and other Siberian peoples, shamans are believed to have been killed by the spirits of their ancestors, who, after 'cooking' their bodies, counted their bones and replaced them, fastening them together with iron and covering them with new flesh."[11]

These are some of the ways in which the Nordic tradition has left its mark in folklore and folk culture. What about the literary transmission of the tradition? Original literary sources are rather few. The main source is the Icelandic literature, the *Edda* and sagas. Here and there other sources have survived by a sheer miracle. For example, one English manuscript about the god Wayland the Smith was found in the binding of a book that turned up in a bookshop in Copenhagen in the nineteenth century. And the only manuscript of *Beowulf* was nearly destroyed in a fire at a country house in England in the eighteenth century—fortunately it was only singed. But, as we shall see in chapter 11, in recent times a new output of epic literature has brought the northern deities and heroes to life again.

Let me turn now to another great branch of the Nordic tradition, namely in the Teutonic realm. First of all the actual word *Teutonic* is interesting. The mythology says that the grandfather of humankind was Tius (simply a variation of the Indo-European word for the Sky God Dyaus). From this name comes *Teutonic*, from which, with a slight variation the adjective *deutsch* is derived. Tius had a son called Mannus, and Mannus in turn had three sons who were the progenitors of the three great Germanic tribes: the Ingaevones, Istaevones, and Hermiones. And Mannus gave his name to the German city of Mannheim.

In the German-speaking lands the written records of the pre-Christian religion are scarce. There is no German equivalent of the *Edda*. One of the very few pieces of written evidence to survive is the so-called *Merseburg Charms*, two tiny texts of about nine lines each, dating from about 900 CE. One of them is a charm for freeing someone from chains. The other describes how Odin or Wotan and two goddesses heal Baldur's horse, which has put its leg out of joint. Although this is such a tiny fragment, it gives us a valuable insight into the mind-set behind it, because this again is shamanic. The horse is one of the traditional shamanic totem animals. It would have been quite normal for a shaman to treat an injured horse by pronouncing a spell over it. The importance of the horse as a sacred animal is demonstrated to this day by the German custom of having a wooden gable in the form of crossed horse heads, especially common in Lower Saxony.

I mentioned earlier the significance of the number seven in the Nordic mythology, and this crops up frequently in the Teutonic world. For example, in Grimms' *Fairy Tales*, there are seven dwarfs, seven-league boots, seven princes turned into seven ravens, and so on. And, if we take the tradition of the three Norns—which is in fact a reflection of a very widespread motif of a triple goddess—we find that it crops up in Germany, in the region colonized by the Romans, as the three Mothers or Matrones. In the Rhineland and the Eiffel there are many shrines to the Matrones, built in the Roman style, and people still leave offerings for them.

The motif of the World Tree is also writ large in the Teutonic world, and there are different variations on it. For example, the Saxons had their own version of the World Tree, which they called the Irminsul, which was cut down on the orders of Charlemagne in the year 772 as part of his Christianization campaign. Another tree that fell victim to Christianization was the great oak sacred to Donar or Thor, which stood at Geismar in Hessen. This was cut down in 760 by the English missionary Boniface.

We still have the tradition of the village tree today—and this is particularly strong in the German-speaking lands, where the village linden (*Dorflinde*) or oak (*Dorfeiche*) is a familiar feature in many villages. Both in the German-speaking world and in England we find the maypole, another incarnation of the World Tree, and there survives a strong tradition of dancing around the maypole on May Day. Yet another variation of the same motif is a custom that is very strong in Germany, although not in England, of the "topping-out" ceremony, the *Richtfest*, as it is called in German. This happens when a new house is nearly complete—that is, when the roof timbers are in place, but the roof has not yet been tiled. They choose that moment to erect what is called a topping-out crown (*Richtkrone*). This has the same basic form as the maypole: a wreath of pine branches encircling a wooden pole. One can see different levels of symbolism here. It surely represents the World Tree as well as male and female, but I believe it is also the axis of the earth, reaching from the south to the North Pole and out to the polar star and surrounded by the circle of the zodiac.

We find the motif of the tree again in the *Völsunga Saga*, where King Völsung has a great hall built around a vast oak tree. The saga describes how Odin, in disguise, comes and drives a magic sword into the tree and says that if anyone can pull the sword out it will make them invincible. Only one person can pull it out, and that is Völsung's son Sigmund. There is a counterpart of this event in the story of King Arthur, who proves his kingship by drawing a sword from a stone.

It is interesting to see how certain themes in Scandinavian mythology metamorphize in the Teutonic realm. Take for example the theme of the Nibelung treasure, which went through several transformations over time, including the version presented by Wagner in the *Ring* cycle. If we trace this back to the Old Norse literature, we find it is mentioned in the *Völsunga Saga*, which tells of a dwarf called Andvari, who lives in a river in the form of a pike and guards a treasure, including a gold ring of magical power. The mischievous god Loki steals the treasure including the ring, whereupon Andvari puts a curse on it, setting off a whole chain of misfortunes.

There is a different version of the story in the great German epic the *Nibelungenlied*, written in the thirteenth century. The Nibelungs were the royal family of the Burgundians, a Germanic tribe who at that time had their capital at Worms on the Rhine. The king of the Nibelungs has a treasure, guarded by a dwarf called Alberich, until Siegfried, a prince of the Netherlands, comes along and steals the treasure. Once again, Alberich puts a curse on it, and again a whole chain of misfortunes ensues.

Then in the nineteenth century Richard Wagner produced his own version of the story in his opera cycle *The Ring of the Nibelung*. Wagner studied the *Edda* and the sagas and took his material from several different sources, stirred it all up, and added his own input. In Wagner's story, the Nibelungs are a race of dwarves. Here again there is a treasure, but it lies at the bottom of the Rhine and is guarded by three Rhine maidens, who are daughters of the Rhine River itself. The dwarf Alberich steals the treasure from the Rhine maidens and makes himself king of the Nibelungs. Then Wotan (or Odin) steals the treasure from Alberich with the help of Loge (i.e., Loki), and again a whole tragic chain of events ensues, leading to the destruction of the gods, the *Götterdämmerung*.

The Rhine maidens are part of the whole mythology of the Rhine. They also appear as mischievous water sprites—beautiful women who sit on the riverbank, combing their golden hair and singing songs that lure young sailors to be shipwrecked on the rocks and drown. One of them was the famous Lorelei celebrated in the poem by Heinrich Heine and the song based on it. She has a rock on the Rhine named after her, and there is a modern statue from the 1980s commemorating the legend.

There is also a whole mythology in Germany connected with elves and dwarves. They are especially associated with mountainous areas where precious metals are mined, such as the Harz mountains, where the dwarves are thought to be the guardians of those precious metals. They are often portrayed as miners, wearing leather aprons and carrying lanterns, picks, and hammers. Typically they are depicted as elusive, quirky, mysterious, unpredictable, sometimes grumpy, but generally likable. They have appeared again and again in various forms in art, fiction, and film—from Grimms' *Fairy Tales* to Walt Disney's *Snow White and the Seven Dwarfs*—and they never lose their ability to engage and intrigue us.

NOTES

1. https://www.iamshaman.com/amanita/inuit.htm
2. http://andy-letcher.blogspot.com/2011/09/taking-piss-reindeers-and-fly-agaric.html
3. Olsen (2017), 16.
4. *Ynglinga Saga*, 7. http://www.sacred-texts.com/neu/heim/02ynglga.htm.
5. Lecture delivered at the New York Open Center conference "An Esoteric Quest for the Mysteries of the North," Iceland, August 2016.
6. Olsen (2017), 14.
7. Olsen (2017), 15.
8. Pennick (2007), 121.
9. Gould, 263.
10. Gould, 267.
11. Eliade, 159.

CHAPTER 6

THE RUNES

In the mossy dampness of a Swedish forest, an old standing stone rises up some three meters high. On the weatherworn surface, partly covered by lichen, some words are written snake-wise—up one side, down the other, and up the middle—in letters made up of vertical, horizontal, and diagonal lines, boldly chiseled in the stone and still clearly legible. The forms of the letters are austerely minimal, yet strangely beautiful and haunting, not to say magical. The inscription explains that the stone was raised by Rolf and Eskil for Livsten, their father, "who died at Skåne by Gårdstånga," and a present-day sign tells us that Gårdstånga was the site of a battle some thousand years ago.[1] In 1816, a farmer in Shropshire, England, ploughed up part of a Viking sundial from about the sixth century CE on which was written, in similar letters to those on the Swedish stone, words to the effect: "Let the pointer show you."[2] On my desk in front of me as I write is a miniature replica of a monument made of reddish granite found at Busdorf in Schleswig-Holstein, Germany, and now kept in the Viking museum at nearby Haithabu. Dating from about 1000 CE, it bears the following dedication, written in the same type of script as the other two examples: "King Sven raised this stone to Skarthi, his vassal, who had set out westwards, but died at Haithabu."

What all of these objects have in common is that they are inscribed in runes, the ancient alphabet of the Germanic peoples.

However, runes are more than an alphabet—they are simultaneously an oracle, a magical system, and a set of glyphs thought to represent universal principles similar to the function of letters of the Hebrew alphabet. Despite being widely frowned upon after the coming of Christianity, the runes survived in certain places as a living script until the eighteenth century and for decorative purposes even later, then were for a long time mainly the province of archaeologists, museum curators, and a few groups of dedicated enthusiasts (of which more later). Now, at the time of writing, they are back with a vengeance. They have become popular as a means of fortune-telling, a method of character analysis, a system of meditation, and even the basis of a kind of physical yoga. Aficionados can attend runic workshops and choose from an abundance of books on the subject. On the Internet they can visit thousands of runic websites and watch innumerable videos on the runes. In Russia, as we shall see later, the runes have attracted a huge following and a commensurate number of eccentric theories.

The runes are an important part of the whole mystique of the North, and it is worth reflecting on what we know of their history and development and why it is that they exert such a fascination in the present age. Let us start with the word *rune* itself, which possesses a number of possible meanings, one being a "secret" or "mystery." The name is apt, as the runes are laden with mysteries. The first mystery is where they came from. Some of the letters resemble prehistoric rock markings; others are more or less identical to some of the Etruscan, Roman, and Greek letters. There are also some similarities to the Phoenician alphabet. Scholarly opinions differ as to where they originated. They may have been carried north by Etruscan traders or by Germanic mercenaries who had served in the Roman army, or they may have arisen independently among the Germanic tribes. We cannot be sure, but a plausible theory is that they are based on north European rock markings, combined with letters adapted from the Graeco-Etruscan-Roman world. The earliest extant runic inscriptions are from about the middle of the second century CE. The original runic alphabet consists of twenty-four letters, arranged in three groups called *aetts* (from the Old Norse word for "eight") (see Fig. 12), and is known as the Elder Futhark—the word *Futhark* being derived from the first six letters: Fehu, Uruz, Thurisaz, Anzus, Raido, and Kenaz.

How did the runes arise? An alphabet, like a language, is usually the result of a long evolutionary process, but the runes appear to have sprung into being very suddenly around the first century CE, if scholarly opinion is to be believed. What are we to make of the already mentioned account in the *Edda* of how the runes were revealed to Odin as he hung on Yggdrasil? I would suggest the possibility that this is a mythologized version of a real event when some Germanic bard or groups of bards were inspired to create a set of symbols to describe the world, act as an oracle, and work magic. He, she, or they would then have shared this revelation with other bards, and so the runes would have been passed on from tribe to tribe.

12. The runes of the Elder Futhark (alphabet). The last two are often shown in the reverse order.

It seems most likely that the runes were a collective creation, as they constitute a far more complex system than most individuals could have conceived. The Norwegian researcher Halvard Hårklau has used sophisticated mathematical methods to analyze the runes of the Elder Futhark and has arrived at some astonishing results. His starting point was the observation that the runes are made up of a maximum of three kinds of stroke: vertical, right-leaning, and left-leaning. It is probably no coincidence that these are the three components of the "Pythagorean Y" (upsilon in Greek), used to symbolize life's course and the point where one has a choice between the virtuous and the decadent paths. By counting the number of vertical, right-leaning, and left-leaning strokes in each of the three *aetts*, he arrived at a grid of numbers in which the diagonals added up to twenty-five (Fig. 13). Proceeding further, he divided the runes into two groups: one consisting of the first, third, fifth, and seventh rune in each row, the other group consisting of the second, fourth, sixth, and eighth rune, again in each row. This yielded two further grids of numbers. Comparing the sums of the diagonals in the three grids, he saw that they added up to nine, sixteen, and twenty-five, respectively, i.e., the squares of three, four, and five—numbers which work for the theorem of Pythagoras (in a right-angled triangle the square on the longest side equals the sum of the squares on the other two sides). When he broke the Futhark down further into subgroups, he found all kinds of symmetries and proportions that could not have been the result of mere chance.

Perhaps the most striking discovery of all was a correspondence between the runes and the Chinese Ba-Gua divination system, which is similar to the I Ching but uses eight trigrams instead of sixty-four hexagrams. Finding the key to matching the runes to the trigrams involved creating number squares from particular groups of runes then doing a complex addition to yield threefold patterns of odd (Yang) and even (Yin) numbers. The resulting correspondences

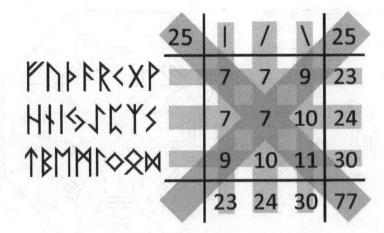

25	│	╱	╲	25
7	7	9	23
7	7	10	24
9	10	11	30
23	24	30	77

13. Numerical analysis of the component strokes of the runes, carried out by the Norwegian researcher Halvard Hårklau. The table shows the number of lines of each of the three types in each row of the runic alphabet. All the lines add up to 77, product of 7 and 11, the smallest and largest numbers in the matrix. Note that the matrix has symmetrical qualities.

between the runes and trigrams are shown in Figure 14. Halvard's account of how he arrived at this solution is highly interesting:

> Regarding the secret of calculating the Ba-Gua from the runes: First, I strove hard to find a solution based on hard maths. I had the intuition it must be a sort of correspondence, and that it should be based on odd versus even numbers. But for a long time, I did not find it. So how did I finally come up with the solution? One early morning, I was having lucid dreaming about the numbers in the matrices, and in this state I could see the solution. Half awake, I went into the office and plotted the formulas into my Excel worksheet—and found that it all worked out neatly![3]

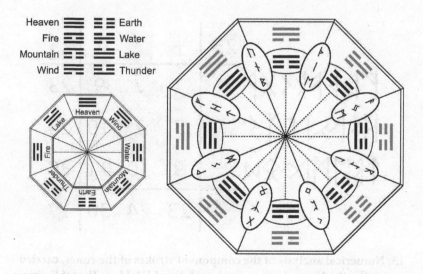

14. Correspondence between the runes and the trigrams of the Chinese Ba-Gua divination system. Halvard Hårklau discovered the key to the correspondences by creating number squares from particular groups of runes then doing a complex addition to yield threefold patterns of odd (Yang) and even (Yin) numbers.

The fact that such complex mathematics lies behind the runes is an indication that they were the outcome of a well-thought-out strategy and that highly sophisticated minds were involved in their creation. Furthermore, the striking correspondence with the Chinese trigrams raises the possibility that the creators of the runes were in touch with Asian traditions. Whoever created the runes, it is astonishing how rapidly and relatively uniformly they spread over a vast swath of northern Europe, encompassing the British Isles, Scandinavia, northern Germany, and extending eastward as far as the Black Sea.

Over time, however, certain variations developed. The Anglo-Saxon Futhark has twenty-nine letters, and in some developments of the runic alphabet there are as many as thirty-three. Later, in about the eighth century, a shorter runic alphabet consisting of sixteen letters was developed. This is now known as the Younger Futhark. Why it was invented is something of a mystery, as it had an insufficient number of signs to cover all phonetic sounds and this meant that in several cases a letter had to serve for more than one sound. Nevertheless, it came to be the standard runic alphabet throughout Scandinavia. As in the case of the Elder Futhark, we do not know who created the Younger, but it may have been the work of a group, possibly made up of representatives from different northern countries. The Anglo-Saxon Futhark has features in common with the other futharks as well as some variations.

The subsequent history of the runes is bound up with the tension between Christianity and Paganism. While runic inscriptions continued to appear on Christian monuments well into the Middle Ages and runic calendar staffs were still in use in certain places in Sweden until the twentieth century, the general tendency of the Christian Church was to discourage or forbid runes in favor of Roman letters. Probably this was not only because of their Pagan associations but also because of their reputation as a divinatory and magical system.

So to what extent were they used for divination and magic? The earliest piece of possible written evidence we have on this subject is provided by the Roman historian Tacitus in his treatise *Germania*. There he writes:

Augury and divination by lot no people practise more diligently. The use of the lots is simple. A little bough is lopped off a fruit-bearing tree, and cut into small pieces; these are distinguished by certain marks, and thrown carelessly and at random over a white garment. In public questions the priest of the particular state, in private the father of the family, invokes the gods, and, with his eyes towards heaven, takes up each piece three times, and finds in them a meaning according to the mark previously impressed on them.[4]

This was written around 98 CE, by which time the runes would have existed for about a century, if they originated as early as the year one, as some scholars maintain. Or possibly Tacitus's description predated the invention of the runes. In that case, what were the "marks" he described? There is no guarantee that they were runes. They might have been some other set of symbols entirely. Therefore, his description must be treated with caution.

There is no doubt, however, that the runes were used for magic, as there is ample evidence for this in both the *Edda* and the sagas. One of the poems of the *Edda* called the *Sigrdrífumál* (*Sayings of Sigrdrífa*) relates how the young hero Sigurd releases the Valkyrie Sigrdrífa (meaning "bringer of victory," an alternative name for Brünnhilde) from the armor in which she is encased. She then instructs Sigurd in rune lore. One verse reads:

Know the victory runes
If you wish to win.
Etch them on the sword-hilt,
Some on the guard,
Some on the blade
And call twice the name of Tyr.[5]

Sigrdrífa goes on to tell Sigurd how to use the runes to help women in childbirth, ensure a safe voyage, heal wounds, speak eloquently, and think cleverly.

There are also many descriptions of rune magic in the Icelandic Sagas. In *Egil's Saga*, the hero Egil is handed a horn full of poisoned ale at a banquet. He stabs his hand with a knife and writes some runes on the horn in blood, whereupon the horn shatters and the poison spills out.[6] In another passage he is called upon to help a sick woman and discovers, hidden in her bed, a piece of whalebone with a curse written on it in runes. He shaves off the runes then carves some healing ones and places them under the woman's pillow, causing her to recover.[7]

Thanks to the Vikings, the runes were carried far and wide—from Greenland to Constantinople, where there are runic graffiti dating from the ninth century carved into the stones of the Hagia Sophia, which was later converted to a mosque and is now a museum. They were probably the work of Norse warriors serving under the Byzantine emperor. After their heyday in the Viking era the use of the runes declined, and by about 1500 they had been largely replaced by Roman letters, except in certain country districts. For most of Europe they appeared to be consigned to a barbaric past that was considered best forgotten.

In the seventeenth century, however, came a new interest in things northern. The runes, which had long slumbered forgotten on their old stones under moss and lichen, now began to attract a different kind of attention from linguists, philologists, and antiquaries. A seminal author in this regard was the Danish physician and antiquary Ole Worm (1588–1654), whose name was often latinized to Olaus Wormius. Fascinated by the runic remains in his own country, Worm published a collection of runic texts entitled *Runir seu Danica literarura antiquissima* (*Runes, or the Oldest Danish Literature*) in 1636, and he followed this up with *Danicorum Monumentorum Libri Sex* (*Six Books on the Monuments of Denmark*), the first proper study of rune stones ever written. It contained many illustrations of rune stones that were subsequently lost.

Another Scandinavian who played an important role in the renewal of interest in the runes was the Swede Johannes Bureus (1568–1652), a royal archivist who became tutor and confidant of

King Gustav Adolph II. Bureus believed that there had been an ancient civilization in the North, possessing a precious Hyperborean tradition of wisdom, a kind of Nordic Kabbalah, which was encoded in the runes and had at some time in the past been transmitted southward and influenced all the main esoteric traditions of Europe. He even believed that the Christian revelation had been foreshadowed in the Nordic pantheon. So, for example, the Trinity was foreshadowed by the three Nordic deities Odin, Thor, and Freya.[8] Bureus created a composite runic symbol that he called the Adulruna, constituting a matrix from which all the runes could be derived.[9]

These Scandinavian scholars paved the way for similar work in other countries. In Britain a dedicated network of old-northern enthusiasts emerged. A leading member of this group was the prominent English clergyman and scholar George Hickes (1642–1715), author of, among other things, a massive work entitled *Linguarum veterum septentrionalium thesaurus grammatico-criticus et archaeologicus* (*A Grammatico-Critical and Archaeological Thesaurus of the Ancient Northern Languages*). Hickes performed a valuable service in this work by including the medieval *Anglo-Saxon Rune Poem*, which would otherwise have been lost to posterity, as the original has disappeared. The poem consists of a series of verses describing each of the runes in turn and explaining their meanings. Hickes's work was much admired among his kindred spirits and helped to fuel the growing scholarly interest in things northern.

In the eighteenth and nineteenth centuries, the revival of interest in the runes gained further momentum. In Germany, Wilhelm Grimm devoted several works to the subject,[10] and John M. Kemble, an English student of Grimm, wrote a seminal essay on *Anglo-Saxon Runes*.[11] George Stephens, an English scholar who emigrated first to Stockholm and then to Copenhagen, was an avid runologist whose magnum opus was *The Old-Northern Runic Monuments of Scandinavia and England*, consisting of four magnificent folio

BEYOND THE NORTH WIND

volumes full of beautiful engravings of rune stones and artifacts with runic inscriptions.[12] Stephens was decidedly anti-German and anxious to combat what he saw as German imperialism in Nordic studies. No doubt he would have been horrified by the scene in Wagner's *Ring* where Wotan's spear is engraved with magical runes.

Thus already the runes were beginning to be linked with national aspirations and to be misappropriated for political ends. This tendency became particularly marked in the German-speaking realm in the late nineteenth and early twentieth centuries with the rise of the ultranationalist "folkish" movement, whose adherents revered the runes as embodying the wisdom of an idealized early Germanic civilization. A seminal figure in this milieu was the Austrian writer and folklorist Guido von List (1848–1919),[13] who claimed that, at the age of fourteen during a visit to the catacombs under St. Stephen's Cathedral in Vienna, he had undergone a conversion to the old gods and made a vow that he would one day build a temple to Wotan. Later he became prominent in folkish circles and founded a Neo-Pagan movement that he called Armanism. In 1902, by which time von List was in his fifties and well known as the author of numerous articles, novels, plays, and folklore studies of a folkish tenor, he underwent a cataract operation, which left him blind for eleven months. During this period he carried out a prolonged meditation on the runes and apparently experienced a vivid revelation of their true nature and meaning. As a result of this experience he wrote a monumental work entitled *Das Geheimnis der Runen* (*The Secret of the Runes*), in which he argued that the true Futhark contained not sixteen or twenty-four but eighteen runes, which he based on eighteen verses in one of the poems of the *Edda* called the "Spell Song."

Up to his death von List remained a revered figure in the folkish movement, which rallied again after World War I and became part of the soil out of which the National Socialist (Nazi) movement sprang. During the Third Reich Heinrich Himmler and the SS made their own eccentric use of the runes, but the mainstream of the Nazi party, including Hitler himself, were scornful of the runologists and of Germanic Pagans in general. Alphabets flutter their way through time and space, and sometimes they come into the wrong hands. One can still point to political misuse of the runes, but the letters themselves cannot be blamed for that.

Today runic aficionados are reading reprints of Guido von List's works, discovering that, if one discards his more disturbing political views and takes some of his more dubious theories with a pinch of salt, there is much fascinating material. Von List's eighteen-rune Futhark is popular among many members of the runic community today.

Another alternative version of the runic alphabet was proposed in the 1930s by the Swedish philologist Sigurd Agrell, a professor at Lund University. In his 1932 work in German *Die spätantike Alphabet-Mystik und die Runenreihe* (*Alphabet Mysticism of Late Antiquity and the Order of the Runes*), he argued that the Fehu rune should come last, making Uruz the first letter. Hence Agrell's alphabet was called Uthark instead of Futhark. While not accepted by the mainstream of runic scholarship, the theory has been taken up by some modern runic practitioners such as the Swede Thomas Karlsson in his book *Uthark: Nightside of the Runes* (2002).

In my novella *Master of the Starlit Grove*, I wrote the following about the runes: "They were used not just for communication but for magic and divination. The Christian priesthood . . . labored fanatically to eradicate the Runes and introduce Roman characters. But many who had officially converted to Christianity continued to use the Runes for gravestone inscriptions, into which they cunningly introduced pagan symbols. Thus the runes survived. They were capsules of magical power, and subtly exerted their influence over the centuries."[14] In my story the runes are part of a Pagan egregore, a collective thought form created during the era of Christianization as a kind of ark to preserve traditions until the time came when Christianity receded. This of course is fiction, but anyone who has worked with the runes knows that there is a remarkable vitality about them as well as an extraordinary versatility.

Consider the many different ways in which the runes are used today. While very few people, apart from the most dedicated enthusiasts, would write a letter in runes, they have a distinct iconic value as a script. Thus one often sees them used for the titles of magazines and websites, woven into robes, carved into ceremonial staffs and tattooed on to skin. Their very archaic nature gives them an advantage over the regular alphabet for such purposes.

There is also their oracular function. Using runes as an oracle is based on the assumption that each rune represents a fundamental principle, a force, a human quality, an aspect of life, or all of these things. The first rune Fehu, for example, means literally "cattle" and, in a derivative sense, "wealth," since cattle were equivalent to wealth for the ancient Germanic peoples. The eleventh rune Isa, as the name suggests, means "ice" and hence a state of frozenness or immobility, whereas the twelfth rune Jera signifies a turning point. These three runes together, therefore, could signify assets which are for the time being bound up in property or in some other way frozen, but which will shortly be released through a change of circumstances. Some of the runes are vertically unsymmetrical and yield a negative meaning when upside down. Thus Fehu upside down could indicate financial difficulties. Rune-readers use a variety of different methods for divination, but a common procedure is the one described by Tacitus in *Germania*, as already quoted. Taking small, flat pieces of wood cut from a fruit-bearing tree and marked with the appropriate symbols, one throws these at random onto a white cloth. Then one offers a prayer to the gods and, looking up at the sky, picks up three pieces, one at a time, and reads their meaning from the signs on them.

Apart from their oracular use, there have been various efforts to develop a system of body movements and postures based on the runes. Whether they were originally used in that way is open to debate, but one possible piece of evidence is the Gallehus treasure: two gold horns found at Gallehus in Denmark and dating from about 400 CE. Apart from bearing runic inscriptions, they also depict human figures in strange bodily positions that could be based on the runes. One eager proponent of runic gymnastics was Friedrich Bernhard Marby (1882–1966), who wrote a series of works on the subject.[15] Marby was one of the followers of the Nordic path who fell afoul of the Nazis. Having survived the war and eight years in concentration camps, he continued his runic work until his death in 1966. Marby's admirer Karl Spiesberger (1904–1992) went on to develop his own complete runic system of mind/body/spirit practice, which included runic yoga as well as the use of the runes in meditation and as mantras.[16] Runic body positions are also included in *Futhark: a Handbook of Rune Magic* (1984) by the prominent American runologist and Odinist, Edred Thorsson (pen name of Dr. Stephen Flowers).

Thorsson/Flowers, who obtained his PhD with a dissertation entitled *Runes and Magic*, founded the Rune Gild in 1984, based in the United States but active internationally. It is centered around a rigorous curriculum of rune work, set out in his book *The Nine Doors of Midgard*.[17] As the author states in the preface to the third edition: "The fundamental work of the *Nine Doors* is that of internalizing the Rune-staves as an inner reality and mentally cross-fertilizing that newly installed symbolic pattern with mythic information drawn from a curriculum of readings in primary and secondary sources."[18]

In the 1990s a Norwegian living in England, Ivar Hafskjold, began teaching what he called Stav, a kind of runic tai chi encompassing body stances, a martial arts method, and a worldview. Hafskjold based the system on an inherited family tradition, extrapolated through the study of Japanese martial arts techniques during a fourteen-year sojourn in Japan. Stav has aroused controversy among runic and Nordic enthusiasts, some of whom have attacked it fiercely as being inauthentic. However, having studied it under Hafskjold's colleague Graham Butcher and having practiced the stances for many years, I can vouch for its beneficial effects.

The runes are used as meditational devices, incorporated into talismans, chanted as mantras, and employed in seasonal rituals and other ceremonies. One can find innumerable books and websites with advice on how to use the runes for such purposes. At the other end of the academic scale there are the university departments of Germanic studies, folklore, and archaeology, where scholars pore over old runic inscriptions and put forward competing theories about the origin of the runes. Sadly, many such departments have disappeared in recent years, but there are some encouraging developments, such as the Woodharrow Institute in Texas, run by Dr. Flowers, devoted to Indo-European and early Germanic studies, including runology.

The runes remain true to their name, a "mystery," but one thing is clear: they have a present and a future as well as a fascinating past.

NOTES

1. Seen by the author in July 2015.
2. Stephens, 114.
3. Quoted from private correspondence.
4. Tacitus, chapter 10.
5. My translation from the Old Icelandic. Tyr is the god of war and supreme bravery.
6. *Egil's Saga*, ch. 44. Smiley and Kellogg, 68.
7. *Egil's Saga*, ch. 73. Smiley and Kellogg, 141.
8. Karlsson, *Götisk kabbala*, 121.
9. Karlsson, *Götisk kabbala*, 140–41.
10. E.g., his *Ueber deutsche Runen* (*On German Runes*) (Göttingen: Dietersche Buchhandlung, 1821).

11. *Archeologia magazine*, Vol. 28, 1840.
12. London and Copenhagen, 1886–1901.
13. For a detailed discussion of von List and his ideas, see Goodrick-Clarke.
14. McIntosh (2014), 95–96.
15. E.g., Marby (1931).
16. Marby's and Spiesberger's books on the runes are at present only published in German. See Bibliography.
17. Revised and expanded edition, South Burlington, VT: The Rune Gild, 2016.
18. Edred Thorsson, *The Nine Doors of Midgard* (South Burlington, VT: The Rune Gild, 2016), iii.

CHAPTER 7

THE VIKINGS:
SAMURAI OF THE WEST

The city of York in northern England, formerly the Viking settlement of Jorvik, is host every year to the Jorvik Viking Festival, the largest event of its kind in Europe, held in February to commemorate the *jolablot* festival, when the Vikings celebrated the end of winter and the approach of spring. For a week the city goes Viking with a vengeance. In the shops and markets you can buy Viking apparel, Viking craft products, and Viking food and drink. There are workshops on everything from Viking falconry to archery and swordplay. The high point of the festival is a battle reenactment, in which two armies—typically Saxon and Viking—confront each other in a park in the city center by Clifford's Tower, the remains of a Norman castle. The majority of the combatants are men, but there are also some women, similarly armed and clad for battle. The two sides process onto the battlefield and take up their positions, making a forest of spears and banners. Helmets and chain mail glint in the winter sunlight, and swords are drummed against colorfully painted shields to heighten the martial atmosphere. Then with a roar the two armies charge at each other, and the scene dissolves into mayhem. It all looks and sounds very realistic, with swords clashing, spears thrusting, everyone shouting their heads off, and the ground becoming strewn with casualties, but everything is played according to careful rules so that no one gets killed or seriously hurt. When it's all over, the corpses stand up none the worse for wear and ready for a pint of beer or a hornful of mead.

Similar battle reenactments and other Viking events take place regularly in many other countries including Norway, Sweden, Denmark, Iceland, Germany, France, Spain, Poland, Russia, the United States, Canada, Brazil, Australia, and New Zealand. The participants are often members of societies dedicated to studying and evoking the Viking culture and way of life. Taking one example at random, l'Arbre Monde (the World Tree) is a group in the Rhône-Alpes region of France, founded in 2013. The website states that the members are "passionate about Scandinavian culture, especially the period of the Viking raids."[1] Activities include reconstructing as accurately as possible the camp life of the Vikings, giving demonstrations of combat techniques and explanations of the different types of weapon and armor, studying the Scandinavian mythology and the sagas, and holding workshops on various crafts such as weaving, stone and wood carving, jewelry making, and cooking.

Clearly the Vikings cast a spell that remains undiminished—or rather has undergone a renewal—a thousand years after their heyday and reaches far beyond their original Scandinavian homeland. Who were the Vikings? Interestingly, their name (probably derived from the Old Norse *vik*, meaning "a bay"), although employed in the sagas, did not come into general use until many centuries after the Viking age. At that time the raiders were referred to by other names, such as Norsemen.

What is it about them that exerts such a fascination? I suggest that part of the explanation coincides with the renewed popularity of the epic genre, which I shall return to in chapter 13. Epics have to do with the heroic, and humans have been telling stories about heroes and heroines since time immemorial. In Jungian psychological terms the hero is an archetype, that is to say, an inherited motif lying deep in the collective unconscious of humanity. It is an archetype that the modern, progressive, rationalist mind feels uncomfortable with, especially when it takes the form of the warrior. But, as Robert Moore and Douglas Gillette point out in their book about archetypes, *King, Warrior, Magician, Lover*: "We can't just take a vote and vote the Warrior out. Like all archetypes, it lives on in spite of our conscious attitudes towards it . . . If the Warrior is an instinctual energy form, then it is here to stay. And it pays to face it."[2] Viking reenactments are one way of engaging with this archetype.

When we gaze across time into the world of the Vikings, we catch a glimpse of something bold and adventurous that part of us wants to reach out to, something lacking in the modern industrialized world. Of course, there is much more to the Vikings than warfare and pillage. From the days of the terrifying Viking raids their image has gone through stages of being feared, vilified, admired, romanticized, idealized, dramatized, and reinvented as each age has created its own version of the legend. At the same time, through archaeological and historical research, more and more has come to light about their way of life and their remarkable achievements.

The dawn of the Viking age is usually considered to be around 793 when Norsemen from Denmark or Norway attacked the monastery of St. Cuthbert on the island of Lindisfarne, off the coast of Northumbria, slaughtering many of the monks, burning the buildings, and pillaging the treasures. An unfortunate beginning to any age, although in defense of the Vikings it has been speculated that the raid was in revenge for Charlemagne's massacre of some 4,500 Saxons at Verden in 782 during his Christianization campaign. Over the next three and a half centuries or so that their age lasted, the Vikings were known as bloodthirsty raiders, but also traders, settlers, and skilled mariners, who established colonies over a large part of the world.

Soon after the raid on Lindisfarne, the Vikings reached Spain. By the second half of the ninth century, they had put down roots in Iceland, penetrated into the depths of Russia, and from there made their way via the Black Sea to Constantinople. Around 900 they colonized Normandy, some decades later reached Greenland, and around

1000 established a short-lived settlement in North America. From Normandy, they colonized Sicily and part of the Italian mainland, where they established a brilliant courtly civilization that encompassed Christian, Jewish, and Islamic cultures. And in 1066, again from Normandy, it was the descendants of Vikings who conquered Britain. Such achievements belie the image of the Vikings as mere primitive barbarians. So what else can we find on the more positive side of the Viking record?

Let us look first at a characteristic that is not normally associated with the Vikings, namely their skill in poetry. The importance attached to poetry in the Nordic culture is attested by the story of the truce concluded after the war between the two groups of gods, the Aesir and the Vanir, as related by Snorri in the *Prose Edda*. Snorri records a conversation between Aegir, the sea god, and Bragi, the god of poetry. Aegir asks Bragi how poetry originated, and Bragi replies that the Aesir and the Vanir sealed their peace accord by both sides spitting into a vat. The account goes on:

> But when they dispersed, the gods kept this symbol of the truce and decided not to let it be wasted, and out of it made a man. His name was Kvasir, he was so wise that no one could ask him any questions to which he did not know the answer. He travelled widely through the world teaching people knowledge, and when he arrived as a guest to some dwarfs, Fialar and Galar, they called him to a private discussion with them and killed him. They poured his blood into two vats and a pot. . . . They mixed honey with the blood and it turned into the mead whoever drinks from which becomes a poet or scholar.[3]

The story goes to relate that the mead came into the possession of a giant called Suttung, who placed his daughter Gunnlod in charge of the precious liquid, which was kept in three vessels. Odin slept with Gunnlod and persuaded her to let him drink one draught from each vessel, but instead he emptied all three. Then he turned himself into an eagle and flew off to Asgard, where he gave the mead to the Aesir and to those skilled in poetry. From this story come various kennings (traditional Nordic metaphors) for poetry including "Kvasir's blood" and "Odin's booty." The story shows how poetry was regarded in Norse culture as the god-given stuff of life, a miraculous elixir made with great sacrifice out of vital fluids—spittle and blood—in a kind of alchemical operation.

The high value attached to poetry is something that the Nordic peoples share with the Japanese samurai, who were formidable fighters but also men of refined culture. One poetic form in which the samurai excelled was the "death poem," a brief reflection on the moment in one's life when death approached. A twentieth-century example in the samurai spirit is the death poem written on March 17, 1945, by General Tadamichi Kuribayashi, the Japanese commander in chief during the Battle of Iwo Jima, in which he is presumed to have been killed in action. In the poem, sent to Imperial Headquarters, the general apologized for failing to defend Iwo Jima against U.S. forces.

The Vikings had a similar propensity for composing poetry even in the thick of battle. Let me quote an example from the *Orkneyinga Saga*, written by an anonymous Icelander in about 1200. One chapter of the saga describes a sea battle between Earl Rognvald of Norway and Earl Thorfinn of Caithness in the north of Scotland. In Thorfinn's boat, along with his warriors, is his court poet Arnor of whom, we are told, he was very fond. The two sides close in on each other, each crew throws grappling ropes over the side of the enemy boat, fierce hand-to-hand fighting begins. In the midst of all this mayhem Arnor composes and declaims a poem:

I saw both my benefactors
Battering each other's men
—fierce was my grief—
Fighting on the Firth.
The sea bled, streamed dark
On the plank-nails, sobbing
With blood on the bulwark-
Shields of the boat.[4]

To compose a poem in such circumstances must have had the effect of investing the moment with a diamond-like sharpness and clarity—a quality that one senses in both the Japanese death poems and in the Viking verses composed in a dramatic or important moment. There are many such moments described in the sagas, involving not only battles but also many other types of event. Take, for instance, *Egil's Saga*. The hero, Egil Skallagrimsson, is an interesting mixture—fierce, rough-hewn, irascible, clever, brave, loyal. He is also an eloquent skald, who is always ready with a verse for the occasion, whether it be a feast, a funeral, a battle, or simply a moment of intense experience. Here he is describing the thrill of setting out on a voyage, as the wind fills the sail and the ship races along:

With its chisel of snow, the headwind,
scourge of the mast, mightily
hones its file by the prow
on the path that my sea-bull treads.
In gusts of wind, that chillful
destroyer of timber planes down
the planks before the head
of my sea-king's swan.[5]

This is also a fine example of the use of metaphors known as kennings: "chisel of snow" for the foam whipped up by the wind, "sea-bull" and "sea-king's swan" for the ship, "destroyer of timber" for the waves. The bards would have carried thousands of such kennings in their memories along with the knowledge of all the complicated rules of meter, alliteration, and poetic structure that were the stock in trade of the skald. Such poetry is not produced by a savage and primitive people.

Another way in which the Vikings left an important mark was in the field of law. The very word *law* comes from the Old Norse word *lög*, and the prefix *by-* as in *bylaw* is from the Norse *by*, meaning "town." Early on, the Vikings had a well-developed legal code, which is exemplified by the case of Iceland. As the historian R. I. Page writes: "Iceland had a sophisticated legal system based on the participation of its free farmers. A legal meeting was called a *thing*, and the great common moot for the whole of Iceland was the *Althingi*, held each summer . . . At the Althingi the free farmers met to record, form and administer the common law of Iceland, civil, criminal and administrative. Its presiding officer was the *lögsögumaðr*, an elected official who served for a number of years."[6] One such *lögsögumaðr* was Thorgeir, who in 1000 made the decision that Iceland should convert to Christianity. Today the leading council of the *Ásatrú* community in Iceland is called the Lögrétta (the law-giving group).

There is much more that can be said about the achievements of the Vikings. Their longboats were wonders of engineering for their time—sleek, clinker-built vessels, flexible enough to withstand fierce gales, able to sail close to the wind, and shallow-keeled so that they could navigate both rivers and high seas. They also made superb weaponry, as well as beautiful jewelry, as witnessed by the silver hoard dating from the late ninth or early tenth century found in 2007 near Harrogate, England, and now in the Yorkshire Museum in York. It contains 617 coins and 65 other objects—necklaces, arm rings, brooches, and a drinking vessel, all marked by fine workmanship. Equally impressive is the hoard of gold ornaments found at Hiddensee, north Germany, in the 1870s and dating from the late tenth century. The collection consists of a braided neck ring, a delicately ornamented brooch, and a set of several filigree pendants that appear to combine the motif of the cross with that of the Thor's hammer.

There is something mysterious about these northern wanderers with their subtle poetry, their superbly engineered ships, and their fine jewelry. Do we perhaps discern in the Vikings another echo of Hyperborea? In chapter 2, I have already mentioned J. G. Bennett's argument that, given the complexity of the proto-Indo-European language, it must have been devised under conditions of prolonged isolation such as would have obtained in the Arctic region at a certain period. Similarly, one could surmise that the people we call Vikings did not invent their poetic system and their shipbuilding and jewelry making from scratch, but developed them on the basis of knowledge inherited from the same civilization that Bennett suggests existed in the far North.

The curator of the Viking Ship Museum in Oslo, Knut Paasche, has said of the Viking ships displayed there, such as the Oseberg ship (Fig. 15): "When you look at a ship like this, you can see that they are not made overnight. It takes thousands of years' experience to make something like this."[7] Note that he spoke of thousands, not hundreds. That means we are talking about knowledge going back at least to the Bronze Age (c. 1800–500 BCE in Scandinavia) and possibly further. This is supported by the existence of Bronze Age cave art in Scandinavia showing boats of a design reminiscent of Viking ships.

Despite their technical achievements, the popular image of these northern seafarers was reflected in a prayer heard all over northern Europe during the Viking age: "From the fury of the Norsemen, good Lord, deliver us." This image remained the norm throughout

15. The Oseberg ship, a Viking vessel discovered in a burial mound near Tønsberg on the west bank of the Oslo Fjord, Norway, and now in the Viking Ship Museum, Oslo.

most of Europe for many centuries, but eventually memories of the raids faded, and the Norse voyagers were relegated to the periphery of the European consciousness. This changed dramatically in the nineteenth century. The scholar of Anglo-Icelandic studies Andrew Wawn points out in his book *The Vikings and the Victorians* that, at the time of Queen Victoria's coronation in 1837, the name of the Vikings would have been familiar to only a handful of people in Britain. "Yet, within fifty years, the word 'Viking' was to be found on dozens of title-pages—of poems, plays, pious fables, parodies, paraphrased sagas, prize essays, published lectures, papers in learned journals, translations, travelogues, scholarly monographs, and entries in encyclopaedias."[8] The Viking as a figure of romance had been born.

My first encounter with the Viking as screen hero was in the 1958 film *The Vikings*, starring Kirk Douglas and made by his own company, a violent story filmed partly in spectacular locations in Norway. This was, in fact, one of a long series of Viking films going right back to the silent screen era and continuing up to the present day. These include some that present a caricature of the Viking, such as *Erik the Viking* (1989), written and directed by Terry Jones and starring John Cleese, members of the Monty Python team. Also in the burlesque genre is the 2006 animated film *Asterix and the Vikings*, based on the Asterix cartoon series by René Goscinny and Albert Uderzo. Here the northerners appear as beefy, boneheaded, wing-helmeted ruffians who drink from human skulls. Subsequent films like *Northmen—A Viking Saga* and *Vikings: The Beserkers* (both 2014) perpetuate the blood-and-thunder aspect of the men from across the North Sea.

Clearly film audiences' fascination with the Vikings remains compelling, and one could fill more than one volume on this topic, but the Viking theme merges with the wider theme of the North in film, literature, and other media, which we shall look at more closely in chapter 13.

NOTES

1. https://larbremonde.wixsite.com/lgam.
2. Robert Moore and Douglas Gillette, *King, Warrior, Magician, Lover* (San Francisco: Harper, 1990), 75.
3. Snorri, 61–62.
4. Pálsson and Edwards, 64.
5. *Sagas of the Icelanders*, 107.
6. Page (2000), 175.
7. Rudgley (2014), 220.
8. Wawn, 3.

CHAPTER 8

NORTHERN MYSTERIES RESURRECTED

The image of the ancient "barbarous" North as a place of marauding tribes, primitive culture, and benighted Paganism was still the predominant one in Europe at the beginning of the eighteenth century, as seen in a poem entitled "The Temple of Fame" by the English poet Alexander Pope (1688–1744). Published in 1715, the poem describes a vision in which Pope sees the temple high up "on a rock of Ice." The structure has four gates, representing the four compass points, each adorned with suitable sculptures. Depicted on the western gate are Perseus, Theseus, Minerva, and other figures from Greek mythology. On the east side are the Magi, Zoroaster, the Chaldaeans, and the Brahmans. On the south is the world of ancient Egypt with its priests, obelisks, and hieroglyphic inscriptions. As for the North, here Pope becomes less flattering:

> Of Gothic structure was the Northern side,
> O'erwrought with ornaments of barb'rous pride.
> There huge Colosses rose, with trophies crown'd,
> And Runic characters were grav'd around.
> There sate Zamolxis with erected eyes,
> And Odin here in mimic trances dies.
> There on rude iron columns, smear'd with blood,

The horrid forms of Scythian heroes stood,
Druids and Bards (their once loud harps unstrung)
And youths that died to be by Poets sung.[1]

It is interesting to see that, although Pope knew about the runes and the story of Odin's ordeal on Yggdrasil, he was unable to rid himself of the disparaging view of the North typical of his era ("rude iron columns, smear'd with blood" and "horrid forms of Scythian heroes"). But even as Pope wrote these words, a different view of the North was emerging with works such as Bishop George Hickes's monumental *Linguarum veterum septentrionalium thesaurus grammatico-criticus et archæologicus* (*A Grammatico-Critical and Archaeological Thesaurus of the Ancient Northern Languages*), published in 1703–5, of which there will be more to say in the next chapter.

By the early eighteenth century, there were also a few small signs that the northern deities were beginning to awake from hibernation. They began to turn up in unexpected places, such as the park of Stowe in Buckinghamshire, laid out from 1718 for Richard Temple, Viscount Cobham (1675–1749) and later for his nephew and heir. In the midst of a carefully created Arcadian landscape, full of Palladian architecture and classical imagery, there stands the Gothic Temple. An imposing, turreted building in red brick, it is a testament to Lord Cobham's admiration for Germanic vigor and love of liberty, transplanted to Britain by the Saxon invaders. Over the entrance to the Temple is a quotation from Corneille's play *Horace*: "Je rends grace aux Dieux de n'estre pas Romain" (I thank the Gods that I am not a Roman). Surrounding the building (but now in a different position) were statues depicting seven Saxon deities corresponding to the days of the week: Sunna, Mona, Tiw, Woden, Thuner, Friga, and Seatern (the first, second, and last being attempts at Saxon versions of the Sun, Moon, and Saturn).

Over the course of the eighteenth century and into the nineteenth, a dedicated group of scholars and writers continued to produce work celebrating and emulating the literary heritage of the North. One of them was the English poet Thomas Gray (1716–1771), who in 1768 published two odes that were translations via Latin from Old Norse originals. One was "The Fatal Sisters," derived from a text in *Njal's Saga* describing Valkyries singing about the outcome of a battle. The second was "The Descent of Odin," based on the story of Balder and his dream predicting his own death. The "descent" of the title is Odin's journey into the underworld to reawaken a dead seeress and question her about Balder's premonition. Here is the first verse of the poem:

Uprose the King of Men with speed,
And saddled straight his coal-black steed;
Down the yawning steep he rode,
That leads to Hela's drear abode.
Him the dog of darkness spied,
His shaggy throat he opened wide,
While from his jaws, with carnage filled,
Foam and human gore distilled:
Hoarse he bays with hideous din,
Eyes that glow and fangs that grin;
And long pursues with fruitless yell
The father of the powerful spell.
Onward still his way he takes,
(The groaning earth beneath him shakes,)
Till full before his fearless eyes
The portals nine of hell arise.[2]

This emerging interest in things northern manifested itself differently from one country to another. In Britain, the North for many people meant the Celtic North, famously celebrated by the Scotsman

James Macpherson (1736–1796), who in the 1760s published a series of volumes of poetry purporting to be translations from manuscripts containing the songs of an ancient Gaelic bard called Ossian. Doubts about the authenticity of the poems were confirmed after Macpherson's death when it became clear that, apart from a few genuine Gaelic fragments, they were Macpherson's own creation. But meanwhile the poems had become a literary sensation, and Ossian was hailed as the Scottish Homer. These were not simple folktales but epic descriptions of heroic grandeur, conveyed in vivid and often eloquent language. They were seen as a triumphant rebuttal of the view that a "primitive" people like the ancient Scots were incapable of producing such poetry. Ossian thus helped to do for Gaelic culture what the *Edda* and the sagas did for Norse culture. Moreover, many Icelanders, enthused by the example of Ossian, were inspired to rediscover their own ancient literature.

The Ossian phenomenon stimulated a wave of Celtomania and a new admiration for the "folk" and their culture. The works appeared in translation in all major European languages and were admired by, among others, Lord Byron, William Blake, Samuel Taylor Coleridge, Johann Wolfgang von Goethe, the philosopher Johann Gottfried Herder, and the French writer and historian François-René de Châteaubriand. Even Napoleon was a fan. The Ossianic poem *Fingal* was his favorite reading, and he commissioned the artist Jean-Auguste-Dominique Ingres to create a series of paintings of scenes from the poems.[3] Ingres was one of many artists who evoked the world of Ossian in their works. Typically, the man himself was portrayed as a robed figure, seized by poetic frenzy, long gray hair and beard blowing in the wind, standing on some bleak clifftop by a stormy sea.

The new celebration of folk culture, which the Ossian poems helped to stimulate, went hand in hand with a romantic glorification of the nation-state and of national symbols, heroes, myths, and traditions, which came to the fore in Europe in the nineteenth century. Countries like Scotland and Ireland could celebrate their Celtic heritage. In England, despite the traces of Viking, Danish, and Saxon influence, and despite the dedicated coterie who admired the Norse sagas and Eddic poems, these did not provide the icons of national mythology. King Arthur and his knights held more charm in England than Odin and the warriors in Valhalla.

In Germany, the situation was rather different. The first German translation of the *Edda*, by Jacob Schimmelmann, was published in Prussia in 1777, and from then on Germany produced much excellent scholarship in the field of Scandinavian studies, runology, Nordic mythology, and the like. In the early part of the nineteenth century the tone was set by the Brothers Grimm, Jakob and Wilhelm. They are best known for their collection of fairy tales, but this was only part of their gigantic output. One of their first collaborative works was a new edition of the first volume of the *Edda* (1815). In 1821 Wilhelm Grimm published a pioneering study entitled *Über deutsche Runen (On German Runes)*, and in 1835 they published their joint encyclopedic work *Deutsche Mythologie* (German Mythology).

All of this fell on ripe soil in a Germany that was not so much a nation as a people in search of one. Even the loosely knit Holy Roman Empire of the German Nation had come to end with Napoleon's invasion, and so the map of the Germany lands looked like a china plate cracked into hundreds of pieces, large and small. A powerful national ethos with appropriate myths and symbols would be needed to glue them together. The working out of this ethos would lead in the twentieth century to an overweening nationalism that climaxed in the maelstrom of National Socialism. However, in case it should be thought that there is something inherent in the northern heritage that leads to political extremism, it would be as well to remember that the same heritage was innocuously celebrated in countries such as Sweden and Denmark, and out of a similar need for a renewal of their national spirit.

In Sweden, the way had been prepared in the seventeenth century by Olaus Rudbeck with his theory of a Swedish Atlantis and by Johannes Bureus with his mystical and eclectic conception of the runes, as mentioned in chapter 2. By the early nineteenth century, many Swedes were calling for a national renewal, and in 1811 a group of officers and civil servants founded the Götiska Förbundet (Gothic Association) to revive the freedom-loving spirit, bravery, and upright character of the ancient Goths.[4] The association published a journal entitled *Iduna*, after the Nordic goddess who guards the apples of eternal youth, and the members took on the names of Norse epic heroes and quaffed from capacious drinking horns during the meetings.[5]

A similar spirit pervaded the work of the Swedish artist Carl Larsson (1853–1919), who in the early twentieth century tried to start a project for a Swedish Pantheon in Uppsala, inspired by the Valhalla monument in Bavaria. This was to be partly a re-creation of the old Pagan temple at Uppsala and would have incorporated both Pagan and Christian elements. This is what Larsson wrote about the project:

> On one of the mounds at Gamla Uppsala a Pantheon shall
> be built. In this vicinity existed the old temple which,
> according to Adam of Bremen, was entirely gilded and
> housed the images of Frey and Thor. Outside it stood the
> sacred grove. Here all of the North used to gather, here at
> this admired sacred site. . . . For me, and probably for you as
> well, this place is still sacred. Let us bury our dead here! . . .
> It will be called *The Temple of Memory*, and the grove, which
> we'll cultivate once more, will be called *The Grove of Life*.[6]

Larsson failed to raise enough money for the project, so it never got off the ground, but he left a number of paintings with distinctly

Pagan themes, especially one called *Midvinterblot*, a vast canvas which hangs in the National Museum in Stockholm depicting the practice of sacrificing the king at midwinter to ensure the fertility of the crops in the following year.

A similar celebration of the Nordic heritage took place in Denmark, where one of its seminal figures was Nikolai Frederik Severin Grundtvig (1783–1872), most famous as the founder of the Danish Folk High School movement. Grundtvig, although a Protestant pastor and theologian, had a great admiration for the Nordic myths, which he saw as a prefiguration of Christianity. In his book *Nordic Mythology*, he projected elements of the mythology onto current events. For example, in the Schleswig-Holstein conflict with Prussia in 1840 he identified Denmark with Heimdall, the god who guards the rainbow bridge to Asgard and sounds a horn when danger is at hand. Thus Denmark became the Watcher of the North, whereas Prussia was identified with Fenris Wolf who is destined to destroy the world at the Ragnarök.[7]

These were some of the early signs of a revival of Nordic Paganism that essentially can be divided into two phases. The first phase, which played out in its most vigorous form in the German-speaking world, began in the nineteenth century, reached a peak in the 1920s and '30s, and largely collapsed in the Nazi period and World War II, although some strands of it continued into the post-war period and beyond. The second phase, which will be examined in detail in chapter 10, began essentially in the 1970s and has continued to the present day.

A crucial moment in the first phase was when the works of Richard Wagner (1813–1883) burst onto the German scene, causing a cultural earthquake whose tremors would be felt around the world. As mentioned in chapter 5, Wagner studied the old Scandinavian literature carefully and reworked the mythology to create his massive four-part opera cycle *Der Ring des Nibelungen* (*The Ring of the Nibelung*), consisting of *Das Rheingold* (*The Rhinegold*), *Die Walküre* (*The Valkyrie*), *Siegfried* and *Götterdämmerung* (*Twilight of the Gods*). The first part premiered in 1869, and the rest followed at intervals until the cycle was performed for the first time in its entirety in 1876 in the new Bayreuth Festival Theatre, paid for partly by Wagner's benefactor, King Ludwig II of Bavaria.

Wagner's mythical characters, as they appeared on stage in the early performances, have helped to shape our conception of what Nordic deities should be like: formidable, autocratic Wotan with his winged helmet, the stern Valkyries brandishing their spears and shields, the dwarf Alberich brooding in his gloomy cave. Today, as they appear in early photographs, they seem like parodies, and yet they presented the Nordic gods and goddesses vividly to the collective mind of the age. In a sense they were the Marvel Comic characters of their time, but on a deeper level they spoke to an atavistic longing that was widely felt in the German lands.

By the mid-nineteenth century, voices in Germany were calling for a new national religion to replace Christianity. Prominent among these was the orientalist Paul de Lagarde, the adopted name of Paul Anton Bötticher (1827–1891). Lagarde, however, offered no concrete alternative to Christianity. That task fell to various Neo-Pagan groups that began to emerge in Austria and Germany, especially in the years between the turn of the twentieth century and World War I. These included the Wodan-Bund (Wodan League), the Gesellschaft Wodan (Wodan Society), the Urda Bund (Urda League), and the Germanische Glaubensgemeinschaft (Germanic Faith Community). Many members of these groups also belonged to the Guido-von-List-Gesellschaft (Guido von List Society), founded in 1908 to further the study of the works of von List, such as his writings on the runes (see chapter 6).[8] For further reading matter, they had periodicals such as *Heimdall*, named after the Nordic watchman god, and *Iduna*, possibly inspired by the earlier Swedish journal of that name, as well as books like *Allvater (Wotan) oder Jehovah?* (*Allfather [Wotan] or Jehovah?*) by the Austrian writer Adolf Weber and published in 1906.

Politically this milieu tended to be bound up with what was known as the *völkisch* (folkish) movement, which perhaps needs some explanation. The adjective, which originally simply meant "belonging to the *Volk* (people)" began to be used in the nineteenth century in the sense of "national," and from 1900 onward it was increasingly applied to groups adopting a racial-chauvinist ideology. The role some of these groups played in contributing to the climate that led to National Socialism has been examined in detail by other historians, notably Nicholas Goodrick-Clarke in his classic study *The Occult Roots of Nazism*, first published by the Aquarian Press in 1985. It would be redundant for me to go over the same ground here. Instead I would like to focus on some of the other reverberations from this early Pagan revival in the German-speaking world.

A number of the avatars of this milieu were prominent in the cultural and artistic sphere. One of them was the artist Hermann Hendrich (1854–1931),[9] who was part of a movement to create a healthy, life-affirming art as a counterbalance to what was seen as the decadence of modernist art. This movement crystallized in the Werdandi-Bund (Verdandi League), founded in 1901 and named after the second of the three Norns of fate, the Norn of the present.

Hendrich had become enamored of the old Germanic gods, partly through a passion for the operas of Wagner—and here we see another example of how seminal Wagner's influence was. In addition to producing a series of paintings on Germanic mythological themes, Hendrich, in the spirit of Wagner's concept of the Gesamtkunstwerk (total work of art), created four temples, each of which combined art and sacred architecture with the function of a numinous space. Two of these were destroyed in World War II. The two that remain are the Nibelungenhalle (Hall of the Nibelungs) in Königswinter, built in homage to Wagner, and the Walpurgishalle (Walpurgis Hall), erected in 1901 on a spot called the Hexentanzplatz (Witches' Dance Arena), on a clifftop high above the town of Thale in the Harz mountains (Fig. 16). The Walpurgis Hall could well be part of a Wagnerian stage set. Its entrance portico, supported by massive pillars of crudely hewn stone, is dominated by a huge head of bearded, one-eyed Wotan/Odin wearing a winged helmet, flanked by his ravens and wolves. Inside is a series of paintings by Hendrich showing scenes from the Walpurgis Night episode in Goethe's *Faust*.

Hendrich found a kindred spirit in the writer Ernst Wachler (1871–1945), an activist in the Neo-Pagan scene and cofounder of the Wodan Society. Enchanted by the Walpurgis Hall and its dramatic setting, Wachler was inspired to create an open-air theater close by. The Harzer Bergtheater (Harz Mountain Theater), as it was called, was intended to use drama as a means of disinterring the spirit of the German nation, which had lain buried for centuries. It

16. The Walpurgishalle at Thale in the Harz Mountains, Germany, designed by the artist Hermann Hendrich and erected in 1901. It was intended to combine art and sacred architecture with the function of a numinous space. Photograph by Axel Seiler.

was inaugurated in 1903 with Wachler's play *Walpurgis—ein Spiel zur Frühlingsfeier* (*Walpurgis: A Play in Celebration of Spring*).[10] The theater still stands today, an impressive amphitheater overlooking the valley of the river Bode, and is regularly used for plays, operas, and musicals.

Another frequent visitor to the clifftop surroundings of the Walpurgis Hall was the painter, poet, and dramatist Ludwig Fahrenkrog (1867–1952). It was there in 1913 that Fahrenkrog together with kindred spirits, held a key meeting of the recently founded Germanic Faith Community in order to draw up a new constitution with guidelines regarding organizational matters, seasonal festivals, and rituals for confirmations, weddings, and funerals. The previous year in a different location Fahrenkrog was one of the organizers of a five-day Pagan festival that included an invocation to Wotan, probably the first large-scale Neo-Pagan ritual ever held in Germany. Fahrenkrog's organization, the Germanic Faith Community, is still active at the time of writing.

Today the old Germanic deities are once again celebrated in Thale in the form of the Mythenweg (Mythological Way), created in 2004, an itinerary through the town marked by a series of some thirteen sculptures of the various deities and figures of Nordic myth, executed by different artists in a variety of styles, ranging from traditional to semiabstract. Set in a park there is a graceful stone statue of the three Norns (Fig. 17), nearby there is Odin's eight-legged horse Sleipnir in filigree ironwork, and in a central position in front of the Town Hall is the Fountain of Wisdom with a larger-than-life-size bronze statue of Odin, pouring water from a drinking horn.

The old gods are also much in evidence at a place deep in the Lüneburg Heath near the town of Jesteburg. Here lies the remarkable Bossard Temple (now a museum), created by the Swiss-born sculptor and painter Michael Bossard (1874–1950) and his wife Jutta (1903–1996). Bossard acquired the property in 1911 and built a house and

17. Statue of the three Norns in a park at Thale in the Harz, Germany—part of the Mythenweg (Mythological Way), an itinerary created in 2004 and marked by sculptures of figures from Nordic mythology.

studio. After his marriage in 1926, he and Jutta, who was an artist and musician, set about creating a Gesamtkunstwerk in the Wagnerian spirit, comprising architecture, sculpture, painting, and horticulture. One of the main buildings is the Edda Hall with an interior decorated with murals, reliefs, and sculptures representing motifs from Nordic mythology. Many of the works depict Odin, with whom Bossard identified, his having lost an eye as a child from scarlet fever.

18. *Lebensbaum* (*Tree of Life*), a sculpture by the architect, sculptor and artist Bernhard Hoetger, which formerly hung on the wall of the Atlantis House in the Böttcherstrasse, Bremen, erected in the years 1930–31. It depicts Odin hanging on the Yggdrasil, the World Tree, to receive the secret of the runes. Photograph courtesy of the Landesamt für Denkmalpflege, Bremen.

A contemporary of Bossard was the industrialist Ludwig Roselius (1874–1943), inventor of decaffeinated coffee and a generous patron. His name is linked with the Böttcherstrasse in Bremen, an ensemble of striking brick architecture in what is sometimes described as an expressionist style built between 1922 and 1931. Roselius, like his architect Bernhard Hoetger, was enamored of the world of Nordic Paganism. One of the striking features of the street was a huge wooden statue of Odin hanging on Yggdrasil and surrounded by a circle of runes (Fig. 18). The statue was destroyed during the bombing of World War II and never replaced, but the rest of the street was lovingly restored after the war.

The Nordic-Pagan revival in Germany that I have described was devastated by the German tragedy of the midtwentieth century. Some fragments of it survived the war, but essentially a new revival, which I shall explore in chapter 10, began around the 1970s. The country that played the leading role in that revival was Iceland, to which the next chapter is devoted.

NOTES

1. https://www.poemhunter.com/poem/the-temple-of-fame/.
2. Posted on website https://en.wikisource.org/wiki/The_Descent_of_Odin ._An_Ode.
3. Herman, 283.
4. Feindt et al., 79.
5. Ibid., 81.
6. Michael Moynihan, "Carl Larsson's Greatest Sacrifice," in *Tyr*, No. 3, 2007, 225–26.
7. Feindt et al., 84–85.
8. For detailed information on these groups, see: Daniel Junker, *Gott in uns!* (Hamburg: Verlag 2002) and Nicholas Goodrick-Clarke, *The Occult Roots of Nazism* (Wellingborough: Aquarian Press, 1985).
9. See the article "Hermann Hendrich" by Thomas Lückewerth in *Heidnisches Jahrbuch* 2006, 197.
10. See Markus Wolff's article "Ludwig Fahrenkrog," in *Tyr*, No. 2, 2003–4, 225.

CHAPTER 9

ICELAND: THE NORTHERN SANCTUM

Iceland is a time capsule. It is as though long ago the gods planned that it would remain for centuries a half-forgotten place on the edge of the Arctic Circle, remote, difficult of access, hiding its mysteries. But around the seventeenth century, the time capsule gradually started to open up, and the contents began to go forth. They have been going forth ever since, and Iceland's cultural treasures have continuously enriched the world. If Iceland had never existed, we would have no *Edda* and no Icelandic sagas, there would be no *The Lord of the Rings*, no Marvel adventures of Thor, and I would not be writing this book.

Iceland has only been inhabited since relatively recently. Although a few Irish monks had lived there briefly in the eighth century, it was Viking adventurers who opened the country up for Scandinavian settlement. Sometime in the second half of the ninth century, a Viking named Floki set sail from Norway in search of a mysterious land that was said to lie somewhere in the North Atlantic. Just as the ancient Greeks used to consult an oracle before founding a new colony, so Floki, before leaving Norway, conducted an elaborate ritual (*blót*) before an assembled throng involving three ravens, birds sacred to Odin. At the place where the ritual had been held, he built a cairn of stones, indicating the profound importance attached to the ceremony, which involved the notion of the *hamingja*, the guardian spirit of the tribe or community. Then he and his crew set sail, taking with them livestock and supplies for a long stay. As the Danish scholar Wilhelm Grönbech (1873–1948) writes:

> He knew his way to the Shetlands and the Faroes, but as soon as the last reef had vanished from view he sent the ravens forth. . . . No other example among the Germanic peoples shows us so clearly the powerful human gift to unite one's soul with an external soul and to control the latter like a part of oneself. . . . The man drew the essential characteristics of the alien *hamingja* [i.e., presumably the *hamingja* of the ravens] into himself . . . while projecting himself into the other—and so the raven-man flew with unerring instinct over the sea.[1]

Thus the very first Viking expedition to Iceland was attended by an act of shamanic magic involving a shaman projecting his soul into a totem animal. After the three ravens had been released, one of them flew back to Norway, the second circled around and landed back on the ship, and the third led the way to the new land, which turned out to be verdant and relatively hospitable in climate. Floki and his men settled in and built a homestead. Unfortunately, distracted by the excellent fishing in the rivers and coastal waters, they neglected to make hay for the coming winter, with the result that all of the animals died. After two years Floki decided the time had come to return home. Before departing, he climbed a mountain, sighted some ice drift in a distant fjord, and decided to name the country Iceland, thinking that it would discourage further settlement.

He was wrong. Word soon spread about the pleasant and verdant island, and in 874 CE the first permanent settler, Ingólf Arnarson, arrived from Norway with his entourage. Nearing the coast, they followed an old Viking practice and threw overboard a pair of high-seat pillars, the decorated wooden posts that flanked the seat of honor in a Norwegian house. Wherever they were carried ashore by the waves would be taken as the best place to settle. This turned out to be a bay on the southwest coast, which Arnarson named Reykjavik (the Smoky Bay) on account of the steam from nearby hot springs, which he took to be smoke.

The discovery of Iceland coincided with a period of turbulence in Norway when King Harald "Finehair" was busy attempting by force of arms to turn the country from a collection of independent fiefdoms into a single kingdom under his rule. Many Norwegians left Norway for a new life in Iceland rather than submit to Harald's autocracy. Thus began a wave of emigration that continued for the next five centuries or so, initially from Norway and later from other places, notably Ireland, where the Vikings stopped en route to capture slaves.

The emigrants claimed land, established homesteads, and survived through fishing or keeping livestock. They could be violent and bloodthirsty when feuds arose, as often happened, but they had their own code of honor and legality, they placed a high value on hospitality, and they were fine craftsmen and poets. Their society was also remarkably democratic. In the year 930 they established a national assembly called the Althing (in Icelandic *Alþingi*)—from *al* ("general") and *þing* ("assembly")—which could arguably be described as Europe's first parliament.

The assembly was held at the Thingvellir (Place of the Thing), lying about forty kilometers northeast of Reykjavik, the present-day capital of the country. It is located in the middle of a long, narrow gorge that lies directly on the seam between the two continental plates of Europe and North America. On either side loom rugged cliffs, thrust up many millennia ago through the two plates pressing together. A waterfall, dropping down like a skein of shimmering white silk, feeds into a stream that runs for some distance down the middle of the gorge before feeding into the largest lake in Iceland, the Thingvallavatn, which stretches away to the south. Today's parliament is still called the Althing, but now has a building in Reykjavik.

It was at the Thingvellir in the year 1000 that the decision was taken for Iceland to become Christian. Previously Paganism had been deeply woven into the social fabric, customs, values, and way of life of the Icelanders. The most important and influential men in the country were thirty-six powerful landholders, who held the title of *goði* (pronounced go-thee), meaning roughly "priest-chieftain" (plural *goðar*). Their duties ranged from participating in the Althing to carrying out religious observances in their home districts, which would often have a Pagan temple where the *goði* would officiate.

What did the Pagan Icelanders actually believe? Perhaps the most fundamental element of their worldview was the belief in fate, which was profoundly connected to everything else in their lives. We have already encountered the Norns, goddesses of fate: Urd, Verdandi, and Skuld, who represent past, present, and future, respectively. Urd spins the thread of fate, Verdandi weaves it into cloth, and Skuld cuts the thread when death, the ultimate moment of fate, is at hand. The Norns sit beneath Yggdrasil by the spring or fountain of fate, which is named after Urd, since the past contains the present and the future.

In Old Norse, there are two words for fate, which have different connotations. There is *urðr*, named like the first Norn, signifying the trajectory of a person's destiny as is laid down at their birth, and there is *ørlög*, which means something more like the universal law or the general order of things. It is on account of *ørlög* that certain actions will lead to certain consequences. Hence the individual builds their own *ørlög* as they go through life. Thus *urðr* and *ørlög* are like the warp and weft of Verdandi's loom.

The Icelanders believed that each person carries his or her own destiny, which has to be accepted stoically. Hence they were constantly on the alert for signs and portents of what fate held in store. There were seeresses, the *völvar*, who could foretell the future and had an important role in Icelandic society. It is significant that the first poem in the *Edda* is the *Völuspá* (*Sayings of the Seeress*). There were also the runes that could be consulted as an oracle, and there were various uncanny phenomena that heralded a fateful event—for example the *fylgja*, a kind of tutelary spirit that accompanied each person throughout their lives, often in the form of an animal (here again we have a shamanic feature). The *fylgja* was normally invisible. When it showed itself, you knew that the person to whom it belonged was close to death. One example of this comes in *Njal's Saga* when Njal and his friend Thord are walking together and Thord sees a goat. "Methinks," he says "the goat lies here in the hollow, and he is all one gore of blood." Njal says that Thord must be a "fey" man, i.e., one near to death. "Thou must have seen the fetch that follows thee, and now be ware of thyself." Thord replies that being careful would do him no good "if death is doomed for me."[2]

The sagas are full of instances where the concept of fate plays a key role, and in some cases there are shamanic elements involved. *The Saga of the People of Vatnsdal*, for example, tells of a powerful Norwegian Viking called Ingimund, who has been told by a Lapp seeress that he will settle in Iceland. As proof of this she says that a silver amulet with the image of the god Frey, which he had been given by the king, is missing from his purse and now lies in a wood in Iceland at the place where he will settle.[3] Uncertain whether to believe the seeress, he sends for three other Lapps, who come specially from the North at his summons. The Lapps are shut away in a shed and spend three nights on a trance journey to Iceland, where they confirm the amulet is to be found. Ingimund then holds a feast and announces to the guests that he is going to Iceland "more because of destiny and the decree of mighty forces than out of any personal desire."[4] The saga goes on to relate that he duly went to Iceland, chose a site for his homestead, and built a great temple. When digging holes for the high-seat pillars, he found the amulet as prophesied.[5]

The importance attached to fate by the Icelanders affected their attitude to the gods, who were not called upon to intercede in order to change or mitigate the dictates of fate. Indeed the gods and goddesses themselves were subject to fate. They could, however, provide encouragement and guidance in meeting the challenges that fate presented. They were not remote, impersonal beings, nor were they free of moral failings. They were like respected elders of the community who were also personifications of qualities in the world and in human beings. Odin was the personification of wisdom; Frey and Freya of erotic passion; Thor of willpower, force, and drive; Loki of mischief and trickery.

For over a century, the majority of Icelanders remained Pagan. Christians were few and for the most part lived peacefully alongside the Pagans. Then toward the end of the tenth century, Christian missionaries began a concerted effort to convert the country. Iceland resisted until the year 1000, when the Norwegian king Olaf Tryggvason, a zealous convert, threatened to kill or maim all Icelanders living in Norway unless Iceland accepted Christianity. Under this pressure, the Icelanders convened a meeting of the Althing, and a much respected *goði* named Thorgeir was asked to make a decision. The outcome is described in *Njal's Saga*. Thorgeir spent a whole day meditating under a bull's hide, as the tradition was on such occasions, and came back with the decision that the country should accept Christianity. Worship of the old gods was to be forbidden, unless it was done in private.

Even that small concession was too much for the more zealous missionaries, and over the next few centuries they repeatedly tried to exterminate the old religion, but these attempts never fully succeeded. Iceland was far from the heart of Europe, orders from

Rome took a long time to arrive, and when they did, the Icelanders were clever at delaying their application. Furthermore, even some of the clergy were willing to compromise with Paganism to a degree. Nevertheless, over time the old beliefs went underground. They ceased to be part of any systematic religious practice, but they lived on in the hearts and minds of the Icelanders.

A number of things helped to keep the Pagan worldview alive in Iceland. One factor was the belief in the existence of the elves—the elusive, mysterious folk who inhabit the wild places of the country along with various nature spirits and guardians of the land. These beings are regarded half with fascination, half with wary caution. To this day many Icelanders believe that the Huldufólk ("hidden folk"), as they are called, become dangerous when their territory is infringed on by construction projects. There are even certain people who are prepared to negotiate with them to avoid this danger. One of the most famous of these in recent times was Erla Stefánsdóttir (1935–2015), who became the country's de facto envoy to the elves. As a result of her negotiations, building sites were shifted and roads diverted to avoid trouble from the Huldufólk. When I was in Iceland in 2016, I read in a newspaper of a case where a bulldozer had shifted a large boulder that turned out to have a special significance for the elves and it had to be carefully put back in its original position. On an earlier trip, I met a couple living in a remote area who had applied to build an extension to their house. When two building inspectors from the local authority came to call, one of the first questions they asked was whether there were any elves living on plot. As the answer was no, the inspectors went away satisfied and the permission was granted.

Traditions like that of the elves are deeply rooted in the soul of Iceland as is the Icelanders' love of their ancient literature, notably the *Edda* and the sagas, which have always had a sacred character for the Icelanders, so that when families emigrated they always took a copy of the *Edda* with them. The *Edda* (whose name is said to mean great-grandmother) is the main source for what we know today about the old Nordic deities.

There are essentially two versions of the *Edda*. One is the *Younger* or *Prose Edda*, often called the Snorri *Edda* after Snorri Sturluson, who composed it in the thirteenth century. Snorri was a larger-than-life character—a politician, wheeler-and-dealer, poet, historian, and libertine, who became caught up in a turmoil involving political intrigues, family quarrels, and an acrimonious dispute over a proposed union with Norway. In the midst of all this he managed to write, among other things, two great books: the *Prose Edda* and the *Heimskringla*, a history of the kings of Norway. The *Prose Edda* is basically a handbook for poets, combining accounts of the old myths and legends with quotations from an earlier collection of Icelandic poetry. This earlier source, which came to light in the seventeenth century, is now called the *Poetic* or *Elder Edda*.

Several versions of the *Poetic Edda* exist. The most complete manuscript, the so-called *Codex Regius*, was kept for centuries in Denmark along with other ancient Icelandic manuscripts such as the *Flateyjarbók*, containing a collection of heroic sagas. The presence of these manuscripts in Denmark was long a bone of contention between the two countries, but after long negotiations, the Danes finally agreed in 1971 to return them to Iceland. Their arrival by ship at Reykjavik was a cause for national celebration. When they were carried ashore, a brass band played, jubilant speeches were given by leading politicians, and a cheering crowd of thousands lined the harbor. It was a striking demonstration of how precious these writings are to the Icelanders. They are now preserved, along with other historical manuscripts, in the Culture House, an exhibition center in Reykjavik.

Snorri's *Edda* reveals the extraordinarily rich and complex poetic tradition of Iceland, with its kennings, its store of imagery and mythological references, and its ability to convey different levels of meaning at the same time.

Iceland's bardic riches were what really drew the country to the attention of the world. Admittedly it had been a trading partner with Europe since the Middle Ages, exporting fish, cloth, falcons, and other goods. Then in the sixteenth century there had been an abortive proposal for Britain to acquire Iceland, which by that time had become a colony of Denmark. The proposal was reconsidered in the eighteenth century with a view to using Iceland as a penal colony, but again the idea came to nothing.[6]

Meanwhile from the mid-seventeenth century, Swedish and Danish scholars began bringing the old Icelandic and other Scandinavian literature to light, using Latin as their scholarly medium. One of the most diligent of these scholars was the Danish historian Peder Resen (1625–1688), who published editions of the Snorri *Edda* as well as the *Hávamál* and *Völuspá* from the *Poetic Edda*, complete with Latin translations of the texts. Other Scandinavian scholars of around the same era produced Old Norse grammars and dictionaries, works on the runes, treatises on Nordic customs and antiquities, and the like. Soon their work stimulated similar efforts in other countries, including Britain, where Bishop George Hickes in 1703–5 produced a monumental work entitled *Linguarum veterum septentrionalium thesaurus grammatico-criticus et archaeologicus* (*A Grammatico-Critical and Archaeological Thesaurus of the Ancient Northern Languages*), a treasure-house of a book, comprising an Icelandic grammar, poetry in Icelandic and English translation, summaries of the sagas, information on runic inscriptions, and much else. It also included an Old English text called the *Anglo-Saxon Rune Poem*, thus preserving the text for posterity after the original manuscript had been lost.

Another seminal work was Thomas Percy's *Five Pieces of Runic Poetry* (1763), bringing together Icelandic texts taken from various sources, along with English translations. Percy's contemporary, the poet Thomas Gray (best known for his "Elegy Written in a Country Churchyard"), was inspired by the northern epic literature to write two "Norse Odes": "The Fatal Sisters" and "The Descent of Odin" (both published in 1768).

The British scholar of Old Norse literature Andrew Wawn has explored the remarkable way in which the northern sagas and epic poetry were taken up in Britain. He writes:

> It was Thomas Percy's *Five Pieces of Runic Poetry*, along with his *Northern Antiquities* (1770), and the splendid 1768 Norse Odes of Thomas Gray, which put the seal on the arrival of the old northern literary sensibility. These were the texts that rolled the pitch for the opening bowlers of Victorian old northernism, and established the canon of old northern texts that guided paraphrasers and imitators for most of the nineteenth century.[7]

One of these "bowlers" was George Dasent, professor of English language and literature at King's College, London. In 1861, he published his translation of *Njal's Saga* under the title *The Story of Burnt Njal*, which became, as Wawn writes, "the work through which many Victorian readers made their first acquaintance with the specifically Icelandic as opposed to Scandinavian old north."[8] Few works in the literature of the world can rival the human depth, epic sweep, and heroic grandeur of *Njal's Saga*, and its sensitive rendering by Dasent helped to give rise to a flood of writings on Iceland and the Vikings from the second half of the nineteenth century onward. These included scholarly works, novels, poetry, and travel writings.

Of the many nineteenth-century travelers to Iceland, two in particular are worth mentioning because of their totally contrasting reactions to the country. The first was Victorian England's

Renaissance genius William Morris (1834–1896)—poet, novelist, textile designer, printer, publisher, translator, and dedicated socialist—who visited Iceland in 1871 and again in 1873. Morris, emotionally shattered on account of his wife's love affair with his fellow artist Dante Gabriel Rossetti, sought and found solace in Iceland, its warmhearted people, its raw, unencumbered landscape and its beautiful, subtle language, which he knew well enough to be able to translate Icelandic literature. Starting in Reykjavik, he and three companions went around the coast and through the interior of the country, traveling on Icelandic ponies, identifying the sites described in the sagas, visiting the famous Geysir and its hot springs, and marveling at the beauty of the fjords, mountains, waterfalls, and glaciers. On the way, Morris kept a travel diary and wrote much poetry. Enchanted with Iceland, he returned there two years later. His love of Iceland and the North had been foreshadowed in his early poem "The Dedication of the Temple" (1855), which contains these lines:

> I cannot love thee, South, for all thy sun,
> For all thy scarlet flowers or thy palms;
> But in the North forever dwells my heart.
> The North with all its human sympathies,
> The glorious North, where all amid the sleet,
> Warm hearts do dwell, warm hearts sing out with joy;
> The North that ever loves the poet well.[9]

The year after Morris's first visit another English traveler went to Iceland, namely Richard Francis Burton (1821–1890)—daredevil explorer, soldier, spy, diplomat, and veteran of a famous pilgrimage to Mecca in the guise of an Arab. But not for Burton was the Iceland of poetry and legend, of gods and elves, of bards and seeresses and Viking heroes. Instead he wrote in minute detail about the climate, the geography, the geology, the architecture, the way of life, the clothes, the food. For example, here is his description of the standard footwear for men:

> It is a square piece of leather—sheep, calf, seal or horse—
> longer and broader than the foot; the toes and heels are
> sewn up, the tread is lined with a bit of coloured flannel,
> and the rim is provided with thongs like our old sandals.
> ... It is one of the worst chaussures known; it has no hold
> upon snow; it is at once torn by stone; being soleless, it gives
> a heavy, lumping, tramping, waddling gait; it readily admits
> water; and being worn over a number of stockings, it makes
> the feet and ankles look Patagonian, even compared with
> the heavy figure.[10]

How different from Morris's moody observations, yet Burton's account has its own fascination and is often witty. In their rough-and-ready hotel in Reykjavik, he and his companions were "serenaded by the monotonous croon of the nurse above" who sometimes broke out into the musical hall song "Champagne Charley"—"with the true British 'rum-ti-tiddy' style of performance."[11] Burton had not only a sharp wit but also a scientific mind. Where other travel writers might have been content to say that Iceland has some periodically active volcanoes, Burton observes:

> Let a piece of one of the igneous rocks be heated to
> redness, and permit the vapour of sulphur to pass over it.
> The oxide of iron is decomposed; a portion of the sulphur
> unites with the iron which remains as sulphuret; the liber-
> ated oxygen unites with the remaining sulphur, and forms
> sulphurous acid. Let the temperature of the heated mass
> sink below a red heat, and then let the vapour of water be
> liassed over it: a decomposition of the sulphuret before

formed is the consequence; the iron is reoxydised, and the liberated sulphur unites with the free hydrogen to form sulphuretted hydrogen.[12]

Meanwhile Iceland's volcanoes had fired the imagination of the French novelist Jules Verne, who featured one of them in his science fiction classic *Journey to the Center of the Earth*, first published in French in 1864, in English in 1871, and subsequently in many other languages. The novel tells the story of the Hamburg professor of mineralogy Otto Lindenbrock, who comes across a coded message on a piece of paper slipped into a runic manuscript of Snorri's *Heimskringla* (*History of the Kings of Norway*), which Verne erroneously calls the "Heims Kringla of Snorre Turlleson." The message on the slip of paper, when decoded, turns out to have been written by a sixteenth-century Icelandic alchemist with the improbable name of Arne Saknussemm, revealing that he has been to the center of the earth via a volcano in the Snaefells Peninsula in the west of Iceland. Lindenbrock and his nephew Axel travel to Iceland and, accompanied by an Icelandic guide called Hans, they climb the volcano and descend into the depths of the earth. After a long journey involving encounters with prehistoric monsters and various other perils, they finally emerge via the Stromboli volcano off the coast of Sicily. In the 1959 film version of the story the professor, played by James Mason, is a Scotsman, and his companion on the journey is Alec, his student at the University of Edinburgh. Later versions include a 1977 remake with Kenneth More in the role of the professor.

Iceland has continued to inspire fiction writers up to the present day. As I write I have before me a novel by the British writer Michael Ridpath entitled *Where the Shadows Lie*,[13] a riveting detective story involving several murders, a long-lost Icelandic saga, Tolkien's *The Lord of the Rings* and one particular ring of sinister power—all played out against the myth-laden scenery of Iceland. The novel is the first in a series called *Fire and Ice*, all set in Iceland. Another book on my desk is a German translation of another novel set in Iceland,[14] namely *Bericht über Sámur* (*Report on Sámur*[15]) by the Swedish writer and politician Per Olof Sundman (1922–1992), a tale of murder and feud in the manner of an old saga but set in the twentieth century. In Iceland itself, although there are disproportionately many writers in relation to the population, not many are internationally known. One of the few is Halldór Laxness (1902–1998), poet, dramatist, short story writer, novelist, and until now the only Icelander to become a Nobel laureate (he won the Nobel Prize for Literature in 1955). Another exception is Sveinbjörn Beinteinsson (1924–1993), farmer and poet in the ancient bardic tradition of Iceland. Sveinbjörn, however, is better known internationally for another reason, namely for his seminal role in the revival of the ancient Pagan religion of the North. The next chapter will describe this revival in detail.

NOTES

1. Grönbech, Vol. II, 201. My translation from the German.
2. Dasent, 80–81.
3. *Sagas of the Icelanders*, 205.
4. Ibid., 208.
5. Ibid., 211.
6. Wawn, 16.
7. Wawn, 24.
8. Wawn 142.
9. Quoted by Wawn, 249.
10. Burton, 376–77.
11. Burton, 368.
12. Burton, 67–68.
13. London: Corvus, 2010.
14. The others being *66° North* (2011), *Meltwater* (2012), and *Sea of Stone* (2014), all published by Corvus, London.
15. Berlin, GDR: Volk und Welt, 1979. Originally published as *Berättelsen om Sâm* (Stockholm: Norstedt, 1977).

CHAPTER 10

OLD GODS, NEW AGE

If there is one place that is most intimately linked with the revival of the old Nordic gods it is the Thingvellir in Iceland. It was here, as already described in the previous chapter, that in the year 1000 the Icelanders made the decision to accept Christianity, and it is here that the followers of Ásatrú, a present-day Pagan movement in Iceland, hold their annual Thing or Midsummer assembly.

In June 2003, I attended a particularly important Thing, which involved the installation of the present Allsherjargoði (chief goði, or priest, of Ásatrú), Hilmar Örn Hilmarsson, a long-standing friend. A crowd of followers and spectators, including press and broadcast media, watched from the grassy slopes of the gorge. Many of the followers wore Viking age costumes, and a forest of flagpoles with colorful banners had been planted in the ground, some bearing the symbols of the assembled goðar (plural of goði), others depicting the four guardian creatures of Iceland—bull, dragon, eagle, and giant—as the protectors of the four compass points of the country. The newly elected Allsherjargoði along with a dozen or so leading goðar all dressed in traditional costumes ascended a natural podium of rock facing the crowd. Torches and a fire bowl blazed in the soft, undying light of the northern summer. The goðar stepped forward in turn to give speeches of welcome and to read from the Edda and the ancient Icelandic laws. Then the new Allsherjargoði took his oath, drank from a mead horn, and delivered his inaugural speech.[1]

This event (Fig. 19) coincided with the thirtieth anniversary of the official recognition of Ásatrú as a religion in Iceland, an achievement largely due to the initiative of one man, Sveinbjörn Beinteinsson (1924–1993). A sheep farmer, born on the family farm at Grafardalur in the west of Iceland, he was also a renowned poet in the ancient bardic tradition. He published two volumes of his own verse and also wrote a remarkable guide to traditional Icelandic poetry composition, describing the many complex styles, metric forms, rhyming conventions, and so forth. Along with his seven brothers and sisters, he learned the art of *rímur*, the traditional way of chanting poetry, from his father and became the most famous *rímur* chanter in Iceland—there exist various recordings of him chanting verses from the *Edda* in a strangely hypnotic tone. An impressive-looking man with an enormous white beard, in his later years he became something of a star, appearing at rock concerts and featured on pop music albums.

Sveinbjörn's friend Jónína K. Berg, a leading *goði*, writes in an article about him:

> The poetry of those brothers and sisters from Grafardalur differs from person to person, but something that consistently shines through is an intense love of nature and the land, combined with a respect for its *landvættir* (protective spirits) and *huldufólk* (hidden beings). Like those entities of a parallel and often invisible world, the poets also become the protectors of our pure Icelandic water, air, soil, and our nature in general.[2]

Sveinbjörn believed firmly in the old gods and recounted that he had once met Odin himself while walking in the countryside.

19. Installation of Hilmar Örn Hilmarsson as Allsherjargoði (head of
the Ásatrú community in Iceland) at the Thingvellir in 2003.

While highly respectful toward other religions—his best friend and neighbor was a Christian priest—he often, as Berg writes, lamented the fact that the Icelanders had been forced to adopt something alien to their ancient roots, when they already had a tradition as beautiful and ethical as Ásatrú.[3]

In due course, he conceived the idea of forming a religious association based on the old beliefs and with the same rights and obligations as other religious confessions in Iceland. After initial discussions with a few close friends, he called a meeting of twelve women and twelve men at a hotel in Reykjavik on April 20, 1972—the first day of summer in the old Heathen calendar—to begin work on the project. Another meeting followed, at which the Ásatrúarféligið (Ásatrú Fellowship) was formally declared and Sveinbjörn chosen as leader, Allsherjargoði. Two months later at the summer solstice the members of the new association held a *blót* (Heathen ritual) at Sveinbjörn's farm, which aroused much interest among the press.

In December of that year, Sveinbjörn and his friend the poet Þorsteinn Guðjónsson visited the minister of justice and church affairs, having already sent him a letter requesting the legalization of Ásatrú. The minister received them politely, but evidently thought they were not serious. After asking them to provide further details and documentation, he walked them to the door. As they left the building, there was a sudden thunderstorm, and lightning struck an adjacent building, causing a power failure and plunging the ministry into darkness. As Berg relates: "Afterwards, people used to say both seriously and humorously that with this lightning the god Þor (Thor) was taking action because of the delay of the Ásatrúarféligið getting approved or legalized."[4]

Formal legalization followed in May 1973. This was accomplished without any constitutional change, as the constitution was found to contain a somewhat vaguely worded clause allowing for the recognition of Ásatrú—from the Danish word Åsetro, probably of nineteenth-century coinage, which until then had been rarely used and means roughly "loyalty to the Aesir" (one of the two groups of Nordic gods, the other being the Vanir). Using the name Ásatrú turned out to have far-reaching consequences, as it has since been adopted by followers of the Nordic religion all over the world.

It should be emphasized that Ásatrú, as exemplified in Iceland, is a religion of peace and tolerance. To quote Berg again: "Sveinbjörn said that he was hardly ever aware of any real animosity toward paganism or its background and the legalization. He and the Ásatrúarféligið have always tried to avoid extremists, never attacked other religions, never tried to convert others and never tried to tell others that Ásatrú is the only right faith."[5]

The present Allsherjargoði, Hilmar Örn Hilmarsson, joined the organization at the age of sixteen in 1974 when there were only some thirty members. At the time of writing, there are over four thousand, that is to say well over 1 percent of the population, and the number is growing steadily. The membership includes many prominent people including university professors, journalists, artists, writers, and politicians. The Allsherjargoði himself is an internationally celebrated musician and composer of film music, who has written the scores for such films as *Children of Nature*, *Cold Fever*, *In the Cut*, and *Beowulf and Grendel*. He actively performs on various instruments. The combination of avant-garde music with traditional poetry and ancient mythology is one of the exciting features of the present-day Ásatrú scene in Iceland.

Currently a new purpose-built temple is being constructed for the Ásatrú Fellowship. Designed by Magnús Jensson, himself a member of the Ásatrúarféligið, it is located on a wooded hill called the Öskjuhlíð overlooking a bay on the outskirts of Reykjavik. The temple is a streamlined structure, reminiscent of a Viking ship, with an annex for offices, lecture rooms, and other facilities. While incorporating sacred numbers and the golden section, the design is emphatically modern. It was felt that, if the Vikings were designing it, they would have wanted to use the best and most up-to-date technology available.

The Ásatrúar celebrate four main annual festivals, coinciding approximately with the equinoxes and solstices, as well as a number of smaller ones. The most important festival, at the summer solstice, is also the annual Ásatrú assembly, the Thing. There are also weddings and funerals, which the *goði* are legally empowered to conduct. In addition, the Ásatrú Fellowship provides spiritual care for people in an emotional crisis or suffering a bereavement.

While Iceland has played a central role in the modern renaissance of Nordic Paganism—particularly by having originated the name Ásatrú which would become the general designation for the religion—it was not the single source of the revival. By some process of morphic resonance similar movements began independently in other parts of the world, as though the old gods and goddesses had suddenly decided that they were ready to return or, to put it another way, the Nordic egregore had been reactivated. Thus from the 1970s onward, Nordic Pagan movements sprang up not only in Iceland but in Britain, the United States, Canada, Germany, Norway, Sweden, Denmark, France, Spain, and many other countries. The religion goes under a variety of different names from one country or group to another. These include Asatru or Ásatrú, Vanatru, Odinism, Germanic Heathenry, Norse or Nordic Paganism, Northern tradition, Anglo-Saxon Heathenry, among others. No single name is acceptable to all groups, but for convenience I shall tend to fall back on Heathenry. Although originally practically a synonym for Pagan, this term has come to be fairly widely accepted as a generic term for the worship of the old Northern deities, especially following the revival of the 1970s, which can be seen as part of a broader resurgence of Pagan and nature-oriented religious movements. For example, the Pagan Federation International (PFI) is represented in over thirty countries at the time of writing.

British anthropologist Richard Rudgley, who has written extensively about Heathenry and related movements, has called this revival the "second Odinic experiment,"[6] as distinct from the first one, which took place mainly in the German-speaking realm in the late nineteenth and early twentieth centuries, as described in chapter 6. In the interim there were a few manifestations of the earlier, folkish type of Odinism. One of them centered around the Australian lawyer Alexander Rud Mills, who was influenced by the writings of Guido von List. His Anglecyn Church of Odin, founded in 1934, was a curious combination of Odinism with a liturgy based on that of the Church of England. In a similar vein, and strongly influenced by Mills, was the Odinist Fellowship, founded in Canada in 1969 by the Danish émigré couple Else and Alex Christensen. There was also a small-scale continuation of some of the German folkish currents from before World War II. Essentially, however, the revival that began in the 1970s has represented a fresh start, generally unencumbered by xenophobic associations, notwithstanding a few extremist groups that flaunt Nordic names and symbols, often more out of a desire to *épater les bourgeois* than from a genuine understanding of the Northern tradition. Journalists often like to write about this faction because it makes better copy, ignoring the fact that this minority is by no means representative of Heathenry as a whole. As the American scholar of religion Michael Strmiska has written:

> The majority of modern Nordic Pagans are both enthusiastically devoted to Northern European cultural heritage and firmly opposed to Nazism and racism. The minority of Nordic Pagans with Neo-Nazi leanings are firmly denounced by most modern Nordic Pagans as members of fringe groups

that they wish to have nothing to do with. The pride in ethnic heritage felt by Nordic Pagans should not be mislabeled
as racism, nor should devotion to Nordic culture be flatly
equated with Nazism.[7]

By the 1970s, the New Age movement was also in full swing
and many people were searching for alternative forms of spirituality and could take their pick of any number of proffered ways to
wisdom and enlightenment: astrology, Kabbalah, Rosicrucianism,
Golden Dawn magic, transcendental meditation, Wicca, Thelema,
the Gurdjieff work, and other isms. While many followers of the
Heathen path would vehemently disavow any connection with the
New Age, there is no doubt that there was and is an overlap between
the two, and many people have come to Heathenry via one or
another of the New Age movements.

A case in point is Freya Aswynn, author of a seminal book on
the runes entitled *Leaves of Yggdrasil*[8] and a friend since our days
as neighbors in London more years ago than I care to count. As
she relates in the introduction to *Leaves of Yggdrasil*, she grew up
in the Netherlands and embarked on a spiritual quest in her twen-
ties. Having tried spiritualism and Rosicrucianism, she moved to
England in the early 1980s, joined a Wicca coven, and then became
involved in various magical groups in the Golden Dawn tradition.
"One day," she writes, "a young man who was a fellow member of
the coven took me down to Surrey to introduce me to a woman who
was considering joining the Craft. . . . This woman turned out to be a
dabbler in the runes and she offered to do a reading for me. She had
a series of flat pieces of clay on which the runes were inscribed and
a piece of paper on which their meanings were written. She invited
me to lay the runes out in a circle and as I touched them something
big happened. I knew with a powerful certainty that the runes were
mine." A few months later came the experience that finally led her

to embrace the Northern gods during a period when she was struggling with a relationship crisis. "I cried out to Wodan in my despair and he answered. From that moment on I was totally committed to his service."[9]

A very different path to the Nordic gods was followed by Stephen McNallen, founder of three successive Asatru organizations in the United States, most recently and lastingly the Asatru Folk Assembly. In his book *Asatru: A Native European Spirituality*, he writes that he decided to follow the gods of the Vikings around 1968 or '69. "This pagan epiphany," he explains, "did not spring from the leftist/hippy/Age-of-Aquarius counter-culture of the 1960s. Quite the opposite. I was attracted to the Vikings by their warlike nature, their will to power, and their assertion of self."[10]

He went on to found the Viking Brotherhood, which he believes to have been the first organization in the United States devoted to the elder faith of the Germanic peoples. It was recognized as a tax-exempt religious organization in 1972—that is to say, in the same year as the inaugural meeting of the Icelandic Ásatrúarféligið, but entirely independently of it. It was only in 1976 that he learned of the term Ásatrú from the book *Hammer of the North* by the Icelandic scholar Magnus Magnusson. "At last," he writes, "I had a name for my beliefs!" Soon the Viking Brotherhood became the Asatru Free Assembly. The latter was dissolved in 1986, and McNallen went on to found his present organization, the Asatru Folk Assembly (AFA).

While the AFA regards Asatru as a sort of Northern tribal religion, it would not be correct to describe it as ethnically chauvinist or supremacist. As McNallen writes: "Just as there is a Native American religion and a native African religion, so there is a native European religion—and Asatru is one of its expressions."[11] McNallen has made it clear that he does not rule out people of non-European background joining Asatru, but he would argue that it usually makes more sense to follow the religion of one's roots.

A more universalist view is taken by another American Asatru group called Hrafnar (from an Old Norse word meaning "ravens"), founded in 1988 by Diana L. Paxson, author of historical fantasy novels, many of which deal with Nordic Pagan themes, as well as books on Asatru, Odin, and the runes. The website of the organization states: "Hrafnar practices inclusive Heathenry. We welcome all, whatever their religious or ancestral background, physical ability, gender identity or sexual orientation, who wish a relationship with our Gods and Goddesses, their own ancestors, and the spirits of this land."[12]

A perennial debate exists between the various Heathen groups as to whether the religion should be inclusive or selective, tribal or universal, and fierce words of condemnation fly back and forth between opposing factions. Among the many Heathen organizations now active in the United States and elsewhere it is possible to find every shade of opinion on these issues.

One of the most influential U.S. Heathen groups is the Troth (originally the Ring of Troth), founded in 1987 by Edred Thorsson (the alias of Dr. Stephen Flowers) and James Chisholm. Like the AFA, it has a trained clergy who can provide counseling and carry out weddings, funerals, coming-of-age rituals, and the like. The Ring of Troth includes the Red Hammer program, which provides aid and support to victims of natural disasters and other tragedies. Flowers/Thorsson, author of many books related to the runes and the Nordic tradition, has also made a valuable contribution to academic work in this field. One of his initiatives is the Woodharrow Institute for Germanic and Runic Studies, a research and teaching establishment based in Texas, which publishes a scholarly journal of early Germanic studies entitled *Symbel*. The creation of the Woodharrow Institute has helped to shore up the declining old Germanic and Scandinavian studies in American universities, which had been weakening over the past half century or so.

Canada too has a flourishing Heathen scene with "kindreds" or "hearths," as regional groups are often called, in many cities such as Halifax, Toronto, Calgary, Edmonton, and Ottawa. One dedicated Canadian Asatruar, Daniel Updike, recalled in an interview how he came to Asatru.[13] As a child of four, he found himself one day spontaneously doodling some curious signs on a piece of paper, much to the anger of his fervently Christian father. Many years later in a bookshop he came across a book on the runes and realized that what he had drawn was part of the Anglo-Saxon runic alphabet. This led him into the whole world of the Nordic tradition.

Across the Atlantic in Britain, Heathenry took root early on. There the Committee for the Restoration of the Odinic Rite, which later became simply the Odinic Rite, was founded in 1973 by John Yoewell and John Gibbs-Bailey. It was they who compiled the set of principles called the Nine Noble Virtues, based on the *Edda*, namely: courage, truth, honor, fidelity, discipline, hospitality, industriousness, self-reliance, perseverance. These have since been adopted by Heathen groups all over the world. So, for that reason among others, the Odinic Rite has had a seminal influence.

Following the early example of Iceland, Britain, and the United States, Heathen groups have been formed in many European countries, often fragmenting into different factions on doctrinal grounds. In Sweden, for example, a split arose between one faction that insists on adhering as strictly as possible to the evidence available from the *Edda* and other original sources, and another group that sees their religion as part of a living and continuously developing folk tradition. There, as well as in Norway and Denmark, political differences have arisen within the Heathen community. In these three countries the standard designation for Nordic Paganism is from an Old Norse term meaning the "old way": *Forn Sed* in Norway and Sweden, *Forn Siðr* in Denmark. In all three the religion is now officially recognized, meaning that *goðar* can carry out marriages, funerals and so forth.

In addition, Denmark has taken a pioneering step in establishing a Pagan cemetery.

Another country that has seen a strong Heathen revival is Germany. This includes a modest survival of some elements of the prewar Heathen movement, as well as many new national and local groups that have sprung up as part of a wider Neo-Pagan movement in the country. These groups have for the most part successfully shaken off the chauvinistic associations of earlier times. They are vibrant, outward-looking, and ecumenical, as witnessed by their regular participation in the Long Night of the Religions (*Lange Nacht der Religionen*), an annual interfaith event in Berlin, alongside Catholics, Protestants, Muslims, Jews, Hindus, Sikhs, and many other religious communities.

The Heathens and other members of the wider Pagan community in Germany attracted attention in the media through a series of demonstrations held over several years from 2012 at the town of Fritzlar in Hessen, where in 724 the English missionary Boniface cut down an ancient oak sacred to Donar/Thor. In 1999, a bronze statue of Boniface, axe in hand, was erected in the Cathedral Square in the center of the town. One resident, who sympathized with the demonstrators, reported that on the day the statue was erected a mighty thunderstorm and a monsoon-like downpour broke loose, resulting in an avalanche from a nearby hill, which blocked the main road through the town.[14] Evidently Donar was not amused by the statue.

The aim of the demonstrators was to have a plaque or stone stele expressing the Pagan point of view on the destruction of the oak placed in the square. Accordingly, a letter was sent to the Hessian Ministry of the Interior and Sport requesting that such a sign be installed, bearing the message: "In memory of the ancestors and gods whose sanctuary once stood here. May the different religions in future live peacefully with one another." The ministry wrote back rejecting the request on the grounds that "the installation of the proposed plaque or stone in the Cathedral Square was not consistent with the purpose of the square nor with the views of the great majority of the citizens."[15] Correspondence with the Catholic bishop of the diocese had equally little effect. At the time of writing the campaign is on ice, but no doubt its time will come again.

The number of countries where Heathenry is represented is surprisingly large, as revealed by a Worldwide Heathen Census, carried out in 2013 by the German-American researcher Dr. Karl Seigfried.[16] The census, advertised on various social media sites over a three-month period, was extremely simple. Participants merely had to select their country from a drop-down menu and click "submit." Altogether 16,700 responses were received from a total of 98 countries. The survey revealed that, apart from the predictable results in Europe and North America, Heathenry was represented on all continents of the world. Who would have thought, for example, that there are Asatru followers in countries like Peru, Israel, Lebanon, Taiwan, and Zimbabwe? These findings rather belie the notion that Asatru is exclusively northern and xenophobic.

Let me now attempt to throw some light on what Heathens actually believe and practice. Any religion can essentially be characterized under four headings, which can be described as the "four Cs," namely: creed (the beliefs held by the religion), cult (the observances and ritual practices), code (the moral principles and rules), community (the things that bind the followers and the way they interact with each other). Here is a brief attempt to describe the essence of Heathenry under these headings.

CREED

Heathenry is polytheistic. It assumes the existence not just of one deity but many (see the appendix for a list of the Nordic gods and goddesses). Stephen McNallen makes a useful distinction between "hard" and "soft" polytheism. In the hard variety, the deities "are assumed to be real, distinct and separate" although allowing for "some sort of underlying unity or power." The soft variety, exemplified by Hinduism, teaches that the gods and goddesses "are manifestations of some greater and ultimately unknowable source."[17] One could also make a distinction between literal and metaphorical polytheism. Some Heathens believe that the gods exist in a literal sense as beings whom one might encounter, just as Sveinbjörn Beinteinsson recalled having encountered Odin during a walk in the country. Others take the view that they are metaphors for forces in the world and in ourselves. Others again would regard them as what the psychologist C. G. Jung called archetypes, motifs located in the collective unconscious of humanity. Yet another view is that they are thought forms or egregores, created by us human beings thinking and talking about them. All of these conceptions and many variations of them are to be found in Heathenry.

Similarly, there is a variety of ways in which the cosmology and cosmogony are interpreted, and it must be borne in mind that there is no single, unified account of these. Snorri's *Prose Edda* tells us that in the beginning there was a vast, formless place called Ginnungagap containing two contrasting elemental worlds of fire and ice. Out of the interaction of these came a giant called Ymir from whose sweat the progenitors of the giants were created. Ymir was nourished by a cow called Audhumla, who then, by licking rime-covered rocks, created a being called Buri, the grandfather of the gods. He in turn fathered a son called Bor, who married the giantess Bestla, and they had three sons who were the gods Odin, Vili, and Vé. These three killed Ymir, using his body to make the earth, his blood to make the lakes and seas, and his skull to make the heavens. From the maggots feasting on Ymir's flesh came the dwarfs, who became skillful artificers and made precious things for the gods, such as Odin's spear, Thor's hammer, and Frey's magic ship.

Human beings, it is related, were created from trees. One day three gods (Odin, Vili, and Vé in the *Prose Edda* or Odin, Lodur, and Hoenir in the *Poetic Edda*) were walking over the still deserted earth and came upon an ash and an elm, which they turned respectively into a man (Ask) and a woman (Embla), from whom proceeded the entire human race. In addition to gods and humans, there are also numerous other beings such as various nature spirits and the tutelary spirits known as *fylgjur* (fetches). Furthermore, the spirits of the ancestors are always present and can be communicated with, as can the elves and nature spirits.

The mythology also speaks of the cosmos as a vast tree, the World Ash or Yggdrasil, as described in chapter 5, with its nine worlds, its three springs or fountains, and the beings who live in and around it: the Norns, the messenger squirrel Ratatosk, the dragon Nidhogg who gnaws at the roots, the four stags who nibble at the leaves, and the cock who perches at the top and warns of impending danger. And it was through hanging on Yggdrasil that Odin obtained the secret of the runes.

Time, as described in the mythology, is cyclical. The entire cycle is described in the *Völuspá* (*Sayings of the Seeress*) in the *Poetic Edda*. After the world has been created by the gods, a golden age ensues. The early humans arrive and set about creating a civilization, building altars and temples, forging tools, and making precious jewelry. They also gather on a field called Idavöll to play games of skill. Then a war arises between the two groups of deities, the Aesir and the Vanir, and subsequently the enemies of the gods—the Fenris Wolf, the Midgard Serpent, and the fire giant Surt—attack in great fury. Everything descends into chaos and the world goes up in smoke. But after a while a new world arises, the earth greens again, the waters flow, and the ancestors resume their games on the Idavöll, and the eagle circles again in the sky.

What are we to make of this mythology? At first it sounds like a leftover from a childlike phase in the evolution of humanity, but it must be remembered that the Nordic bards were accustomed to expressing themselves in metaphors, using names that were clues to a deeper meaning. The Norwegian scholar Maria Kvilhaug (alias the Lady of the Labyrinth), in her writings and in a series of lectures posted on the Internet, has produced some highly interesting interpretations of the myths. For example, she suggests that the name of the giant Ymir is cognate with the Old Norse word *ymr* meaning "a big sound" and that Ymir is a symbol for the primal sound of the universe.[18] And, if one takes a Jungian approach, the Nordic mythology offers endless layers of meaning. Yggdrasil, for example, could be seen as a map of the human mind, with the root-gnawing Nidhogg representing the fears and traumatic memories that lurk in the unconscious.

The rationalist might ask whether Heathens really believe all the stories in the *Edda*, to which the Heathen might reply that Heathenry is not a matter of belief but of experience and that, if one approaches the mythology experientially, in a spirit of openness, it will yield important truths and insights.

CULT

Just as Heathenry is a matter of experience rather than belief, so the essential aspect for most Heathens is the active exercise of the religion through ritual and other practices. The general word that Heathens use for ritual is *blót*, meaning "offering" or "sacrifice." *Blóts* are held to mark the equinoxes and solstices and also on other occasions when the need arises, such as for handfastings (weddings), funerals, the blessing of children, and coming-of-age ceremonies. For preference they are held in the open air but can take place indoors if necessary. The form of the ritual differs from one group to another and depending on the purpose, but a seasonal blót might take its course roughly as follows.

The celebrants enter the ritual space and form a circle around a ring of stones within which a log fire waits to be lit. One of the group acts as *goði* (priest). Others are assigned various parts in the ritual. The *goði* or one of the other participants circumambulates the ritual space, raising a hammer of Thor at each of the four compass points and in the center and calling upon the spirits of each one to hallow the circle and keep watch. There follows a speech greeting the gods, goddesses, nature spirits, and ancestors and inviting their presence at the ritual. One member of the group is assigned to light the fire and does so while reciting some words honoring the fire element. A song or two may be sung as the fire comes to life. Then some words may be spoken on the subject of the seasonal festival being celebrated, and the appropriate deity or deities may be invoked. More songs may follow. Then comes the moment when personal offerings are made in the form of fruit, flowers, or other objects, which the celebrants have brought with them. Each places his or her offering in the fire while saying, if they wish, to whom or what purpose they are making the offering. A loaf of bread, sometimes in the form of a horse (as a symbolic sacrifice), is passed around. Each person eats a portion and throws a piece into the fire as a further offering. A mead horn circulates three times and each person can speak a toast or say some thoughtful words. The first round is for the gods and goddesses, the second for the ancestors, and the third for anything else one may wish to speak about. The gathering ends with some words of thanks to the gods, goddesses, spirits, and ancestors for their presence at the rite, followed by a formal closing of the circle.

Every seasonal ritual can be regarded as an opportunity for each participant to reflect and share their reflections on any significant things that may be happening at that season, and also to think about where they are in the greater cycle of their own life, what tasks and challenges they face, what things they are grateful for, and which deities are particularly important for them at that moment.

CODE

In Heathenry there is no religious authority looking over one's shoulder and threatening dire punishment or damnation in the hereafter if one commits some transgression or other. This does not mean that Heathens are amoral, but rather that they observe a shared morality, rooted in the traditions of their community and set out in certain texts such the Eddic poem called the *Hávamál*, meaning the "Sayings of the High One" (i.e., Odin himself). This contains a set of guidelines for living wisely and responsibly: be hospitable, cultivate friendship, give generously, don't drink to excess, "don't trust the ice until you have crossed it."[19] One of the most frequently quoted verses reads:

> Cattle die,
> Kinsfolk die,
> You too shall one day die;
> Yet the good name and reputation
> That you have earned
> Shall never die.[20]

Based on this text and others in the *Edda*, the Odinic Rite in England drew up the already mentioned set of Nine Noble Virtues—courage, truth, honor, fidelity, discipline, hospitality, industriousness, self-reliance, perseverance—which have since been accepted by Heathen groups in many countries. These are not the equivalent of the Ten Commandments but rather principles on which to base one's life in order to act courageously, truthfully, honorably, etc., in relation to one's fellow humans and before the gods.

COMMUNITY

The notion of community is important for Heathens, but is interpreted very differently from one Heathen group to another. For many practitioners it means the group with which they regularly perform rituals. For others it is what is known in England as the "pub moot" and in Germany as the *Stammtisch*, i.e., a regular gathering of kindred spirits in a pub, café or restaurant. It can also mean the Heathen or Asatru movement as a whole or the wider Pagan movement. Many Heathens feel themselves to be part of a worldwide Pagan community that includes the Native American medicine man, the African sangoma, the Siberian shaman, and the Cuban Santeria priest. Earlier in this chapter I dealt with the debate about whether the northern tradition can be shared by people whose roots are in other points of the compass. The answer is clearly provided by the survey of Dr. Seigfried, described above. The North now also calls to the South, East, and West. And we should remember that in countries such as the United States one individual may have roots derived from many different regions.

Let's now consider whether it is possible to revive a religion after more than a thousand years and, if it is possible, how it can be done and to what extent. Again, there are widely differing views on these questions. Some Heathens would regard their religion as a direct continuation from former times. Others would see it as a reconstruction or reinvention. Some advocate adhering strictly to the old sources; others believe in adapting them and introducing new elements. On the basic question of whether a revival is possible, let's consider the example of the prime symbol of Asatru: the hammer of Thor. The importance of the hammer is repeatedly emphasized in the *Edda*. In the poem called the *Þrymskviða*, for example, there is a story about how the hammer is stolen by the giant Thrym, who then demands the goddess Freya in exchange. Following a ruse thought up by Loki, Thor disguises himself as Freya and is accepted by Thrym as his bride. At the wedding feast the giant, following an old Nordic custom, orders that the hammer be placed in the lap of the bride as a fertility charm. Thor then promptly slays the giant with the hammer and returns home.

The use of the hammer in connection with weddings evidently went back many centuries. A piece of rock art discovered at Tanum in Sweden and dating from about 1000 BCE shows what appears to be a marriage scene in which a tall man with an enormous phallus is holding a hammer (or possibly an axe) over the couple, apparently in an act of blessing. At any rate, the practice of placing a hammer in the lap of the bride was followed in Scandinavia until the nineteenth century, and has recently been revived in Sweden, as mentioned in chapter 5. There are other uses of the hammer for ritual blessing or consecration, of which a number of examples can be found in the Old Norse literature. Therefore, it is entirely consistent with ancient tradition that Asatruar use the hammer of Thor today in consecrating a sacred space before a ritual, as described in our sample of a blót.

Another ritual object mentioned in the old literature is the oath ring. In the *Eyrbyggiasaga*, for example, an account of the settlement of the Snaefells Peninsula, there is a description of a Pagan temple with the following passage: "At its inner end was a room resembling what is now the choir in a church, and there stood a stone in the middle of the floor like an altar. Upon it lay a penannular ring weighing twenty ounces. On the ring all oaths must be sworn. The temple priest had to wear it on his arm at all formal meetings."[21] Such rings are commonly used at Ásatrú handfastings today. When the couple makes their vows, they and the *goði* all grasp the ring together and swear in the name of Vár, goddess of oaths and contracts.

Reconstructing the old religion from such elements is rather like putting together a jigsaw puzzle with some pieces old and worn and others missing. One has to fill in the gaps as best one can, with the help of research, guesswork, and a fair bit of imagination. The end result may be rather different from the original, but it is no less meaningful to the modern Heathen.

NOTES

1. See also my article "Iceland's Pagan Renaissance" in *Tyr*, vol. 3, 2007–2008, 249–58.
2. Jónína K. Berg, "Sveinbjörn Beinteinsson: A Personal Reminiscence" in *Tyr*, vol. 3, 2007–8, 263.
3. Ibid., 268.
4. Ibid., 270–71.
5. Ibid., 271.
6. Richard Rudgley, *Pagan Resurrection* (London: Century, 2006).
7. Michael F. Strmiska and Baldur A. Sigurvinsson, "Asatru: Nordic Paganism in Iceland and America" in Michael F. Strmiska (ed.), *Modern Paganism in World Cultures* (Santa Barbara: ABC-CLIO, 2005), 128.
8. First edition, London: limited edition by the author, 1988.
9. Aswynn, xii–xiii.
10. Stephen A. McNallen, *Asatru: a Native European Spirituality* (Nevada City, CA: Runestone Press, 2015), 61.
11. McNallen, 12.
12. https://hrafnar.org/.
13. https://www.youtube.com/watch?v=ppJ5usXICX8.
14. Report on the demonstration at http://www.voenix.de/press/Stimmen-zur-Aktion-in-Fritzlar-am-16-6-2012/27/index.html.
15. Ibid.
16. See the website http://www.norsemyth.org/2014/01/worldwide-heathen-census-2013-results.html.
17. McNallen, 12.
18. See her YouTube lecture on "Soundwaves and the Big Bang in the Poetic Edda": https://www.youtube.com/watch?v=evE6aLg-_Q8&list=PLxDBGYdDmm2n7-nYh49d9qMJRZB8Z1qSa.
19. *Hávamál*, verse 81, my translation.
20. *Hávamál*, verse 76, my translation.
21. Quoted in Page, 29–30.

CHAPTER 11

THE EAST TURNS NORTHWARD: RUSSIA AND THE NORTHERN SPIRIT

East is East and North is North, but the twain meet in Russia, which has a larger share of the Arctic coast than any other country. Russia is a country of soul-searchers. For centuries the Russians have been asking themselves the same questions repeatedly: Who are we? What are our roots? What are our virtues and vices? What is our relationship to God or the gods? Do we have a mission in the world? If so, what is it?

This mood of questioning introspection pervades Russian literature from Pushkin to Solzhenitsyn. Bolshevism sought to present itself as the final answer and convince its subjects that no further soul-searching was necessary. Then came the great upheaval of the 1990s, and suddenly a thousand different isms became available to fill the spiritual vacuum left by the fall of communism. These present a bewildering picture, in which religion, spirituality, ideology, and politics are often mixed up together and the old boundaries—right/left, capitalist/socialist, nationalist/internationalist, traditionalist/radical—are no longer hard and fast. The scene is like a constantly shifting kaleidoscope, but I shall attempt to provide at least a swift impression of it and how the theme of the North fits in.

The Russians are pursuing various different paths in their attempts to discover or rediscover a sense of meaning and identity. Some are turning to the Orthodox Church, which once again has full congregations and a respected place in the life of the nation. Others look back nostalgically to the Soviet days, parading through the streets with portraits of Stalin, while in Red Square uniformed guards stand reverently beside the embalmed body of Lenin like priests bravely perpetuating some long-obsolete cult. Another group is turning to a variety of alternative forms of spirituality such as Theosophy, Buddhism, Rosicrucianism, Freemasonry, and the teachings of Nikolai and Helena Roerich. And yet another group looks much further back into the past—to pre-Christian times and the earliest settlement of the Russian territories. These are of course crude categories, and there is a good deal of overlap between them. The theme of nationalism is one that is very pervasive in the whole Russian discourse about the search for meaning, and this applies particularly to the last group that I have mentioned. To understand these developments, we must make a brief excursion into Russian history.

Long before Russia there was Scythia, the name given by the Greeks to a kingdom that reached its height around the fourth century BCE. Its heartland was located roughly in what is now Ukraine, but at one time it had an empire that extended from the Black Sea to Central Asia and from the Urals to the Persian Gulf. Scythia's partly nomadic people were ferocious and often cruel (the Greek historian Herodotus describes how they blinded their slaves), but they were formidable horsemen and superb jewelers and goldsmiths, and their kingdom was efficiently administered.

The Scythians disappeared from history in around the second century BCE—or did they? In today's Russia, there are those who look back with admiration to the Scythians and believe that Russia urgently needs a revival of the Scythian spirit. A group calling itself the New Scythians takes inspiration from the work of the ethnologist Lev Nikolaevich Gumilev (1912–1992), author of a magnum opus called *Ethnogenesis and the Earth's Biosphere*. The essence of Gumilev's theory is that each of the world's peoples has a life cycle of some 1,200–1,500 years, beginning with the impact of some passionate idea or impulse, which causes the formation of an "ethnos"—or "superethnos" in the case of a group of peoples possessing ties and common causes. There follows a period of flourishing and then of decline and collapse. When a new ethnos arises, it can draw inspiration from remembering the glorious achievements of its predecessors, which it can take over and further develop.

Gumilev is considered one of the seminal thinkers of Eurasianism, a movement which argues that Russia should be part of a community of sovereign nations stretching from the Baltic to the Pacific. The most prominent advocate of Eurasianism is Alexander Dugin (b. 1962), one of Russia's leading political philosophers and a highly influential figure. Dugin, who has over the years developed from a rebellious hippie into a radical conservative, is widely seen in the West as a guru of the right, but in fact he cannot be so easily categorized. Labels that are common currency in the West can easily come unstuck in the topsy-turvy Russian political scene. Dugin seeks to invoke Hyperborea as part of the historical foundation for Eurasianism. In an essay entitled "Hyperborea and Eurasia"[1] he proposes an interesting dynamic between North and South. The former he calls Turan, an old Persian name for a region in Central Asia that the Persians identified with the North. He writes:

> Ancient civilizations were formed under the influence of
> impulses coming from the North, but these only crystallized
> and took shape south of a particular geographical feature:
> the chain of Eurasian mountains which stretches from the
> Pyrenees to Manchuria. Civilization arose within this mys-
> terious paradigm. From north of these mountains flowed
> raw manpower, which settled and froze into specific forms
> in the south. . . . What lies to the North . . . is a shadowy
> unknown sphere, the world of barbarism, the otherworldly
> abode of infernal beings—Picts, wild Germanics, Turanians.
> This two-fold model of sacred geography was described in

particular detail by the ancient Iranians. . . . The North Eurasian belt, from France to the Amur, forms a single zone, Turan (which, in fact, represents Hyperborea or at least the threshold of Hyperborea).

Dugin goes on to say that the ancient civilizations of the south were constantly being invaded by the Turanians, who brought not only destruction, but also new life, new blood, and fresh energy to the southern peoples.

For Dugin Genghis Khan is a northern figure under whom "North and the South were themselves integrated into a single unit of Eurasian territory, subordinate to the will of the North in a planetary, continental sense. This is the grand Nordic restoration of sacred geography, which was achieved by Genghis Khan through his empire." Metaphorically Genghis Khan "erased the mountains" between North and South, an endeavor which is also central to Dugin's Eurasian vision.

Another advocate of Eurasianism is Pavel Zarifullin, writer, ethnographer, public figure, and director of Moscow's Lev Gumilev Center. Zarifullin is also a leading ideologue of the New Scythian movement. In a speech at the Gumilev Center in March 2012, Zarifullin called for the emergence of a new Russian consciousness inspired by the heroism, achievements, and vital spirit of the Scythians. Using Gumilev's terminology, he spoke of the Scythian superethnos as a manifestation of the ideal of the brotherhood of the Eurasian peoples and went on to say that, in the context of today's crisis of ideology, Scythianism can act as a unifying force for Eurasia.[2] He further elaborates these ideas in his book *The New Scythians*.[3]

While Scythia for many Russians remains a name to conjure with, others look back to a different heritage, namely that of the Vikings, who also played a formative role in Russian history. The very name *Russia* is derived from the Rus or Rhos, a tribe most probably of Scandinavian origin, although many Russians argue that they were in fact Slavic. The Rus were also called Varangians, from the Norse word *væringi*, meaning something like a "sworn comrade." Under their chieftain Rurik (c. 830–879), they invaded from the north and settled initially in the vicinity of Novgorod, founding what became the Rurik dynasty. Rurik's successors then moved the capital south to Kiev, establishing the state of Kievan Rus as the nucleus for what later became the Russian nation, which was ruled by members of the Rurik dynasty until the early seventeenth century. From their Kievan kingdom, the Rus made perilous journeys down the Dnieper River to the Black Sea, braving rapids and hostile tribes, and then proceeded to Constantinople where they engaged in trade. Some of them remained as an elite guard for the Byzantine emperor. The memory of Rurik and the Rus is still celebrated in Russia, and a famous painting by the twentieth-century artist Nikolai Roerich, entitled *Guests from Overseas*, shows Viking ships making their way up an estuary into Russian territory.

The debate about whether the Varangians were Nordic or Slavic is characteristic of the way in which the Russian sense of identity has vacillated between contrasting modes. At the dawn of the eighteenth century Peter the Great sought to drag the country kicking and screaming down the path of modernization and westernization. In the same spirit he transformed a desolate swamp on the Baltic coast into his shining new capital of Saint Petersburg in 1703. But the old Russia refused to go away. Saint Petersburg and Moscow became symbolic poles in a cultural and spiritual tug-of-war between innovation and traditionalism, rationality and irrationality, the urban and the rural.

While many members of the educated classes admired all things western, their hearts remained rooted in their native land. The west meant the Enlightenment, progress, reform, democracy, commerce, the industrial revolution, modernity. The east meant the Russian motherland, its cherished traditions, the unending vastness of its rural depths, the Eastern Orthodox Church and its compelling liturgy, the Russian language with its incomparable resonance and subtlety. In short, the motherland exerted a powerful tug, which is reflected again and again in Russian literature. The nineteenth-century poet Mikhail Lermontov expressed it poignantly in his poem "Native Land":

> I love my native land but with a strange love,
> . . . I love—why, I do not know—
> The cold silence of her steppes,
> The swaying of her boundless forests,
> Her overflowing rivers, sea-like;
> I love to gallop along a country track in a cart
> And, with slow gaze, piercing the shadows of the night
> And sighing for a shelter, to come upon by the wayside
> The flickering lights of sad villages.[4]

While it was natural to think of Russia as lying to the east of Europe, in the early eighteenth century there arose a new tendency among the Russians to associate their country with the North. This was closely bound up with the building of Peter the Great's magnificent new northern capital of Saint Petersburg. The subject of Russia and the North is interestingly examined by Otto Boele in his book *The North in Russian Romantic Literature*.[5]

Although the North was perceived as cold, rough, and inhospitable, over time these very attributes came to be prized by the Russians, as they were held to breed the qualities of endurance, bravery, determination, and inventiveness. Boele writes that already "in the first half of the eighteenth century the North acquired a heroic character which was specific to the national consciousness of that time. . . . [S]ince Russia was a *young* nation, the North was an appropriate spatial symbol, signifying its youthful and untainted identity."[6]

Consequently "it became common practice in Russia to refer to some outstanding compatriot . . . by picking the most obvious equivalent in world history or classical mythology, and by simply adding the adjective 'Northern'. . . Thus Empress Catherine II became known as the 'Semiramis of the North', while the new capital was called the 'Northern Rome' or the 'Northern Palmira.'"

By the end of the eighteenth century the glorification of the North had become a prominent theme in Russian literature. To quote Boele again: "The discovery of Germano-Scandinavian mythology, the struggle against the allegedly artificial literature of Classicism, the quest for 'real' poetry—that is, poetry which was supposed to reflect a nation's unique spirit—all these processes which dominated the second half of the eighteenth century in Europe had their effect on intellectual life in Russia as well."[7]

To the writers of this era the North meant not only the Germano-Scandinavian peoples but also the Celts—in fact, often no attempt was made to differentiate between them. As we have seen, the poems of the alleged Gaelic bard Ossian caused a sensation throughout Europe in the late eighteenth and early decades of the nineteenth century. In Russia they fell on particularly ripe soil, and some Russian poets even claimed that Ossian, when translated into traditional Russian meter,[8] sounded even better than the original. The image of the Hebridean poet, with his harp, windblown beard, and tales of heroism, glory, and tragedy set in wild, storm-lashed landscapes, was something with which the Russians could easily identify. It accorded with the view that they were essentially a northern people, with all the force and ruggedness which the North gave them.

The early nineteenth century also saw the work of Vasiliy Kapnist, already mentioned in chapter 3 as a champion of the Hyperborean theory. Kapnist's claim that the Russians were descended from the Hyperboreans was to have wide repercussions, which continue to the present day, as we shall see.

In the course of the nineteenth century Russian writers and scholars continued to take an interest in Scandinavian history, literature, and mythology, and parts of the *Edda* and the sagas began to appear in translation. Their reception of Nordic mythology was partly filtered through Germany, with which Russia had long-standing ties—it had even been ruled for a time by a German monarch in Empress Catherine the Great. The country was full of German settlers who had greatly contributed to the economic development of the country, and German literature in translation was widely read. The Russians therefore had reason to be grateful to the Germans, even though they sometimes complained about the Teutonic traits of assertiveness and drive. Both countries have shared a tendency to soul-searching introspection and both have struggled with the tension between the polarities of east and west, north and south, culture and barbarism, rationality and irrationality. Between the two nations there is a kind of symbiosis, which has even survived the trauma of World War II.

This Russo-German symbiosis was demonstrated spectacularly by the reception Richard Wagner's work got in Russia. Wagner first visited Russia in the early 1860s, giving concerts in Saint Petersburg and Moscow to spellbound audiences, and after his death the wave of Wagnermania in Russia reached new heights. The complete *Ring* cycle was first staged in Saint Petersburg in 1889, followed by a command performance in Moscow for the tsar. Many further performances were staged, and Wagner's influence in Russia on music, theater, and the arts in general was enormous. Inevitably the popularity of Wagner's *Ring*, with its dramatic depictions of Wotan, Brünnhilde, Siegfried, and Alberich, brought with it a new fascination with the figures of Nordic mythology and their world. Enthusiasm for Wagner even survived the advent of Bolshevism, as evidenced by Sergei Eisenstein's production of *Die Walküre* (*The Valkyrie*) at Moscow's Bolshoi Theatre in 1940.

On the whole, during the communist years Russia had other preoccupations than the gods of the North. However, interest in the mystique of the North reawakened as a part of the mood of spiritual searching that emerged after its fall in 1989. To understand this development, we need to glance back briefly at the general history of esoteric and alternative spiritual movements in Russia.

Already in the eighteenth century Russians were being exposed to esoteric ideas partly through works by western European mystical writers translated into Russian and partly through Russian writings in a similar vein. Such works continued to filter through society throughout the nineteenth century along with imported western movements such as Freemasonry, Martinism, and Rosicrucianism. The visit to Russia of the French occultist Papus (alias Dr. Gérard Encausse) in 1905 was symptomatic of this traffic of ideas.

Another key movement that should be mentioned here is Theosophy, which, although it was officially founded in New York in 1875, was created by a Russian, or rather a Russo-German, woman: Helena Petrovna Blavatsky (1831–1891), a highly charismatic visionary, who claimed to reveal in her writings an ancient wisdom that underlay all world religions. She proclaimed that the present human race is the fifth in a succession of root races, the four previous ones having appeared at various times in the history of the earth, each occupying a different continent. In her magnum opus, *The Secret Doctrine*, Blavatsky speaks of the North and Hyperborea in connection with the first two races. The first and sublimest of the races occupied what she calls the "Imperishable Sacred Land," which she connects with the polestar: "Of this mysterious and sacred land very little can be said, except, perhaps . . . that the pole-star has its watchful eye upon it, from the dawn to the close of the twilight of 'a day' of the GREAT BREATH." The inhabitants of this land were immortal and had ethereal rather than physical bodies. Furthermore, this continent, unlike those of the second, third, and fourth races, was never destroyed and would one day produce a "divine mortal" who would be "the future seed of humanity."[9]

Blavatsky then goes on to talk about Hyperborea, the home of the second race:

> The "HYPERBOREAN" will be the name chosen for the Second Continent, the land which stretched out its promontories southward and westward from the North Pole to receive the Second Race, and comprised the whole of what is now known as Northern Asia. Such was the name given by the oldest Greeks to the far-off and mysterious region, whither their tradition made Apollo the "Hyperborean" travel every year. *Astronomically,* Apollo is of course the Sun, who, abandoning his Hellenic sanctuaries, loved to visit annually his far-away country. . . . But *historically,* or better, perhaps, ethnologically and geologically, the meaning is different. The land of the Hyperboreans . . . was neither an ideal country, as surmised by the mythologists, nor yet a land in the neighbourhood of Scythia and the Danube. It was a real Continent, a *bona-fide* land which knew no winter in those early days, nor have its sorry remains more than one night and day during the year, even now. The nocturnal shadows never fall upon it, said the Greeks; for it is the *land of the Gods,* the favourite abode of Apollo, the god of light, and its inhabitants are his beloved priests and servants. This may be regarded as poetised *fiction* now; but it was poetised *truth* then.[10]

Blavatsky's *Secret Doctrine*, along with the Theosophical movement as a whole, has found its way to her homeland and has long since been available in Russian translation. Her remarks about the Second Continent are much quoted by Russian Hyperborean enthusiasts.

By the early twentieth century Russia was teeming with esoteric and spiritual movements of one kind or another. Within this phenomenon various different strands could be observed. There were those who focused on esoteric traditions such as Rosicrucianism, Freemasonry, Gnosticism, Theosophy, Kabbalah, and the Tarot. Another group attempted to unite occultism and science in pursuit of a dream of infinitely expanding human potential. Typical of this group were the followers of Konstantin Tsiolkovsky (1857–1935), who dreamed of creating, by technology and eugenic selection, a race of superhumans that would eventually colonize other planets. Others turned to religions like Buddhism or to the Graeco-Armenian sage G. I. Gurdjieff with his quasi-Manichaean teaching that human beings are asleep but can be taught to wake up with the right shock methods.

Surprisingly, some of these movements continued after the Russian Revolution even into the period of the most severe repression in the 1930s, albeit in great secrecy and under constant threat of imprisonment or death,[11] but almost all of them had been crushed by the end of the Stalinist terror, and only in the 1950s, with the partial thaw under Khrushchev, did similar movements begin to emerge again. During the 1960s to the 1980s they enjoyed a tenuous revival, and after Perestroika and the events of 1989 they began to mushroom. The advent of the Internet has enabled them to flourish and multiply as never before.

One particular ism that has flourished anew in the postcommunist era is nationalism. Under communism it was officially discouraged in favor of internationalism, although it was from time to time taken out of the cupboard for tactical reasons, as when Stalin appealed to patriotic feeling in order to mobilize the country against the German invasion. After the collapse of communism, Russian national fervor came back in full force. "Workers of the world, unite!" is a fine-sounding slogan, but, in the end, it was no match for the love of the motherland and Lermontov's "flickering lights of sad villages."

Among the various isms and "-osophies" of the postcommunist era, the old theme of light from the North is back and flourishing. As we have seen, it has a history going back three centuries or more, so when it reemerged at the end of the twentieth century, the ground was already prepared. It now manifests itself broadly in four areas: in ideology and politics; in the cultural sphere, e.g., literature and art; in the Neo-Pagan scene; and in alternative archaeology and research into prehistory—although to a great extent these four domains overlap.

The northernists within the ideological-political sphere draw inspiration from various earlier writers on the theme of the northern mystique, in particular two whom I have already mentioned in chapter 2. One of them is Bâl Gangâdhar Tilak, whose book *The Arctic Home in the Vedas* is published in Russian translation and frequently quoted by believers in the notion of a Russian Hyperborea. Tilak's name features prominently on many Russian websites devoted to the theme of Hyperborea,[12] and it is striking how his argument, drawn from the Vedas, has become grist to the mill of so many Russian proponents of the Hyperborean theory. Another writer much quoted by the same faction is René Guénon (1886–1951), the main founder of the "traditionalist" school of thought and a proponent of the notion of Hyperborea as the original source of the primordial tradition. As such, he is congenial to Russian traditionalists such as Alexander Dugin, who also quotes with approval the work of the Dutch-German writer Herman Wirth (1885–1981).

By now it should be apparent that in Russia the light from the North shines on an intriguing, multifarious, and sometimes troubling world—troubling because some of the groups operating within it evince tendencies to xenophobia, anti-Semitism, and other forms of racial prejudice (here be dragons again) and certain of these groups have even been prosecuted or banned for that reason. Entering this world, one encounters a mind-set that harbors notions of a vanished Aryan civilization in the far North, the Russians as its successors, and the new golden age that awaits them if they can awaken to who they really are and reclaim their true heritage.

This mind-set is typified by the group Dyerzhava Rus (roughly translatable as "the sovereign power of Russia"), which straddles the ideological-political sphere and Neo-Paganism and alternative prehistory. According to its website,[13] the Russians are descendants of a race that arrived in an intergalactic spaceship many millennia ago and went via Asia (the country of the As, as the godlike invaders were called) to the region of the North Pole, where they settled in a continent called Daaria, meaning "gift to the Aryans." As a result of a great natural catastrophe 111,820 years ago (a curiously precise figure!), this continent disappeared and the inhabitants emigrated to the region of the Urals and became the Russians.

The concept of *dyerzhava* is explained as

> a form of collective organization in which the people deter-
> mine their own everyday life. . . . . All aspects of life are
> discussed at the *Vyeche*, that is the assembly of the Rus, a
> people sharing one language, one belief, one culture and
> one tradition. . . . The spiritual basis of *dyerzhava* is the
> Slavianic faith, which covers every facet of life. . . .[14] For the
> rebirth of the *dyerzhava* . . . it is essential to have the cor-
> rect knowledge, which brings correct action and correct
> living. It is also essential to get rid of such foreign words as:
> "mayor, president, federal district" etc. We have plenty of
> our own. It is unnecessary to invent words when we have
> terms like "head" [голова] and "foreman" [старшина]. . . .
> The whole system is in our genes, in the folk memory, it is
> only necessary to recall it.

The site contains an eclectic list of deities, including the Russian gods Perun, Veles, and Kupala, but also Odin and Thor and the Hindu god Agni. There is also the full text in Russian of the Icelandic *Ynglinga Saga*, which treats Odin as a real historical figure who ruled a city called Asgard in the eastern country of Asaland, before settling in the North with his tribe. This ties in conveniently with the already mentioned account of how demigods from space called the As originally landed in a country called Asia.

The mental universe characterized by such websites has also given rise to a genre of literature, sometimes called "metahistory," which mingles fact and fiction with the most extravagant theories in a heady mixture capable of attracting a large readership. One of its most prominent exponents was Vladimir Shcherbakov (1938–2004), an engineer and technical journalist turned author. During and after the Soviet period he produced a stream of stories, novels, and nonfiction works, characterized by a colorful style and lively imagination. Typical of his writings in the metahistory genre is an extraordinary work entitled *Asgard—City of the Gods* (1991),[15] which vividly illustrates the Russian fascination with Nordic mythology. At times the reader is unsure whether it is fiction or nonfiction, but it makes a compelling read.

The narrative starts with the author relating how he came close to drowning in the Black Sea and had a near-death experience in which he found himself ascending through a tunnel and seeing a beautiful walled city with a great silvery dome, a columned temple, and a grove full of trees with golden leaves. Only later, reading the *Prose Edda*, did he recognize what he had seen as the home of the gods in Asgard, and he set out on a quest to find out where Asgard had been located. In describing the quest, he draws partly on his wide knowledge of history, mythology, archaeology, etymology, and geography and partly on flights of fantasy and imagination, bringing in extraterrestrials and the gods themselves. His concept of metahistory evidently means perceiving higher, unseen forces at work behind historical events. He includes, for example, a startling interpretation of World War II in which Hitler, ignorant of the cosmic dimension of the struggle, forfeited the support of the gods by attacking the Russians as the successors to Asgard. At the same time, Hitler unknowingly allied himself with the main enemy of the Aesir, the Fenris Wolf, naming his eastern headquarters the Wolf's Lair. Thus, on one side, together with the Germans, were the Fenris Wolf, Jörmungand (the Midgard Serpent), and Surt (the destructive fire giant), while on the other side were the Aesir and Vanir, now allied and fighting side by side with the Russians. The predictable outcome was a victory for the latter.

Buried in Shcherbakov's book are some intriguing, if unconvincing, theories. For example, he examines the word *Idavöll*, the name given in the *Edda* to the field where the survivors of Ragnarök (the great apocalyptic cataclysm) will assemble before beginning to build a new world. The name means roughly "splendid plain," but Shcherbakov argues that the phoneme *-völl* is cognate with the Russian word *valun*, meaning "a rounded stone," and links this with a game in which balls made of gypsum were rolled over a field. Such a game was evidently played at the ancient city of Nisa in what is now Iran, so Shcherbakov concludes that Nisa was the central city of Asgard and it was there that the Aesir gathered to confer and play bowls with the gypsum balls.

The northern light also permeates a number of works that belong more decidedly in the fiction category. One of the best-known authors in this genre is Sergei Alexeyev (b. 1952), an impressive, gray-bearded figure cast in the mold of a rustic sage from a Tolstoy novel, who sometimes gives interviews from his home in the country. Alexeyev is of the national-patriotic persuasion, which comes across strongly in his writings. These include a series of novels under the title *The Treasure of the Valkyrie*, of which seven volumes have appeared at the time of writing.[16]

The narrative, whose hero is an army officer called Col. Rusinov, repeatedly glorifies a northern Aryan civilization and its Slavic descendants, who are pitted against an evil conspiracy bent on establishing a world dictatorship, destroying the remnants of the northern culture and uprooting the Russian people. In one passage, Rusinov reflects on the bond between Russia and Germany, which has survived devastating wars and much bloodshed:

> This attraction lay outside the sphere of politics and ideology . . . it was a spiritual bond of a cosmic order like a tree with one indivisible root. This root was nourished by the juice of the Northern earth and, no matter where its shoots took root, the North remained the ancestral home of the Aryans. This is why there existed in India a legend that the gods live there in the cold country and that they are blond and blue-eyed.[17]

Alexeyev's books are extremely popular, reaching editions of over 400,000 copies, and are eagerly read by both right and left.[18] In order to appreciate the significance of writers like him, one has to realize that there is a tradition in Russia of treating writers as sages and gurus. Dostoyevsky, Tolstoy, Bulgakov, Pasternak, Solzhenitsyn, and many others have been regarded in this way. Thus, the popularity of a series like *The Treasure of the Valkyrie* is an indication that the ideas in it are profoundly appealing to its readers.

So far, I have mentioned how the idea of light from the North manifests itself in Russia in the political and in the literary sphere. Another area in which this is evident is in the world of Neo-Paganism, which is a relatively new phenomenon in Russia, dating essentially from the 1990s, although there are certain indigenous forms of Paganism that have survived here and there since pre-Christian times, such as that practiced in the Mari Republic and among a few native shamans in Siberia. Russian Neo-Pagans worship the old Slavic deities such as Perun, god of thunder, and Veles, god of the earth and of cattle, but there are some groups that have adopted the Norse pantheon and use the name Asatru, which, as we have seen, was chosen by Icelandic Pagans to denote their faith and has since come to be used by Nordic Pagans in many different countries. There are now a number of Asatru groups active in Russia.

Russian Asatru followers, when asked what place Asatru has on Russian soil, can say that, apart from the fact that there are up to a million ethnic Germans living in Russia, there is a long history of interpenetration between the Germanic and Slavic cultures, going right back to the time of the Viking settlers and that the two pantheons can live quite peacefully with each other.

Another aspect of the Northern tradition, namely the runes, has proved popular in Russia as a divinatory and magical system. Numerous books are available on the subject, both by Russian authors and by western authors translated into Russian, such as Edred Thorsson's *Futhark*. There are also a number of websites offering fortune-telling services using the runes. One of the most serious Russian experts on the subject is Leonid Korablev (b. 1971). In addition to being a sculptor and graphic artist, he has written many books on the runes as well as on Iceland and its mythology and lore, and has the advantage of knowing Icelandic and being able to study the *Edda* and the sagas in the original. Through his books, lectures, and television broadcasts on Iceland, he has done much to promote interest in the country among the Russians.

Alongside the Scandinavian runes, one also sees Russian runic alphabets, mostly of rather doubtful provenance. There is, for example, the so-called *Book of Veles*, written on wooden boards in a rune-like script and purporting to be an ancient Pagan text, Veles being the Slavic god of the earth and of cattle. It is widely thought to be a forgery, but to many people in the Slavic world, it is holy writ.

A name that has already cropped up in connection with Russia is Hyperborea, the fabled Northern land that has exerted such fascination since the time of the ancient Greeks. In Russia the notion of Hyperborea has become a powerful motif that has captured the imaginations of many and inspired some astonishing visual art. This again is a territory where we shall find some dragons. It is also one that needs to be examined in some depth and breadth, so the next chapter will be devoted to the subject of Hyperborea in the Russian context.

NOTES

1. Posted on the website entitled *The Fourth Political Theory*: http://4pt.su/de /node/158.
2. Reported on the website http://baznica.info/article/novye-skify -uchredili-dvizhenie-v-solnechn/.
3. *Новые скифы* (*Novi Skify*) (Saint Petersburg: Limbus Press, c. 2013).
4. Reproduced in Dmitri Obolenksy (ed.), *The Penguin Book of Russian Verse, 2nd ed.* (Harmondsworth: Penguin, 1965). Translation mine.
5. Boele (1996).
6. Boele, 23–24.
7. Boele, 26.
8. Boele, 41.
9. Blavatsky (1888), 6.
10. Blavatsky (1888), 7.
11. See Konstantin Burmistrov's article "The History of Esotericism in Soviet Russia in the 1920s–1930s" in Menzel (2012).
12. E.g., http://slavyanskaya-kultura.ru.
13. http://derzhavarus.ru/.
14. I use the coined word *Slavianic* to translate the root славян-, which is used to designate the old belief of the Rus.
15. *Асгард город богов* (*Asgard – gorod bogov*) (Moscow: Molodoya Gvardia, 1991).
16. *Сокровище валькирии* (*Sokrovischey Valkyrii*), in 7 parts (Moscow: various publishers, 1995–2012).
17. *Сокровище валькирии* (*Sokrovischey Valkyrii*), Part 1, 65. Online version: http://knijky.ru/books/stoyashchiy-u-solnca?
18. Schnirelman, 80.

CHAPTER 12

A RUSSIAN HYPERBOREA?

In 1765, on the orders of Empress Catherine the Great, a secret naval expedition set out from the northern Russian port of Archangel and sailed via the estuary of the Dvina River out into the White Sea. Masterminded by the great scientist and polymath Mikhail Lomonosov, it was led by Admiral Vassily Chichagov, whose official mission was to find a northeast passage and search for whaling grounds. But, as later recorded by Chichagov's son, the admiral carried a sealed letter to be opened after he had set sail, ordering him to head for the North Pole. Two attempts were made in successive years, but both times the ship failed to break through the ice and had to return to Archangel. There is still much speculation about the real purpose of the expedition, but there are those who firmly believe it had to do with the search for Hyperborea. One such was the archaeologist and Hyperborea enthusiast Valerii Dyomin (1942–2006), who speculated that, in ordering the expedition, the empress was motivated by the prospect of discovering the elixir of eternal youth, which was said to have been invented by the Hyperboreans.[1]

Such rumors surrounding the expedition tell us less about its real purpose than about the way in which the Hyperborean motif has taken hold in Russia. As we have seen, it appeared again in the early nineteenth century when it was taken up by Count Vasiliy Kapnist with his book *A Short Survey on the Hyperboreans* (1815), claiming that the Russians were descended from the Hyperboreans, the carriers of the "Northern light."

In 1921 another Russian expedition was mounted, this time to the Kola Peninsula between the Barents Sea and the White Sea in Russian Lapland. Its leader was Alexander Barchenko, a fascinating figure who was largely unknown until the extraordinary story of his life began to be unearthed in the late 1990s by the Russian historian, philologist, and Tibetologist Alexander Andreyev.[2] Barchenko was a scientist, author, and parapsychological researcher much influenced by the writings of the French mystic Joseph-Alexandre de Saint-Yves d'Alveydre. He was fascinated by the notion that various advanced civilizations had existed in the distant past and remnants of them and their superior knowledge could be found in certain remote, hidden places in the world, such as the fabled lands of Agartha and Shambhala that have captured the imaginations of so many esotericists. Later this fascination was to lead Barchenko into a scheme to link the dream of Shambhala with the Bolshevik cause.[3] For Barchenko, Hyperborea was another such source of ancient wisdom, so the hope of finding traces of it must have been very much in his mind when he set out for the Kola Peninsula, although the main purpose of the expedition was to investigate some mysterious outbreaks of mass hysteria that had been occurring among the Sami, the indigenous people of that region.

The expedition set off for Murmansk in the spring and by August had set up its base at the Lovozero (the Lake of Lov) at the center of the peninsula and surrounded by a bleak landscape of tundra, pine forests, and bare, rocky hills. There were only a few small settlements, and the inhabitants lived mostly by fishing and keeping reindeer. Soon after their arrival, the expedition members asked the local fishermen to take them by boat to a small island in the lake, but the fishermen refused point-blank, explaining that only shamans could go there. They also described a whole island covered by reindeer horns. Evidently these had been placed there by magicians of the surrounding tribes as a tribute to the spirits of the place, and to move them would be to invite misfortune. After a few days, the son of the local shaman agreed to take them over in his sailing boat, but when they approached the island, a gust of wind ripped the sail and broke the mast.

Exploring the area of marshy tundra around their campsite on the south side of the lake, they found a paved road, extending for about one and a half kilometers and ending at a curious platform from which they could look across the lake to a rock face on which carvings of gigantic human figures were faintly visible. They also found pyramid-shaped mounds, cubic stones, and fallen columns, yellowish-white in color like massive candles, which the local Sami worshipped like gods.

The expedition also studied the Sami themselves, who were a fascinating mixture in terms of religion. While they followed the observances of the Russian Orthodox Church, they continued worshipping their ancient sun god and offering bloodless sacrifices at their menhirs in secret. They also had remarkable powers of healing, as demonstrated when Barchenko had a severe heart attack. Lying on the ground, he was treated by a female shaman called Anna Vasilievna, who whispered something in his ear and then pointed a dagger at his heart, making short, poking movements. The pain in Barchenko's heart grew intense, and he felt that he was about to die. Instead he fell into a deep sleep. When he awoke the next morning, the pain was gone, and the heart problem never came back.

After spending a year in the area making a detailed study of the remains and talking to the Sami, the team came to the conclusion that they had discovered Hyperborea, and Barchenko was convinced that the Sami shamans were the successors to the priests of the Hyperboreans. That people had, he believed, flourished in the north until the fifth millennium BCE and then had been forced by climatic change to migrate south and then east, eventually reaching India.[4] His scenario is therefore comparable to that proposed by, for example, Felice Vinci (see chapter 1), but with some differences—e.g., for Vinci the migration took place about two thousand years later.

The account of the Barchenko expedition is reminiscent of the uncanny world of H. P. Lovecraft with his tales of the "Old Ones" and their monstrous remains, and one can imagine what Lovecraft would have done with the theme of the mass hysteria among the Sami. However, Lovecraft's ancients evoke only horror, whereas Barchenko believed he had encountered the remnants of a superior civilization. Tragically, Barchenko was executed in 1938 during the Stalinist terror, but his torch was taken up again three-quarters of a century later when another expedition set out for the Kola Peninsula. Entitled "Hyperborea 97" it was followed a year later by "Hyperborea 98." The leader was the previously mentioned Valeriy Dyomin. A team of four volunteers made up the first expedition. By the second the group had grown to several dozen, drawn from many different cities and regions of the country.[5]

The Dyomin team found the same Lovecraftian megalithic remains that Barchenko had described and more. There were defensive earthworks, regularly shaped stone slabs carved with mysterious signs, and what appeared to be the remains of a kind of giant astrolabe with a fifteen-meter-long groove carved in a rock face, apparently for marking the times of particular astronomical alignments. Ascending a mountain, they found a large number of stone pyramids. Dyomin reported that there had been others down by the lake, but communist zealots had destroyed them in the 1920s and '30s. He also found ten labyrinths made up of stones laid out in spiral form and reported that further labyrinths had been destroyed, presumably also by the communists.

Dyomin, like Barchenko, was convinced that he had found Hyperborea—or rather one of its strongholds. In his conclusions, he supports the familiar Hyperborean theory of the North having been once inhabited by an advanced civilization but puts it much further back in time than Barchenko or Vinci. He claims that samples taken from the megalithic remains on the Kola Peninsula indicate that the Hyperboreans lived there about 12,000–14,000 years ago. He mentions with approval Bâl Gangâdhar Tilak's book *The Arctic Home in the Vedas*, which is now being eagerly read in Russian translation. The Hyperboreans, he says, were sun worshippers, as indicated by the rock carvings showing solar symbols found in the Murmansk area of the peninsula. Apollo, the sun god, was said to have been born in the far north, then traveled south, but returned regularly to his homeland—hence his sobriquet, the Hyperborean Apollo. Furthermore, when the Greeks established the shrine of Apollo at Delphi, his first prophet was called Olen—a Russian, totemic name meaning reindeer![6]

Labyrinths of the kind that Dyomin found on the Kola Peninsula are also present in the Karelia Republic of the Russian Federation bordering Finland and on the Solovetsky Islands in the White Sea. Dyomin also observes that spiral labyrinths are found practically throughout the world. In northern Russia they are called "Babylons," which he speculates might be a corruption of the name Avalon, the enchanted land of Arthurian legend. He also points out that, in many northern traditions and legends, stone spirals are connected with elves, gnomes, and similar inhabitants of the subterranean world. He believes that the tradition of making labyrinths began in the north and spread out from there over time.[7]

The ancient remains in the north of Russia have attracted continuing attention from other archaeologists, such as Sergei Golubev. Starting in the year 2000, Golubev has led a series of expeditions to the Kola Peninsula and the islands in the White Sea under the auspices of the Russian Geographical Society. Their discoveries have led Golubev to conclude:

On the islands in the White Sea stood the oldest sacred
center of humankind. . . . The more we try to understand
the astonishing constructions of the Arctic or Hyperborean
culture, the more we are convinced that they represent not
only a national Russian treasure but also a unique monument in the history of humanity—no less amazing and
probably older than the famous Stonehenge in England and
the pyramids of Egypt and Mexico.[8]

In addition to labyrinths and pyramids Golubev's team found
dolmens, menhirs, and other relics. They came to the conclusion that
one of the Solovetsky Islands had been a kind of Elysium to which
the inhabitants of the surrounding settlements had sent their dead.
Another island, Kuzova, they believed to have been a sacred place
where people came to conduct weddings and other ceremonies,
to bring offerings to the gods, or to ask for their support in battle
or trading expeditions. One of the striking features they found on
Kuzova was a huge throne, roughly twice human height, carved out
of solid stone.[9]

Perhaps even more mysterious than the remains on the Kola
Peninsula are the extraordinary stone spheres found on the unin-
habited island of Champ, located far to the north of the Arctic Circle
at a latitude of 80.67 degrees. The spheres, ranging in diameter from
a few millimeters to several meters, are so perfect that it is hard to
believe they were not shaped by human hand, although some geolo-
gists argue that they were formed by nature under water around an
organic core.

Turning from archaeology to the visual arts in Russia, we find in
this domain one of the most striking expressions of the Hyperborean
theme. Interestingly, it was already present to a small degree in the
Soviet era. The prominent sculptress Vera Mukhina (1889–1953),
famous for her monumental statues of striding, forward-pointing

socialist heroes, also created a sculpture entitled *Boreas, the North Wind*, depicting the wind god in the form of a naked athlete, apparently leaping through space like a trapeze artist alongside the crudely shaped figure of a bear—doubtless an allusion to the northern constellation of Ursa Major. Apparently even such a major exponent of socialist realism could hear a whisper of Northern spirit.

That spirit strongly pervades the work of another Soviet-era artist: Konstantin Alexeyevich Vasilyev (1942–1976).[10] Born in the town of Maykop, close to the northeast coast of the Black Sea, Vasiliev as a young boy evinced a remarkable artistic talent. After studying art in Moscow and Kazan, he embarked on a career as a painter and theatrical designer, which was tragically cut short by his death at the age of thirty-four in what was ostensibly a railway accident, but which many believed to have really been an assassination. Today his work has a cult following and its own museum in Moscow. Having been born during the horror of World War II, Vasiliev might have been expected to be anti-German—and indeed many of his canvases glorify the Russian wartime struggle—yet at the same time he clearly felt a profound kinship with the Nordic-Germanic spirit. He avidly studied the Icelandic sagas and Eddic poems, and he learned German so that he could read the texts of Wagner's operas. Many of his paintings reflect these preoccupations, depicting Nordic and Slavic gods, goddesses, and warriors in dramatic, heroic postures.

While in the Soviet period such artists were few and far between, in the new Russia they constitute a flourishing genre with many practitioners. One of the most prolific is Alexander Uglanov, born in 1960 in the city of Tver.[11] Uglanov's powerful, haunting works have something of the French Symbolists and the German Romantics with a pinch of surrealism, and yet are unmistakably Russian. Many of them are pervaded by the Hyperborean theme and by the spirit of what he calls the "Veda" (as in the Indian scriptures known as the Vedas), signifying an ancient wisdom tradition handed down among the Indo-Europeans and present in Russian mythology and folklore. Indeed, one of his paintings is actually entitled *Veda* and depicts a radiant, fair-haired goddess figure standing before a huge, ancient tree with a human face, and surrounded by three sacred animals of northern Russian tradition: reindeer, bear, and swan. Another work, entitled *The Path to Asgard*, shows an enormous Viking ship sailing through the air and appearing dramatically through a curtain of cloud. Other canvases depict a variety of Hyperborean images: shining, snow-covered palaces, sacred groves, angelic figures floating in space over the North Pole. Fig. 20 shows his painting *Salt of the Earth*, depicting a goddess figure holding what appears to be the polestar and hovering over a forest-encircled lake, in the middle of which is a mound with an anthropomorphic tree surrounded by worshippers.

Another artist working in a similar vein is Vsevelod Ivanov (b. 1950).[12] In his work we find again many images of otherworldly Hyperborean landscapes. Typical is his painting entitled *The Exodus from Hyperborea*, showing an endless caravan of sleighs pulled by mammoths, making its way out of a city resembling some northern Babylon, with towering pyramids, domes, and fairy-tale castles—all snow-covered and glistening in the light of the sun setting over a distant ocean. Another, entitled *Coastal Vision of the Hyperborean Goddess*, shows an oceanside cliff face with a shining female face looking out from behind rocks carved into weird human figures. On the shore in the foreground are people, a ship, and several stone spheres of the kind found on the Arctic island of Champ.

Describing himself and his work, Ivanov makes it clear that he has a strong agenda:

> From an early age I knew that the Russian people were
> and are being robbed economically, but an equally dread-
> ful form of robbery is the distortion of Russian history....

20. *Salt of the Earth,* **a painting by the Russian artist Alexander Uglanov.**

Only after many decades has it become possible to publish literature on the early chronicles of the Russian people. . . . I as a schoolboy felt the need to give expression to that splendid heritage. . . . My creative work is a bridge to the radiant and splendid world of our Russian past. In the act of creation I become immersed in that world. And, looking at paintings by artists like Victor Korolkov . . . I experience great joy, knowing that, despite the invention of photography, film and animation, the power of the brush is just as strong as it was 200 years ago. The work of the Russian artist should have an illuminating function. It is necessary to actively oppose the "globalization" of art.[13]

The fellow artist mentioned by Ivanov is also extremely interesting. The paintings of the late Victor Korolkov (1958–2004)[14] are touched by a similar otherworldly spirit, but executed in a more delicate, densely detailed style with subtle coloring, somewhat reminiscent of the fairy-tale illustrations of British nineteenth- and twentieth-century artist Arthur Rackham. Korolkov's main subjects are taken from Russian mythology and fairy tales, but some have a Nordic touch, such as his *World Tree* with a double trunk and two faces, male and female, reminiscent of both Yggdrasil of Nordic mythology and the two primal human beings, Ask and Embla, whom Odin and his two brothers made from trees.

Another artist worth mentioning in this connection is Andrei Klimenko (b. 1956), also known under the curious pseudonym Andriko WenSix, who paints in a forceful, monumental style. Typical is his powerful picture of the Slavic god Veles, dressed in the skin of a bull and riding on a bear. More Nordic is his work showing a flying Viking ship, a motif that appears in a number of paintings of this genre.

These paintings tell us a great deal about Russian culture and the Russian soul. Their creators, in a similar way to the novelists that I have mentioned, regard themselves as having a mission to enlighten, uplift, and inspire. They strive in their works to convey beauty and light. How different from the prevailing orthodoxy in the Western art world, where students are told that art has nothing to do with beauty, tradition is something to be shunned, and anything goes as long as it is provocative or even shocking. The pictures also reveal much about the present spiritual mood of the nation. They have a romantic quality, and romanticism is typically marked by a longing for that which is far away in time or space—remote, elusive, but perhaps not quite unreachable. Many Russians are touched by this longing after the decades of prosaic Marxist doctrine, hence the appeal of the Hyperborean dream that is so vividly conveyed by these artists.

Visionary paintings of the Northern promised land are much in evidence on the Internet. A search there by entering the name Hyperborea in Cyrillic letters reveals innumerable websites with names like "Hyperborea, our vanished homeland." There is even a video game called Hyperborea that can be played online. One particularly informative site is called "Everything about Hyperborea."[16] The period when Hyperborea was inhabited is described there as "a golden age for humanity, an epoch of general happiness, contentment, and well-being" when people lived "in peace and contentment, knowing neither hunger, nor illness, nor any adversity or deprivation." The rediscovery of Hyperborea has brought to light "the sublime treasure house of our ancient culture . . . We are giving back to ourselves our glorious past, and consequently we now have the possibility of a bright future."

Already the Arctic region of Russia is becoming a destination for tourists in search of the Hyperborean light. There is at least one person offering tours of the region, namely Dr. Elena Loboda, a chemist and biologist who has also made an extensive study of different spiritual traditions. She describes herself as "a wisdom keeper of the ancient Veddik tradition of the Northern Lineages of Arctic Gaia." In an essay on the spiritual heritage of northern Siberia, posted on her website, she writes:

It is important to emphasize that Hyperborean esoteric practices which awaken deep wisdom and inner natural goodness do not belong to any single religion or culture. In the territory of the Russian Federation there exist more than 50 different tribes which have been practicing the Hyperborean heritage. Although these tribes are speaking many different languages, some of which are the most ancient living languages on our planet (Paleolithic) they follow the same ageless tradition and perform similar rituals and ceremonies. The wisdom-keepers of the Hyperborean tradition affirm it as an ancient heritage of Shambala-Belovodie-Tule (Tula), the pure land that exists in the highest dimensions.

Some of these spiritual practices have been used through hundreds of hundreds of years in the highest level of training of other traditions and religions like Dzogchen (in Tibetan Bon and Buddhism), Hesychasm (esoteric early Christian tradition), or Bhagti Yoga.[17]

Apart from her Hyperborean tours, Dr. Loboda teaches a whole range of spiritual and health practices based on the ancient wisdom of the North.

For many the Hyperborean idea is not just a northern but also a global vision. The website Everything about Hyperborea states:

At one time there existed in the North of our planet a single, unified humanity and a single, unified language and culture. Rescuing themselves from a great natural cataclysm, the survivors dispersed over various parts of the earth, shaping different countries, peoples, languages. The early myths of various peoples of the world speak about . . . a Golden Age of humanity and a Heavenly Land.[18]

According to one popular school of thought, Russia is the source of a proto-language and a proto-civilization, whose traces can be found everywhere if you know where to look for them. A leading exponent of what one might call Russo-Hyperboreanism is Valeriy Chudinov (b. 1942), a gray-bearded polymath with startling, often outlandish-seeming theories, which he argues engagingly. In an interview posted on the website of the Pagan group Rodnoverie-Rus, he says: "If you take Eurasia, from Britain to Alaska, in the Stone Age it was all Russian. One forms the impression that Russian was the very language of which the Bible speaks, that there was one language before the building of the Tower of Babel and that language was Russian."[19] Chudinov supports his theories with ingenious linguistic arguments. Thus, he argues that the syllable -rus in the word "Etruscan" comes from the same root as -rus in "Russian." Rome, he claims, was originally a Russian state called Rim, as it is in Russian which he points out is the reverse of the word mir, meaning "world" or "peace."

The popularity of the Hyperborean theory in Russia says much about the Russian character. Despite, or perhaps because of, all the traumas of the past century, there is still a streak of fresh idealism in the Russian mind and a willingness to embrace wholeheartedly visions and ideas that give hope and a sense of meaning, even at the risk of overcredulity. Along with all the contradictions and paradoxes in their character, they have retained a vital energy to dream that comes across strongly in the Hyperborean visions we have encountered. The shadow side of these bright visions of a glorious Russian past is an element of chauvinism that can sometimes take on xenophobic forms. "Here be dragons!" But, as we have seen, for many Russians the Hyperborean vision is a universal one that sees the North as belonging to the world as a whole.

NOTES

1. Interview with Dyomin in the newspaper *Argumenty i Fakty*, posted in English translation on *Pravda* online: http://www.pravdareport.com/science /mysteries/29-11-2006/85697-paradise-0/.

2. See Alexander Andreyev's books Время Шамбали (*Vremya Shambali*), 2nd ed. (Saint Petersburg: Nyeva Publishing House, 2004) and also Оккультист Страны Советов (*Okkultist Strany Sovietov*) (Moscow: Yazua, EKSMO, 2004).

3. This story is fascinatingly told by Alexander Andreyev in the two above-mentioned works. For English-speaking readers the subject is dealt with in Andrei Znameski's book *Red Shambhala* (Wheaton, IL: Quest Books, 2011), which draws on Andreyev's work.

4. Valeriy Dyomin, Гиперборея - праматерь мировой культуры (*Hypberborea – Pramater Mirovoi Kultury*) (Moscow: Veche, 2003).

5. The first expedition is described in Dyomin (1997). For the second expedition and his further findings, see Dyomin (2003 and 2011).

6. Dyomin (2003).

7. Dyomin (2011).

8. See article on Golubev's expeditions on the Internet bulletin *File-RF*, April 12, 2011 (file-rf.ru/analytics/627).

9. Ibid.

10. See Schnirelman, 172, and website http://www.bibliotekar.ru/Kvasiliev /index.htm.

11. See website https://vdohnovenie2.ru/bylinnaya-rus-xudozhnik-aleksandr -uglanov/.

12. See Schnirelman, 178, and website http://www.slavs.org.ua/vsevolod-ivanov.

13. Quoted from the website http://www.slavs.org.ua/vsevolod-ivanov.

14. See various websites such as http://web-kapiche.ru/70-viktor-korolkov.html.

15. See Schnirelman, 174, and website http://web-kapiche.ru/210-andrey -klimenko-kartiny.html.

16. www.yperboreia.org.

17. http://www.polarlight.org/heritage-en.html.

18. www.yperboreia.org.

19. http://belvoin.narod.ru/images-a/Chydinov.html.

BEYOND THE NORTH WIND

CHAPTER 13

THE NORTH IN THE AGE OF MASS COMMUNICATION

The American mythologist Joseph Campbell once said that the gods are not to be found in books on mythology "but are right on the corner of Broadway and 42nd Street, waiting for the lights to change."[1] If that is true, then we would expect them to be as confused by the age they find themselves in as the character called Miles in Woody Allen's film *Sleeper*, who is kept in cryogenic suspension for two hundred years and wakes up in 2173. Yet the gods—and certainly the Nordic ones—have adjusted remarkably well to the world of space travel, mass communication, digital media, virtual reality, and modern entertainment. Indeed, not only have they adapted, but they appear to be flourishing as never before.

Let's look at some of the areas of modern culture where the North and its gods and heroes are featured, and let's begin with the realm of literature. I already discussed in chapter 11 some of the Russian fiction featuring Northern and Hyperborean themes. No doubt similar examples could be found in other languages, but here I shall concentrate on works written in English.

The theme of the North as a place of danger, darkness, and terror is one that has often been exploited in literature. At the end of Mary Shelley's novel *Frankenstein* (1818) the famous monster flees toward the North Pole, pursued by his creator Viktor Frankenstein, who is intent on killing the creature. After traveling across the frozen ocean in a dogsled, Frankenstein boards a ship trapped amid the ice and collapses in a fever. While he is lying in his cabin, the monster enters and murders him, then leaps back onto the ice after telling the captain he intends to proceed to the northernmost extremity of the globe and there cremate himself—a bleak ending in the bleakest of places.

The polar theme was picked up again by the young Arthur Conan Doyle in his ghost story *The Captain of the Pole-Star*. The narrator, a medical student called John McAlister Ray, goes on a voyage as a passenger on board a Scottish whaling ship called the *Pole-Star*, bound for the Arctic and commanded by Captain Nicholas Craigie, a wild-eyed man with some intense, private obsession. As the Arctic winter draws in and ice floes threaten to trap the ship, the crew grows increasingly uneasy, especially when they keep seeing a white, ghostly figure moving about near the vessel and hearing eerie, mournful cries piercing the vast, icy silence. McAlister is scornful of these reports until he hears something that shakes him.

> I was leaning against the bulwarks when there arose from
> the ice almost directly underneath me a cry, sharp and
> shrill, upon the silent air of the night, beginning, as it
> seemed to me, at a note such as prima donna never reached,
> and mounting from that ever higher and higher until it
> culminated in a long wail of agony, which might have been
> the last cry of a lost soul. The ghastly scream is still ringing
> in my ears. Grief, unutterable grief, seemed to be expressed
> in it, and a great longing, and yet through it all there was an
> occasional wild note of exultation.[2]

The captain, convinced that the apparition is his deceased fiancée, grows increasingly excited. Finally, he jumps over the side of the ship on to the ice and runs toward the phantom. Later the crew finds him lying dead with a happy expression on his face, and they bury him at sea.

One further example from the nineteenth century will suffice, namely Edgar Allan Poe's story *A Descent into the Maelstrom* (1841). The maelstrom of the title is based on the *Moskstraumen*, a complex of powerful eddies and whirlpools in the ocean close to the island of Mosken in Norway's Lofoten archipelago. In the story, a fisherman tells the narrator how he miraculously survived the maelstrom by tying himself to a barrel, while his brother perished in the whirlpool. Seeing the maelstrom from a clifftop, the narrator describes it as follows:

> Even while I gazed, this current acquired a monstrous velocity. Each moment added to its speed—to its headlong impetuosity. In five minutes the whole sea, as far as Vurrgh, was lashed into ungovernable fury; but it was between Moskoe and the coast that the main uproar held its sway. Here the vast bed of the waters, seamed and scarred into a thousand conflicting channels, burst suddenly into phrensied convulsion—heaving, boiling, hissing—gyrating in gigantic and innumerable vortices, and all whirling and plunging on to the eastward with a rapidity which water never elsewhere assumes except in precipitous descents.[3]

Poe's inspired way with the strange and outlandish greatly influenced the American writer, poet, and artist Clark Ashton Smith (1893–1961), who also exploited the theme of the North. In his short story cycle *Hyperborea* (published sporadically between 1931 and 1958), he adapted elements of the Hyperborean mythology and presented them as fantasy fiction. His Hyperborea is a warm and fertile place which has gone through different stages of settlement. There is a magnificent capital called Commoriom, and various deities with exotic-sounding names are worshipped, such as the toad god Tsathoggua and the elk goddess Yhoundeh. Echoing the legends of a great catastrophe that caused the departure of the Hyperboreans, Smith writes in his story *The Tale of Satampra Zeiros* that Commoriom "was deserted many hundreds of years ago because of the prophecy of the white sybil of Polarion, who foretold an undescribed and abominable doom for all mortal beings who should dare to tarry within its environs." And he goes on to describe Commoriom itself in a way reminiscent of some of the visions of Hyperborea depicted by those Russian artists that we encountered in chapter 12:

> And still it stands, a luster of marble, a magnificence of
> granite, all a-throng with spires and cupolas and obelisks
> that the mighty trees of the jungle have not yet over-
> towered, in a fertile inland valley of Hyperborea. And men
> say that in its unbroken vaults there lies entire and unde-
> spoiled as if of yore the rich treasure of olden monarchs;
> that the high-built tombs retain the gems and electrum that
> were buried with their mummies.[4]

Smith's story cycle, written in his typical rich, purple prose, has the epic quality that runs through much of the literature about the North.

Epic is a term that tends to be used rather loosely, but it has relevance in this context. The original Greek noun *epos* means a word, story, or poem, but the English word *epic*, as a noun or adjective, has acquired an extended meaning, conveying the idea of something grand and heroic. Until a few decades ago literary pundits would have tended to write off the epic as an outmoded genre, of interest only to mythologists, scholars of Old Norse literature, and the like. The poet and literary scholar Frederick Turner, himself a writer of epic poetry, has described how his colleagues in the world of literary scholarship tried to "cage" the epic genre "to make the world safe— safe for reason, for prose, for the marketplace, for revolution . . ."[5] Yet, he writes, a new generation has grown up without such prejudices. "The very word 'epic' is now a live term in their vocabulary for something that is big, exciting, and cutting-edge. The cultural genres of Marvel Comix, gothic, anime, manga, multi-user dungeon gaming, summer superhero movies . . . reprise all the epic themes and motifs. . . ." As examples of modern epics he cites *The Wizard of Oz, Star Wars, Star Trek, The Lord of the Rings, Lost, The Matrix, Superman,* Harry Potter, Narnia, and *Batman.*[6] Professor Turner also points out that, despite discouragements from the scholarly establishment, the epic has continued as a genre within conventional literature from Tolstoy's *War and Peace* and Herman Melville's *Moby Dick* to T. S. Eliot's *The Waste Land* and science fiction epics like Isaac Asimov's *Foundation* trilogy.

There is also a large quantity of popular literature aimed at readers who like hot-blooded adventure stories set in the world of the Vikings and/or the Nordic deities. Books in this category range from those of the "sword and sorcery" variety to well-researched period novels, sometimes based on real historical characters. The book covers of this genre typically feature dragon-headed Viking ships, runic inscriptions, swords, battle-axes, chain-mailed and helmeted warriors, and often a god or two, such as one-eyed Odin or hammer-wielding Thor.

Different writers have used the Nordic material in distinctly different ways. J. R. R. Tolkien's trilogy, *The Lord of the Rings,* for example, is full of motifs, names, and themes taken from the *Edda* and the sagas. Tolkien's "Middle Earth" is borrowed from Midgard, one of the nine worlds of Yggdrasil. The wizard Gandalf is named after one of the dwarfs listed in the *Völuspá (Sayings of the Seeress)* from the *Edda,* and Gandalf also has certain characteristics of Odin. The theme of the cursed ring also comes from Nordic literature. Tolkien vehemently denied that his ring had anything to with Wagner's opera cycle, but probably both of them drew on the same Scandinavian sources, such as the *Völsunga Saga*, where a chain of tragic events is set off by the theft of a gold treasure.

More recently Nordic mythology has been used overtly by the British writer Antonia Byatt in her remarkable novel *Ragnarok: End of the Gods* (2011). The book is essentially a retelling of the Nordic myths, interspersed and connected with the story of an English girl, evacuated to a country town at the age of three at the beginning of World War II. After learning to read, she becomes enamored of the Nordic myths through a book called *Asgard and the Gods*, "a solid volume, bound in green, with an intriguing, rushing image on the cover, of Odin's Wild Hunt on horseback tearing through a clouded sky amid jagged bolts of lightning."[7] There is also an illustration of the Riesengebirge in Germany, depicting rocks half resembling gigantic humanoid figures.[8] Such images give her a sense of energy and power, in contrast to the "cotton-wool cloud of nothingness" that she experiences when trying to pray in the local church during a service.[9] The events in the theater of war, of which she is uncomfortably aware, are paralleled by the story of the gods of Asgard, as they plunge toward the apocalypse of Ragnarök.

Another modern author who has skillfully adapted the Nordic mythology, albeit in a very different way, is Neil Gaiman. His book *American Gods*, published in 2001, has become a huge best seller and given rise to a television series of the same title. The central character is a man simply called Shadow, who is released from prison at the beginning of the book and, while traveling home by air, finds himself sitting next to a mysterious man who introduces himself as Mr. Wednesday—an immediate giveaway if you know that Wednesday is Woden's or Odin's day. Further clues follow: he has one glass eye and a tie pin in the form of a tree, he offers Shadow a draught of mead, and a friend of his calls him a "cold-blooded, heartless old tree-hanger." Shadow reluctantly accepts employment from Wednesday and they set off on a journey on which they soon encounter other gods and goddesses. Some of these are from the Nordic pantheon, but there are also Slavic, Egyptian, African, Native American, and various other deities.

Interspersed with the story of Shadow's adventures are accounts of how these various deities came to America. Odin, for example, was brought there by the first Viking explorers to reach the coast in 813 CE, while the Slavic pantheon arrived with the wave of Russian immigrants in the nineteenth century. It turns out that all of these old gods are preparing for a war with the new gods, that is to say, the gods of the computer, the telephone, the stock market, and the other things that modernity worships. There is, it seems, not room in the world for both sets of entities. The story builds to a dramatic and violent climax.

The author of *American Gods* started his career as a writer for comic books, and it was through comics that he had his first encounter with the Nordic pantheon. He has described how he read a story about Thor in one of the Marvel Comics and thus became infused with a fascination for Nordic mythology.[10]

Thor's appearance in comics in the mid-twentieth century[11] is inseparably linked with the Marvel team of story writer Stan Lee and artist Jack Kirby. It appears to have been Kirby, a man with a fascination for myths and legends, who first brought Thor to the pages of comic books. The mighty hammer-swinger appeared in a three-part story in the comic book series *Boy Commanders*, published by DC Comics during World War II. The story, which was clearly intended as wartime propaganda, culminates in the Asgard Castle in Norway, where a troop of boy commandos, under their adult leader Rip

Carter, confronts a group of Nazis. The heroes, aided by Thor and Odin, prevail, and Thor, with a swing of his hammer, sends the Nazis to the realm of darkness. Kirby's version of Thor appeared again in 1957 in a series called *Tales of the Unexpected*, also published by DC Comics, and in August 1962 he and Lee launched the "Saga of Thor" in the Marvel Comics series *Journey into Mystery*. The cover shows a youthful, hammer-wielding Thor on the roof of a skyscraper, battling with aliens made of green stone. Evidently it was thought that, as a modern super-hero, he ought to have a surname, so in *Journey into Mystery* he is called Thor Odinson and, like Superman and Batman, he has an alter ego in everyday life. Thor's is Dr. Donald Blake, who has a lame leg, walks with a stick, and is altogether unheroic, but when he picks up an old cudgel and knocks it against a stone, the cudgel becomes a hammer and he turns into Thor. Marvel went on to introduce other Nordic gods and goddesses into their comics, including Odin, Sif, Baldur, and the villainous god Loki, but it was Thor who remained the most prominent Nordic figure in comics and later in films and computer games.

Icelandic scholar Jón Karl Helgason, in his book *Echoes of Valhalla* tracing the progress of the Nordic deities from the world of the *Edda* to that of modern mass media, points out that, since the publication of the early Lee and Kirby stories, Marvel has produced hundreds of comics about Thor. Many of the narratives were adapted for the television cartoon series *The Marvel Super Heroes* (1966), and more recent adaptations of this kind are the fantasy action movies *Thor* (2011), directed by Kenneth Branagh, and its sequel *Thor: The Dark World* (2013), directed by Alan Taylor. Both of these films have been exploited for selling spin-off merchandise, ranging from T-shirts and cuff links to alarm clocks and wallets. "Thor's role in the comic series *The Avengers*," Helgason writes "has contributed to his colossal international fame. Offshoots of this material, including

Joss Whedon's films *The Avengers* (2012) and *Avengers: Age of Ultron* (2015), have also made their way into cinemas, televisions, computers and video games consoles."[12]

Among mortal heroes, one of the most popular in recent years has been Beowulf, taken from the epic of that name. Although written down in England in the late tenth or eleventh century, the story is set in Scandinavia. It relates how Beowulf, a gallant warrior from Geatland (the present-day Swedish province of Götaland) comes to the rescue of the Danish king Hrothgar, whose court is being plagued by a monster called Grendel. Beowulf kills Grendel and then goes on to kill Grendel's equally fearsome mother. He returns home and becomes king of Geatland. Then, after fifty years, he fights and defeats a dragon, but is himself killed in the combat.

There have been several film versions of *Beowulf*. One of the best is the animated 1998 film made for British television, which is visually beautiful, true to the story, and with a voice-over that splendidly captures the spirit of the original text with its alliteration and kennings. The following year appeared a very different film version starring Christopher Lambert in the title role. Shot in Romania, it is all blood and thunder and full of over-the-top scenes, as when Beowulf fights with Grendel's mother after she has turned herself from a blond Hollywood vamp into a sort of giant crab.

A rather subtler treatment is the 2007 film *Beowulf*, a British-American production, directed by Robert Zemeckis, written by Neil Gaiman and Robert Avary, and with a cast including Ray Winstone as Beowulf and Anthony Hopkins as King Hrothgar. The film was made using a process called motion capture, which shows the actors as recognizably themselves but half transformed into computer-animated figures. The effect is oddly fascinating and underlines the mythical quality of the subject matter. The screenplay has some interesting variations on the original story. Grendel is a rather pitiful monster, who turns out to be Hrothgar's son by a beautiful water demon. Beowulf in turn is seduced by her and she gives birth to the dragon who eventually kills and is killed by Beowulf.

Yet another interpretation of the story is presented in the 2005 film *Beowulf and Grendel*, a Canadian-British-Icelandic production, directed by Sturla Gunnarsson with Gerard Butler as Beowulf and Stellan Skarsgård as Hrothgar. The haunting soundtrack by Hilmar Örn Hilmarsson provides a moody accompaniment to the dramatic Icelandic locations. In this version Grendel is not a monster of fantasy but a man bent on avenging his father's death at the hands of King Hrothgar. Eventually he is captured by Beowulf, escapes by severing an arm, and dies as a result. Beowulf then kills Grendel's mother, who is a sea hag. In another departure from the original story, there is a beautiful witch called Selma, who has a son by Grendel and becomes Beowulf's lover.

If the gods and goddesses have happily made the transition to the cinema screen, they have become equally at home in the world of pop music. "Immigrant Song," first performed by the legendary British hard rock band Led Zeppelin in the summer of 1970 at the Bath Festival of Blues and Progressive Music, begins with a high-volume celebration of the land of "the ice and snow." Earlier that summer, while the band was touring Iceland, two of its members, Robert Plant and Jimmy Page, were inspired to write the song, which was released in the autumn of that year as a single and then as part of the album *Led Zeppelin III*. While Viking songs were a relatively minor part of the group's repertoire, "Immigrant Song" was a fore-taste of what was to become a distinct genre within the pop music scene. The genre covers a confusing variety of categories and names (Viking metal, Viking rock, Pagan metal, folk metal, neo-folk, etc.). Styles differ widely within a broadly Nordic orientation. For want of a better term, let us call the overall genre neo-Nordic.[13]

Other bands soon followed the example of Led Zeppelin in introducing Nordic and Viking references into their lyrics, although initially these motifs were put there as colorful embellishments rather than out of any deeper interest in what lay behind them. However, with the growth of Nordic Paganism (commonly called Asatru, Odinism, or Heathenry), as described in chapter 10, came a proliferation of bands who explicitly adopted a Nordic image, not only in their lyrics but also in their names, their style of dress, and their album covers. Many of their members were—and still are—followers of the Pagan movement. One of the pioneers of this genre was the Swedish band Bathory, launched in 1983 and dissolved in 2004, whose lyrics and stylistics incorporated both Nordic and provocatively Satanic elements. Other groups, in the same provocative spirit and eager to *épater les bourgeois*, flaunted Nazi insignia.

By the 1990s, there were neo-Nordic bands emerging in many different parts of the world. Typical was the Norwegian heavy metal group Einherjer, founded in 1993 and still going at the time of writing. The name (otherwise usually spelled *einherjar*, meaning "lone fighters") refers to the fallen warriors who reside in Valhalla. The cover of their early album *Dragons of the North* shows the dragon-headed prow of a Viking ship. Another album, *Odin Owns Ye All*, has a cover depicting the face of the one-eyed god along with his two ravens, carved in wood. The videos accompanying their singles are commensurately atmospheric. The one for the elegiac song "Ballad of the Swords" features a procession of figures, silhouetted in black against a bleak landscape, carrying a dead warrior to a pyre, from which he ascends into the sky.

Einherjer's lyrics show an intimate familiarity with Old Norse literature. They sing of Ginnungagap, Yggdrasil, the sacrifice of Odin, the death of Balder, and much else. Sometimes they quote directly from the *Edda*, as in their song "Home," which contains (slightly compressed) the poignant lines from the *Völuspá* (*Sayings of the Seeress*) about the mortality and men and cattle and the immortality of a person's reputation.

Equally Pagan in style and image is the Faroese band Tyr, founded in 1998 and named after the Nordic god who sacrificed a hand in order to capture the Fenris Wolf. Their albums, such as *Ragnarök*, *Eric the Red*, and *By the Light of the Northern Star*, have characteristic covers depicting Viking ships, sword-wielding warriors, and eerie northern landscapes. Their lyrics are heavily influenced by Scandinavian mythology, and their music incorporates elements of Faroese traditional music, adapted to the heavy metal idiom. Their message is proudly Pagan, as in their song "Hold the Hammer High."

Another Scandinavian country, Iceland, has produced the internationally acclaimed band Sigur Rós (meaning "Victory Rose"), founded in 1994 by Jónsi Birgisson, Georg Holm, and Ágúst Ævar Gunnarsson who was later replaced by Orri Páll Dýrason. Kjartan Sveinsson joined the band as a keyboard, flute, and guitar player in 1998. Others have come on board or worked with the group over the years, notably the composer and leader of the Ásatrú community in Iceland, Hilmar Örn Hilmarsson, the traditional *rímur* chanter and baritone Steindór Andersen, and the stone marimba player and sculptor Páll Guðmundsson. Björk, the well-known pop singer, was an early champion of the band.

Sigur Rós has been instrumental in reinvigorating old Icelandic musical and bardic traditions by combining them with modern popular music styles. Characteristic is the album *Rímur* (1991), in which Andersen chants old Icelandic poetry to Sigur Rós's subtle and unobtrusive accompaniment. Another of their productions is *Odin's Raven Magic*, based on an old Icelandic poem. It had a triumphant premiere at London's Barbican Centre on April 21, 2002, performed by the group together with a sizable orchestra, playing music composed by Hilmar Örn Hilmarsson, Jón Þór Birgisson, Georg Holm, Kjartan Sveinsson, Orri Páll Dýrason, Steindór Andersen, and María Huld Markan Sigfúsdóttir. The piece rises gradually to an orgiastic climax of Wagnerian intensity that leaves the listener floating in another realm.

Britain has also produced its crop of neo-Nordic groups. One of the most interesting to appear in recent decades is Fire and Ice, founded by Ian Read in 1991. Its genre is sometimes described as "neo-folk," although Read finds the term inadequate. Read is one of the most creative and eclectic artists working in the Neo-Pagan musical scene. A dedicated follower of the Nordic Pagan path and a rune-master, he regards his songs as a way of conveying his worldview. As he has said in an interview: "My aim is to supply alternative or different doorways for those who wish to walk on the path towards Rûna. These move all people differently because all people have different movements. The message works on various levels like unpeeling an onion layer after layer."[14] The term *Rûna*, referring to the path of Nordic wisdom embodied in the runes, is also the title of one of the Fire and Ice albums. The group's songs are strongly influenced by folk music and many are adaptations of traditional English songs. Typically, they have a wistful, haunting quality.

One European country that has produced a particularly large number of neo-Nordic bands is Germany. Helrunar, founded in 2001, sings mostly in German, Norwegian, and Old Norse. Its poetic quality is much more refined than the average of the genre. The lyrics are based on a detailed knowledge of Old Nordic literature and mythology and use traditional poetic devices such as alliteration and the metaphors known as kennings. In a rather different mode is the group Faun, founded in 1999, whose themes are taken not just from Nordic but also from Celtic, Greek, and other Pagan traditions. The band uses a variety of instruments such as Celtic harp, flute, bagpipes, and hurdy-gurdy to produce a rather gentle, dreamy sound. In a different style again is the music of Heimdalls Wacht (referring to Heimdall, who guards the rainbow bridge to the home of the gods and goddesses) from North-Rhine-Westphalia and active since 2004. The website[15] for the band characterizes the music as "a most distinctive and expressive blend: on the basis of raw and at the same time melancholic and melodic Black Metal . . ." while they describe their mission as follows:

> Heimdalls Wacht is the sound and the fury of our present era, reproaching the modern world in its pervasive conformity and mindless stupidity. Clamoring wrath! Shrieking desperation! Sonic weltschmerz! Withdrawn melancholy! Heimdalls Wacht's music, lyrics, and overall concept provide an outlet for a deep-rooted uneasiness, a discomfort in the face of an empty zeitgeist and the monotony of the masses, treating with contempt today's consumer society that venerates hollow idols and cannot grasp true spiritual richness.

Holland too has its neo-Nordic groups, such as Baldrs Draumar, meaning "Balder's Dreams" (founded 2009). The group is from Frisia and proud of their local roots—they describe their style as "furious Frisian folk metal." The cover of their album *Nordseegermanen* (*North Sea Germanic People*) is shown in Figure 21.

Looking farther afield, we find that the neo-Nordic genre has spread far and wide and is by no means confined to northern regions. In Russia there are bands such as Midgaard, founded in 2006—which has a Nordic focus, as the name suggests—and Ruyan, active since 2010, which looks more to Russian Pagan traditions. Greece has produced Hildr Valkyrie, a largely one-woman show (since 2003) featuring Hildr herself as singer, composer, lyricist, and musician, accompanied by various other instrumentalists. In

21. Cover of the album *Nordseegermanen* (North Sea Germanic People) by the band Baldrs Draumar (Balder's Dreams).

North America there are groups such as Beorn's Hall (U.S., founded 2016) and Dagaz (Canada, founded 2004). Latin America too has its neo-Nordic bands like Mighty Thor (Mexico, formed 2001) and Hordethor (Colombia, formed 2002).

So it seems that the Northern deities are indeed alive and well in the modern world—and not just on the corner of Broadway and 42nd Street, but in the film studios of Hollywood, at pop concerts, and in the pages of comics and best-selling books. And they are no longer waiting for the traffic lights to change. They have already crossed over into our world from their "ultimate, dim Thule."

NOTES

1. Quoted by the psychologist James Hillman in a lecture in 2007 in the Mythic Journeys series under the auspices of the Mythic Imagination Institute. Online at: https://www.youtube.com/watch?v=iFkkQ9eq8qw.
2. The story is posted in full on the website https://www.lang.nagoya-u.ac.jp.
3. Posted on http://www.classicshorts.com/stories/DescentIntoMaelstrom.html.
4. Clark Ashton Smith, "The Tale of Satampra Zeiros" in the collection *Emperor of Dreams*, ed. Stephen Jones (London: Gollancz, 2002), 57.
5. Turner, 4.
6. Turner, 17.
7. Byatt, 10–11.
8. Byatt, 12.
9. Byatt, 13.
10. Recounted by Gaiman in various interviews, e.g., at the Boston Public Library on May 4, 2017, available online at https://www.youtube.com/watch?v=mX7pvtU9m_w.
11. For an account of Thor's career in comics, see Jón Karl Helgasson, *Echoes of Valhalla* (2017), and *The Jack Kirby Collector*, a magazine series published from 1994 by TwoMorrows Publishing.
12. Helgason, 31.
13. For an interesting survey of this genre, see Helgason, ch. 5, "Odin: From Wagner to Viking Metal."
14. http://www.heimdallr.ch/Interviews/2001/fire.html.
15. http://heimdallswacht.de/.

CHAPTER 14

CONCLUSION

In this book I have explored the theme of the North, both as a geographical location and as an idea. I have spoken frequently about the notion of Hyperborea and the role it has played in myth, legend, romance, and even politics. In this concluding chapter I would like to summarize the evidence regarding Hyperborea and finally discuss what significance the Hyperborean legend and the whole current fascination with the North might have for us in the present age.

So, was there a Hyperborea? First of all, for such a place to have existed certain climatic and geographical conditions would have had to exist; that is to say a temperate zone would have had to exist in the Arctic region. While this sounds improbable in view of the conditions in the Arctic today, there are several ways in which it might have been possible.

One factor that affects the dynamics of temperature and climate on the earth is the degree of inclination of the earth's axis of rotation, which is the same as the degree to which the equator is out of alignment with the ecliptic (the path that the sun appears to trace around the earth). The greater this degree—i.e., the more the earth tilts—the more extreme is the variation between summer and winter in terms of temperature and daylight hours. This angle varies over long periods of time between 22.1 and 24.5 degrees, causing commensurate changes. There is even a theory that at one time in the distant past the axis was vertical. This would mean that at the poles the sun never set but circled continually around the earth, half visible above the horizon. As Joscelyn Godwin writes:

> Numerous authorities . . . assure us that in primordial times the earth was not tilted, but spun perfectly upright with its equator in the same plane as the ecliptic. . . . Under these circumstances there would be no seasons of summer or winter, spring or fall; all days would be alike. Near the equator, the climate would always be hot; near the poles, always cold. . . . Nevertheless, the absence of seasons would make the earth habitable, and even comfortable, to much higher latitudes than is the case today. . . . Aided by ocean currents and by the inner heat of the earth, twelve hours of sunlight would permit fertility to a very high latitude.[1]

With that in mind let's look at some evidence from nature. On the island of Spitzbergen, which lies only about seven hundred miles from the North Pole (a day's drive on a good road), researchers have found fossilized remains of water lilies, palm trees, and crustaceans that inhabit only tropical waters. On Canada's Baffin Island, some nine hundred miles from the pole, remains of alder and birch trees have been discovered, pointing to a warmer climate that prevailed there until about 17,000 years ago.[2] And, as already mentioned in chapter 3, remains of trees have also been found on Grinnell Land in the far north of Canada, including yew, elm, lime, birch, poplar, and hazel—all of which would normally require an average annual temperature of +8 degrees Centigrade, instead of the present –20.

The presence of these flora in prehistoric times could be accounted for by the verticality of the earth's axis at that period or possibly by the existence of a freak temperate zone in the midst of the Arctic, caused by warm-water currents and other factors, as suggested by Ewing and Donn, whose research I mentioned in chapter 3.

Something else that should be mentioned is the phenomenon of continental drift, that is to say, the capacity of the earth's crust to move in relation to the planet's core, as though the planet were an egg with a loose shell that could slide this way and that. Thus, over long periods of time, landmasses could have slid either away from the Pole or toward it, while the axis of rotation remained the same in relation to the planet as a whole. This would mean that there could once have been land at the North Pole, albeit many millions of years ago, long before any probable human habitation—unless there have been humans on the earth for much longer than is commonly thought. So probably we have to look to some of the other factors I have mentioned if we are seeking evidence for Hyperborea.

What about the catastrophe that is said to have brought Hyperborea and its golden age to an end? The likelihood that some such catastrophe took place is supported by accounts to that effect in the lore of many different peoples—from the story of the great flood in the Old Testament to Plato's account of the destruction of Atlantis in *Timaeus*. In the Nordic eschatology there is a similar scenario. A wolf swallows the sun, another wolf catches the moon, the stars disappear from the sky, trees are uprooted from the earth, mountains fall, the ocean surges up on to the land and with it the Midgard Serpent.

These accounts tie in with the evidence from research into the prehistory of the northern latitudes. The retreat of the ice age from about the fifteenth millennium BCE appears to have proceeded sporadically, sometimes interrupted by the return of extreme cold, sometimes accelerating and causing rapid melting of the glaciers, sometimes accompanied by intense volcanic activity. One particularly cataclysmic period is believed to have occurred around the eleventh millennium BCE, when an abrupt drop in temperature, temporarily reversing the deglaciation, was accompanied by massive volcanic eruptions, blackening the sky with dust and bringing tidal waves,[3] or—in the words of the *Edda*—causing the wolf to swallow the sun, the stars to disappear, and the Midgard Serpent to be swept ashore. One region affected by this catastrophe was Siberia, where it has been possible to learn a great deal from the corpses of the mammoths who died at that time. So suddenly did the cold descend on them that their bodies were kept in "cryogenic suspension," including the undigested vegetation in their stomachs. This vegetation was found to include grasses, bluebells, buttercups, tender sedges, and wild beans, indicating that Siberia had a mild climate before the catastrophe.[4]

As a possible location for Hyperborea, the areas of Siberia and northern Russia bordering the Arctic Ocean have a certain amount in their favor. Recent archaeological findings suggest that humans were already living there at a very early date. In 2012, an eleven-year-old schoolboy discovered the well-preserved corpse of a fifteen-year-old male mammoth in the Sopkarginsky district on the eastern bank of the giant Yenisei River in northern Siberia. Archaeologists who investigated the discovery found wounds on the body indicating that the animal had been hunted and killed by early humans using weapons made of bone and stone. If this was the case, it means that the area was inhabited at least 45,000 years ago, which is when the mammoth is estimated to have died.[5] That would allow for a period of some 32,000–33,000 years of habitation before the onset of the catastrophe I have described—theoretically more than enough time for an advanced culture to develop.

Possible traces of such a culture are the remains described in chapter 12: the pyramids, dolmens, and labyrinths found on the Kola Peninsula and the mysterious stone spheres on the island of Champ. On the other hand, apart from these remains, what evidence we have of human habitation in that region suggests a hunter-gatherer people engaged in a continuously hard struggle for survival, using simple tools of stone, ivory, and bone—in other words, a far cry from the golden Hyperborean civilization of romance and legend.

Nevertheless, let us try a thought experiment, putting together what we have learned so far. Let us say that at some distant point in time—perhaps 50,000 years ago—an unknown people settled near the Arctic Circle, possibly in the territories that are now the north of Scandinavia, Russia, and Siberia. Over many millennia they developed a culture that included a complex and sophisticated language, a commensurately refined poetic tradition, a religion with shamanic characteristics, advanced mathematical and astronomical knowledge, highly developed technical skills, and perhaps a matriarchal order. Over time they spread out from their homeland, giving rise to Stonehenge, the Callanish Stones, the Platonic spheres of Orkney, the Bredarör tomb in Sweden, the solar observatory at Goseck in Germany, and the ubiquitous labyrinths. With the onset of the natural catastrophe around the eleventh millennium BCE, they abandoned their far northern homeland and moved south through Scandinavia and into the European continent. Some eight thousand years later, a contingent of Indo-Europeans settled in Scandinavia and became the Germanic people, overlapping with the Hyperborean people and inheriting some of their ways and traditions, including shamanism. The encounter with the Hyperboreans might then have been recorded allegorically in Germanic mythology as the story of the war and later alliance between the Aesir and the Vanir. Alternatively, perhaps it is the giants of the *Edda* who are the Hyperboreans.

This is of course speculation, and basically the jury is still out on whether there was a Hyperborea and where it might have been located, but there are many who believe in scenarios that are a good deal more fantastic than the one I have just outlined, as a search on the Internet under "Hyperborea" will reveal. Hyperborea is one of those things that, if it didn't exist, would have to be invented.

We have seen the impact of Hyperboreanism in Russia and how, when the theme crops up, there are sometimes a few xenophobic dragons lurking about, as there are within some of the Nordic Pagan organizations. On this subject, my friend, the writer and philosopher of magical thinking Lionel Snell, has some interesting observations to make. The Nordic pantheon, he says, was driven underground by Christianity, so to speak banished into hell—and he goes on:

> Another way of saying it is that these ancient gods have been driven down into the collective unconscious and abandoned. The effect of doing this is similar to the effect you would get if you drove your cats, dogs and other domestic animals back into the jungle: when you set out to rediscover them several generations later, you would find that they had reverted to the wild, grown feral and fierce. But their essential nature remains unchanged—a cat is still a cat with all its potential.
>
> Something like this happened to the Norse gods. The first attempts to re-contact them this [i.e., the twentieth] century had drastic results. Jung, in his essay on Wotan first published in 1936, describes how the "old god of storm and frenzy, the long quiescent Wotan" is awakening "like an extinct volcano, to a new activity, in a civilised country that had long supposed to have outgrown the middle ages". He describes how the "youth movement" had sacrificed sheep to this old god, and how the same spirit was now stirring in the Nazi movement. Perhaps we should compare the resulting havoc in Germany to what would happen if the people who chased their cats into the wild were to enter the jungle several years later and say "oh look, there's our Kitty! Do

let's take her back home." Half a century later there is still something awesome and wild about the Norse gods.[6]

It is these qualities of the "awesome" and the "wild"—and I would add the "heroic"—that many people would readily associate with the North today. Say the word *North* and they will think of the blood-and-thunder, swashbuckling world of Beowulf, Thor, and the Vikings. Through our computers we can now enter this world with a few mouse clicks and experience vicariously the awesome, wild, and heroic in the safety of our homes.

But there is a less "feral" side of the North that I believe is ultimately of greater significance. More and more people are discovering the amazing riches of the *Edda* and the sagas and the worldview that underlies them: the deities as embodiments of the great forces in the universe and in ourselves, the cyclical view of human history, the ancient shamanic tradition of the North, and the notion of the world as a vast, living tree to which we are all connected.

All this is very different from the idea of the North that I encountered in the world of international development, in which I worked for a number of years. There the North meant the "developed" world—cutting-edge technology, motorways, dams, factories, urbanization, digitalization—while the South meant a deficiency of all those things, which needed to be made good. In this book I have tried to present a different image of the North—one that speaks to a part of us that no amount of technical progress can satisfy. The North is the direction for the explorer with a dream—the seeker after Hyperborea, Belovodye, Agartha, Shambhala, Shangri-La. The musicologist Marjorie Roth, whom I quoted at the beginning of the book, presents an eloquent description of the North as "a shifting idea, always out of reach, always leading to a further north, to an elsewhere" and "a place where you can be truthful to yourself."

As for the relationship between North and South, if Apollo is a god who wanders between the two, as many sources tell us, we can see him as being like the dots in the Yin-Yang symbol—the light dot in the dark North and the dark dot in the bright South—reminding us that the two sides are interdependent and moving together in a continuous dance.

NOTES

1. Godwin, 13–14.
2. Hancock, 478–79.
3. I am summarizing the evidence present by Hancock in chapters 27 and 51.
4. Ivan T. Sanderson, "Riddle of the Quick-Frozen Giants," in *Saturday Evening Post*, January 16, 1960, 82, quoted by Hancock, 216.
5. Article by Anna Liesowska, "The smoking gun 'proving ancient man killed woolly mammoth 45,000 years ago'" in *Siberian Times* online, February 19, 2018.
6. Lionel Snell, foreword to Freya Aswynn, *Leaves of Yggdrasil*, vii–viii.

APPENDIX

WHO'S WHO IN NORTHERN MYTHOLOGY

(Cross-references are shown in italics.)

This is not an exhaustive list but includes the major Nordic deities, heroes, and mythical beings and in some cases their equivalents in other mythologies.

Aegir

God of the sea. His wife is *Ran*, and they have nine daughters who are waves. The similarity of the name to that of the Greek sea god Aegaeon, after whom the Aegean is named, suggests that the two are cognates. See chapter 3.

Aesir (plural of As)

One of the two groups of Nordic deities, the other being the *Vanir*. These groups are thought to derive from two different cultures, that of the Aesir being warlike, and that of the Vanir being peace-loving and benevolent. Some scholars believe that the Vanir were embedded in a more archaic, non-Indo-European culture, indigenous to northern Europe, that was earth-centered and pastoral and gave prominence to female deities (see for example the cult of *Nerthus*). By contrast, according to this theory, the Aesir were the gods of an Indo-European, hunter-gatherer people who migrated from the east and initially came into conflict with the people of the Vanir, but eventually merged with them—viz. the account in the *Prose Edda* which relates that the two groups had been in conflict but then made a truce involving an exchange of hostages. The Aesir sent *Hoenir* and *Mímir* to the Vanir, while the latter sent *Njörd*, *Frey*, and *Freya* to the Aesir. In the *Völuspá* (*Sayings of the Seeress*) in the *Poetic Edda* the outbreak of a new war between the Aesir and Vanir is the beginning of the downfall of the gods.

Agnar

Son of King *Geirröd*. As related in the poem *Grimnismal*, Agnar comes to *Odin*'s aid when the latter is tortured by Geirröd.

Alvis (the "All-Wise")

A dwarf who desires to marry Thor's daughter and is compelled by *Thor* to answer a series of questions to test his knowledge, as related in the Eddic poem the *Alvissmal*. The questions relate to the different names for the earth, sky, sun, moon, sea, etc., in all the various worlds or realms, i.e., those of the Aesir, the Vanir, human beings, giants, and elves. Alvis answers correctly by giving a string of kennings for each word, but to no avail. As he answers the final question, sunlight falls into the hall, turning Alvis to stone. There is perhaps a subtext to this story, relating to poetry, which was a sacred art in the Nordic culture. Thor's daughter is possibly a metaphor for the muse of poetry, whose gift Alvis desires. The message could be that it is not sufficient to know all the correct kennings if one lacks the flame of poetic inspiration.

Andvari ("Careful One")

A dwarf who appears in the Eddic poems *Völuspá* (*Sayings of the Seeress*) and the *Reginsmal* (*Song of Regin*) as well as in the *Völsunga Saga*. Andvari lives in a river in the form of a pike, guarding a hoard of gold, including a magical ring. *Loki* steals the treasure including the ring, whereupon Andvari puts a curse on it, setting off a chain of misfortunes.

Ask (Ash Tree) and Embla (Elm)

The two primal human beings created from trees by three gods. The story varies somewhat between the *Poetic Edda* and the *Prose Edda*. In the former it is *Odin*, *Hoenir*, and *Lodur* who discover the two trees. Odin gives them breath, Hoenir gives them spirit or passion, and Lodur gives them hair and fresh complexions. In the *Prose Edda* Odin is accompanied by his brothers *Vili* and *Vé*. Odin gives not only breath but also life. Vili bestows understanding and emotion, and Vé confers form, speech, hearing, and sight.

Audhumla

The primeval cow, who played a key role in the creation of life. As the *Prose Edda* relates, the primal giant *Ymir*, who arose out of the interaction of fire and ice, was nourished by a cow called Audhumla (how she appeared is not clear) who then, by licking rime-covered rocks, created a being called *Buri*, grandfather of the gods.

Austri (East), Nordri (North), Sudri (South), and Vestri (West)

According to the *Prose Edda*, the four dwarfs of the compass points. The sons of *Bor*, after killing the giant *Ymir* and turning his skull into the sky, placed the dwarfs at the four quarters in order to support it.

Balder (alternatively Baldur or Baldr)

Balder, son of *Odin* and *Frigg*, is the fair, radiant god of light. His mother had extracted a vow from all substances, animals, and plants in the world that they would not harm Balder, excluding only the delicate mistletoe because of its tender age, an omission that was to prove fatal. As an entertainment Balder would stand up in front of the gods and remain unharmed while they shot or threw stones at him. But *Loki* persuaded the blind god *Hödr* (or Hod) to shoot at Balder, his twin brother, with an arrow made of mistletoe, and guided his aim. The arrow flew and Balder fell dead, causing great grief among the gods. As a god of light, Balder shares certain characteristics with Apollo, and it is possible that the two names are cognates.

Beowulf
Hero of the medieval Anglo-Saxon epic named after him. Beowulf comes from Sweden to the aid of the Danish king Hrothgar, whose court is being plagued by the murderous monster *Grendel*. Beowulf kills Grendel and then Grendel's mother. Returning home, he becomes king of Geatland (later the Swedish province of Götaland). Fifty years later he fights and defeats a dragon, but is killed in the fight.

Bestla
A giantess, described in the *Prose Edda* as the wife of *Bor* (son of *Buri*) and the mother of *Odin*, *Vili*, and *Vé*.

Bor or Bur ("son")
Son of the primordial being, *Buri*. He takes the giantess *Bestla* as his wife.

Bragi
God of poetry. His name means "poetry" or "eloquence" and is probably cognate with the pejorative English word *brag*. Bragi is mentioned a number of times in both the *Prose Edda* and the *Poetic Edda*. For example in the *Grimnismal* from the *Poetic Edda* he is referred to as the best of skalds. His wife is *Idun*, goddess of eternal youth.

Brímir ("sea")
A mythological being associated with the sea, whose name is cognates with the English word *brine*. Arguably the name is related to that of the port city of Bremen in north Germany.

Brynhild (alternatively Brunhild, Brünhild, Brunnhilde, Brünnhilde)

Generally considered one of the *Valkyries*, a many-faceted figure, who features in the *Edda* and in other sources In the *Völsunga Saga* and the *Nibelungenlied* she is a deceived woman who plots deadly revenge, and in Wagner's *Ring* cycle her image has become that of a buxom, spear-wielding Amazon. In the Eddic poem *Sigrdrífumál* she appears as Sigrdrífa, a Valkyrie who is sleeping, trapped in a suit of armor, until she is freed by the hero *Sigurd*.

Buri

The primordial being who was created by the cow *Audhumla* licking salt-covered rocks.

Dísir (singular Dís)

Female supernatural figures of indeterminate role, variously depicted as fierce, Valkyrie-like beings, female ancestors, or benevolent tutelary spirits of a person, group, or place.

Dwarfs

Mysterious, somewhat elemental beings who have their own world, but from time to time are called upon to help the gods. According to the *Edda* they arose from the maggots feasting on *Ymir*'s flesh. In time they became skillful craftspeople and made precious things for the gods, such as Odin's spear, Thor's hammer, and Frey's magic ship. Sometimes they are treated as identical to the *elves*, sometimes as a separate species.

Elves

Otherworldly beings of two different kinds: Light Elves and Black or Dark Elves. In the Eddic poem the *Gylfaginning*, as related by Snorri, *Odin* speaks of the elves as follows: "There is one place that is called Alfheim. There live the folk called the light-elves, but dark-elves live down in the ground, and they are unlike them in appearance, and even more unlike them in nature. Light-elves are fairer than the sun to look at, but dark elves are blacker than pitch."[1] However, it is the Dark Elves who help the gods by making the fetter to harness the *Fenris Wolf*.

Embla

See *Ask and Embla*.

Eostre (German Ostara)

A spring goddess who, according to the British chronicler Bede (673–735 CE), gave her name to the Christian festival of Easter. Her German equivalent is *Ostara*. Information on this deity is scant.

Fenris Wolf (Fenrir)

The terrible offspring of *Loki* and the giantess Angrboda. The gods, becoming alarmed at the growth of the creature, have him restrained with a fetter made by the dark *elves* and fashioned out of six things: the sound of a cat's footfall, the beard of a woman, the roots of a mountain, the nerves of a bear, the breath of fishes, and the spittle of birds.[2] At the end of the world, the Ragnarök, the wolf breaks free and devours both the sun and *Odin*. Only the silent god *Vidar* is able to overcome the wolf by thrusting his outsize shoe into the creature's jaws.

Forseti

Snorri writes of this god: "Forseti is the name of the son of Baldr and Nanna . . . He has a hall in heaven called Glitnir, and whoever comes to him with difficult legal disputes, they all leave with their differences settled. It is the best place of judgment among gods and men."[3]

Frey

A fertility god and an important member of the group of deities known as the *Vanir*, Frey is the son of *Njörd* and brother of *Freya*. Frey possesses a magic ship called Skídbladnir and a golden boar called *Gullinborsti*, which pulls his chariot. He was worshipped, along with *Thor* and *Odin*, in the great Pagan temple at Uppsala, Sweden. Illustrations of his statue show him with an enormous phallus.

Freya

A prominent goddess, daughter of *Njörd*, sister of *Frey*, and wife of Od. Like her brother, she belongs to the *Vanir*. She is associated with love and sexuality and has many lovers. In return for sleeping with four dwarfs in turn, she acquired her necklace Brisingamen. She travels in a chariot drawn by cats and is associated with the magical practice known as *seiðr*. There is some doubt as to whether her identity overlaps with that of *Frigg*.

Frigg

Wife of *Odin* and queen of the Ásynjur, the female *Aesir*. She has her own splendid dwelling called Fensalir and her own servants. She makes all things promise not to harm her son *Balder*, omitting only the mistletoe, which causes his death, and she sends Balder's brother Hermod into the underworld to plead for his return. There is some evidence that she may be a variation of *Freya*.

Fylgja (plural Fylgjur)

A tutelary spirit that becomes attached to an individual throughout that person's lifetime, often in the form of an animal—an example of the shamanic nature of much of the Nordic mythology. The *fylgja* was normally invisible. Its visible appearance showed that the person to whom it belonged was close to death. Sometimes the *fylgja* is attached to a family rather than an individual. There is some overlap with the concept of *hamingja*.

Gefion (or Gefiun)

One of the goddesses or Asynjur. Snorri says of her: "She is a virgin, and is attended by all who die virgins."[4] Her name means "the giver."

Geirröd

A king who features in the Eddic poem called the *Grimnismal*. *Odin* arrives at Geirröd's court incognito under the name of Grimnir, and Gerröd tries to force him to reveal his identity by tying him between two fires. Geirröd's ten-year-old son *Agnar* comes to Odin's aid and gives him a hornful of wine to drink, whereupon Odin gives the boy a wealth of knowledge about himself, the gods, and the whole Nordic universe. The *Grimnismal* is therefore an important source of information on the Nordic mythology. When Geirröd discovers Odin's true identity, he tries to make amends, but accidentally falls on his sword and dies.

Giants

Giants play an important part in the Nordic world from its very inception, as the first being to appear out of the primal clash of fire and ice is the giant *Ymir*. He is killed by *Odin*, *Vili*, and *Vé*, who create the earth out of his body, the seas from his blood, and the sky from his skull. But while still alive, he produced three offspring: a man and a woman came from under his left hand, and one foot mated with the other to produce a six-headed son. These, according to the *Vafthrudnismal* from the *Poetic Edda*, became the progenitors of the evil Frost Giants. The giants and giantesses appear in other parts of the *Edda*. They are not always evil but often clumsy and doltish. There is, for example, the story, as related in chapter 10, of how the giant Thrym steals *Thor*'s hammer but is tricked into giving it back when Thor, disguised as *Freya*, pretends to be Thrym's bride and the hammer is placed in his lap.

Grendel

The humanoid monster featured in the medieval Anglo-Saxon epic *Beowulf*, who carries out repeated massacres at the court of King Hrothgar of Denmark, until the hero *Beowulf* arrives from Sweden. Beowulf kills Grendel and the monster's mother and restores peace to Hrothgar's court.

Gullinborsti ("golden bristles")

The golden boar that pulls the chariot of the god Frey.

Gullveig

A mysterious female, apparently an evil sorceress, who is three times killed by the gods and three times comes to life again. She is some-how the cause of the war between the *Aesir* and the *Vanir*, as related in the *Völuspá*:

> The war I remember, the first in the world,
> When the gods with spears had smitten Gollveig,
> And in the hall of Hor had burned her,
>
> Three times burned, and three times born,
> Oft and again, yet ever she lives.
> Heith they named her who sought their home,
> The wide-seeing witch, in magic wise;
>
> Minds she bewitched that were moved by her magic,
> To evil women a joy she was.
> On the host his spear did Othin hurl,
> Then in the world did war first come;
> The wall that girdled the gods was broken,
> And the field by the warlike Wanes was trodden.[5]

Hamingja

A tutelary spirit, similar to the *fylgja*.

Heimdall

A key figure in the Nordic pantheon, Heimdall is the watchman god who guards the Rainbow Bridge to Asgard. His hearing is so acute that he can hear wool growing on the backs of sheep. He has a trumpet that he will sound at the approach of the Ragnarök, the end of the world. In the Eddic poem the *Rígsthula,* where he appears under the name *Ríg,* he is harbored three times by an elderly couple. Each time he sleeps with the woman, and as a result she gives birth to three sons who are progenitors of the three castes of early Nordic society: serfs, free farmers, and nobles. Brian Branston, in his book *Gods of the North,* says that Heimdall corresponds to Agni, the fire god described in the ancient Hindu *Rigveda.* Both are white, strong, and possessing golden teeth; both have acute hearing; Heimdall has nine mothers, while Agni is the son of variously two, seven, nine, and ten mothers; and Agni, like Ríg/Heimdall, is the founder of three castes.[6]

Hel

The name for both the underworld where the dead reside and the goddess who presides over it. Snorri describes her in very somber terms, evidently colored by the Christian conception of her dwelling place:

> Hel he threw into Niflheim [one of the names for the underworld] and gave her authority over nine worlds, such that she has to administer board and lodging to those sent to her, and that is those who die of sickness or old age. She has great mansions there and her walls are exceptionally high and the gates great. Her hall is called Eliudnir, her dish Hunger, her knife Famine, the servant Ganglati, serving-

maid Ganglot, her threshold where you enter Stumbling-block, her bed Sick-bed, her curtains Gleaming-bale. She is half black and half flesh-coloured—thus she is easily recognizable—and rather downcast and fierce-looking.[7]

Helgi
The hero of a series of lays in the *Poetic Edda*. Helgi is the son of King Hjörvard and a beautiful woman called Sigrlinn. At first he is tongue-tied and no name takes hold with him, until one day he is sitting on a hill and sees nine *Valkyries* riding past. The most beautiful of them calls him by the name Helgi, which he accepts and begins to speak. The different lays give varying accounts of his life, which is marked by much fighting and slaughter.

Hödr (or Hod)
A blind god, son of *Odin* and twin brother of *Balder*. Through the trickery of *Loki*, he is induced to shoot and kill Balder with an arrow made of mistletoe.

Hoenir
A god of the *Aesir*, Hoenir's main appearance is the *Völuspá* (*Sayings of the Seeress*) where *Odin*, Hoenir, and *Lodur* create the first human beings from an ash and an elm tree.

Hugin and Munin
A pair of ravens who accompany *Odin* and serve as his messengers. *Hugin* means "thought" and *Munin* "memory."

Idun
Goddess of eternal youth, which she bestows through the miraculous apples that she possesses. She is the wife of *Bragi*, god of poetry.

Jörd

Goddess of the earth, daughter of Night and mother of *Thor*.

Kvasir

A figure who features in the story of the creation of the mead of poetry, which came about as a result of the peace made after the war between the *Aesir* and the *Vanir*. To seal the accord, both sides spat into a vessel and from their combined spittle a man called Kvasir was created, who was rich in knowledge and wisdom. Kvasir was slain by two *dwarfs*, Fjalar and Galar, and his blood was made into the mead of poetry. "Kvasir's blood" is often used as a kenning for poetry.

Líf ("life")

A woman who survives Ragnarök along with another person, Leifthrasir. The *Vafthrudnismal* in the *Poetic Edda* says that they will hide in Yggdrasil, subsisting on morning dew, and from them the new race shall arise.

Lodur

Probably another name for *Loki*. Lodur appears in the *Völuspá* (*Sayings of the Seeress*) as one of the trio (*Odin*, *Hoenir*, and Lodur) who animate an ash and an elm tree to create the first human beings.

Loki

The malevolent troublemaker and trickster among the gods, Loki is one of the most ambiguous as well as fascinating figures in the Nordic mythology. He represents a type of destructive, mischief-making god found in many mythologies, such as the Egyptian god Set and the demonic Lempo in Finnish tradition. He is the father of the *Fenris Wolf*, the *Midgard Serpent*, and the goddess *Hel*, ruler of the underworld. He is constantly mocking the gods, cutting them down to size, and finding ways to cause misfortune. It is Loki who persuades the blind god *Hödr* to shoot at *Balder* with an arrow of mistletoe, thus causing Balder's death. On the other hand, Loki sometimes uses his cunning to extricate the gods from difficult situations. For example, when the giant Thrym steals *Thor*'s hammer with the idea of exchanging it for the goddess *Freya*, Loki devises a plan whereby Thor dresses as Freya and pretends to be Thrym's bride. At the wedding feast, following an old custom, the hammer is placed in Thor's lap as a fertility charm, and Thor promptly slays the giant with it. Another instance of Loki coming to the rescue of the gods is the episode of the building of the walls of Asgard. A master mason from among the giants promised to build impregnable walls in return for the sun, the moon, and the hand of Freya, and the gods agreed provided that the mason finished the job in one winter. If he failed, he would forfeit his reward, which is what the gods hoped would happen. The giant set about the job, helped by his stallion Sviðilfari, and it began to look as though the task would be finished on time, so the gods turned to Loki to find a solution. Loki, in the form of a mare, distracted Sviðilfari from the job and coupled with him. Thus the giant was cheated of his wages, and Loki gave birth to a mare with eight legs called *Sleipnir*, which became *Odin*'s horse.

Magni

See *Móði and Magni*.

Mannus

In his *Germania* the first-century Roman historian Tacitus writes of the Germanic people: "In their ancient ballads, their only form of recorded history, they celebrate *Tuisto*, a god sprung from the earth, and they assign to him a son called Mannus, their progenitor through his three sons."[8] The sons in turn became the progenitors of three Germanic tribes: the Ingaevones, Hermiones, and Istaevones.

Midgard Serpent

The horrifying sea monster who will come ashore at Ragnarök and wreak havoc. The serpent is the offspring of *Loki* and the giantess Angrboda. *Thor* is a particular antagonist of the serpent and on one occasion goes out in a boat, hooks the monster with an ox head, and almost succeeds in landing it.

Mímir

A somewhat mysterious figure, embodying wisdom. The well or fountain of Mímir at the base of the World Tree Yggdrasil, is where *Odin* sacrifices an eye in order to gain clairvoyant vision.

Móði and Magni

Two sons of *Thor* by a giantess called Jarnsaxa, Móði and Magni will inherit Thor's hammer Mjöllnir. The names are probably cognates with the English words *might* and *main*, which in turn are related to two Old Norse words *mott* and *megin*. The former implies muscular strength, while the latter describes a fluid vital energy, similar to chi in the Chinese tradition.

Nerthus

A goddess personifying the earth. The first-century Roman historian Tacitus writes of her cult among several of the Germanic tribes as follows:

> In an island of the ocean stands the wood *Castum*: in it is a chariot dedicated to the Goddess covered over with a curtain, and permitted to be touched by none but the Priest. Whenever the Goddess enters this her holy vehicle, he perceives her; and with profound veneration attends the motion of the chariot, which is always drawn by yoked cows. Then it is that days of rejoicing always ensue, and in all places whatsoever which she descends to honour with a

visit and her company, feasts and recreation abound. They go not to war; they touch no arms; fast laid up is every hostile weapon; peace and repose are then only known, then only beloved, till to the temple the same priest reconducts the Goddess when well tired with the conversation of mortal beings. Anon the chariot is washed and purified in a secret lake, as also the curtain; nay, the Deity herself too, if you choose to believe it. In this office it is slaves who minister, and they are forthwith doomed to be swallowed up in the same lake. Hence all men are possessed with mysterious terror; as well as with a holy ignorance what that must be, which none see but such as are immediately to perish.[9]

Njörd

A god of the sea and father of *Frey* and *Freya*. Snorri writes of him as follows: "He lives in heaven in a place called Noatun. He rules over the motion of wind and moderates sea and fire. It is to him that one must pray for voyages and fishing. . . . Njörd is not of the race of the Aesir. He was brought up in the land of the Vanir, but the Vanir gave him as a hostage to the gods. . . . He came to be the pledge of truce between the gods and the Vanir."[10] Snorri goes on to relate that Njörd had a wife called Skadi, but they disagreed about where they should live. Skadi wanted to stay in the mountains where she grew up, but Njörd wanted to be in his home close to the sea. They tried a compromise whereby they spent nine nights alternately in each place, but neither was happy with the arrangement and they went their separate ways.

Norns

The three goddesses of fate, Urd, Verdandi, and Skuld—corresponding to past, present, and future—who sit by the well or fountain of fate by the foot of Yggdrasil, the World Tree. See chapter 5 for further information on the Norns.

Odin

Odin (Old Norse Óðinn, English Woden, German Wotan) is not only the supreme god of the Nordic pantheon but also the most many-faceted and many-named—a chameleon among gods and a master of disguise. He is the frenzied, warlike leader of the wild horde. He is renowned for his great wisdom. He is a psychopomp or guide of souls on their journey to the land of the dead—a function he shares with Mercury, with whom the Romans identified him. He is the god of eloquence (another Mercurial characteristic) and of poetry and song. He is a shaman who sacrificed an eye by throwing it into the well of Mímir in return for clairvoyant vision and who hung for nine days and nights on the World Tree to gain the secret of the runes. He is also not above a certain amount of trickery and deception in order to gain an advantage.

The name *Odin* is thought to be derived from the old German root *wuot* ("fury" or "frenzy"), which is cognates with the modern German word *Wut* ("anger") and probably with the old English *wood*, meaning "furious or wild," as in *woodwose*, the wild man of myth and heraldry. Brian Branston, in *Gods of the North*, points out the similarity between Odin/Woden and the Hindu god Vâta, Lord of the Wind in the *Rigveda*. He concludes that the two names are cognates and both gods are descended from an Indo-European god of the wind.[11] It is tempting to link the name Odin, the one-eyed god, with the identical-sounding Russian word *odin*, meaning "one," but the similarity is probably coincidence. Some of Odin's many other names are listed in the Eddic poem called the *Grimnismal*. They include the following: Grímr (the masked one), Gangleri (wayweary), Sangetall (truthful), Fjölsviðr (wide in wisdom), Síðhöttr (broad hat), Síðskegger (long beard), Alföðr (All-Father), Atríðr (rider), Göndlir (wand-bearer), Hárbar (graybeard), Váfuðr (wanderer).[12]

Snorri Sturluson believed that Odin was a deification of a real historical figure. In his prologue to the *Prose Edda* he writes that Odin came from a Trojan dynasty. Following a prophecy that he would become famous in the northern part of the world, he traveled via Germany and Denmark to Sweden. "There was there a king whose name was Gylfi, and when he learned of the arrival of the men of Asia (who were called Æsir), he went to meet them and offered Odin as much power in his realm as he wished himself." Note Snorri's interesting claim that the words *Asia* and *Aesir* are cognates. Snorri goes on to relate that Odin established a kingdom with the same system of rulership as in Troy with twelve chiefs to administer the laws of the land. He then proceeded farther north and made his son Sæming king of Norway. Another son called Yngvi he made king of Sweden, "and from him are descended the family lines known as the Ynglings."[13]

Odin is one of the most frequently portrayed of the Nordic gods, and there are several stereotypical images of him. One is the gray-bearded wanderer with staff and rustic hat, as in the familiar 1886 portrait by Georg von Rosen (Fig. 22). Another is the throned figure with winged helmet and spear, attended by his two ravens and two wolves. Yet another is the leader of the wild horde on his eight-legged steed, charging across a stormy sky. And of course there is the classic Wagnerian image—again with winged helmet and spear. Odin remains a god of many faces and personae.

22. *Odin, the Wanderer*, as portrayed by the Swedish artist Georg von Rosen in 1886.

Ostara
See *Eostre*.

Ran
Wife of the sea god *Aegir*. Her name appears in a number of kennings such as "Ran's way" for the sea.

Ratatosk
The squirrel that runs up and downs Yggdrasil bearing messages.

Ríg
An alternative name for *Heimdall*. He is progenitor of the three castes in ancient Nordic society—serfs, free farmers, and nobles—as related in the Eddic poem the *Rígsthula*.

Sif
A goddess renowned for her golden hair, which she acquired in the following way. *Loki*, out of mischief, had cut off all of Sif's hair. When her husband *Thor* found out, he threatened to break every bone in Loki's body unless he arranged for the Black Elves to make Sif a head of golden hair. Loki obeyed and the Black Elves duly made the golden hair, which took root as soon as it touched Sif's head. Brian Branston, in *Gods of the North*, argues that the golden hair is a metaphor for ripe corn and Sif is a northern version of the Greek goddess Ceres. In connection with the marriage of Sif and Thor, Branston relates a beautiful folk tradition from the north of England, according to which "the beneficent sheet lightning of summer flashed over the swollen ears of corn in order to ripen them."[14]

Sigmund
Son of King Völsung and an important figure in the *Völsunga Saga*, which describes an incident that is paralleled in the story of King Arthur and Excalibur. King Völsung has a hall built around a great

oak tree, and *Odin*, in disguise, drives a magic sword into the tree and says that the person who can pull out the sword will become invincible. Only Sigmund succeeds in pulling the sword out of the tree.

Sigrdrífa

See *Brynhild*.

Sigurd

A classic Nordic hero, son of *Sigmund* and his wife Hjördís. Sigurd features prominently in the *Völsunga Saga* and also in the Eddic poem the *Sigrdrífumál* as the rescuer of *Sigdrífa/Brynhild*.

Skadi

A winter goddess, married to *Njörd* until they disagreed about where they should live, Njörd preferring the seaside and Skadi preferring her home in the mountains. Skadi travels on skis and has a hare as her animal. There is a Norwegian Stone Age rock carving believed to depict her, showing her as a hare on skis. See also *Njörd* and chapter 5 for further information.

Skuld

See *Norns*.

Sleipnir

Odin's eight-legged horse, sired by the stallion Sviðilfari out of *Loki* in the form of a mare. See also *Loki*.

Surt

A mighty fire demon. One of the destructive beings who will attack the gods at the Ragnarök.

Thiazi

A giant, father of *Skadi*. Thiazi is killed by the gods after the episode of his abduction of the goddess Idun. See also *Loki*.

Thor (German Donar)

Son of *Odin* and *Jörd*, Thor is the epitome of physical strength and bravery. Next to Odin he is the most prominent of the Nordic pantheon and has at times been seen as the supreme northern deity. Thor has many different facets. He is the god of thunder and hence was identified by the Romans with Jupiter. His day of the week is Thursday (German Donnerstag). He is also a god of war and renowned for his prowess in slaying giants. He figures frequently in lore, legend, and literature because of his courage and larger-than-life character, and in today's media he is probably the most portrayed of the Nordic gods (see chapter 13). He lives in a great mansion called Bilskirnir with 540 halls and a roof of silver. He drives a chariot drawn by two goats, who are slaughtered and eaten each day but regenerate themselves overnight. His main hallmark is a great hammer called Mjöllnir, which never misses its mark when thrown and always returns to its owner. In the northern tradition the hammer is not only a weapon but a ceremonial object used to perform rituals, solemnize agreements, and consecrate marriages. Thor has often been considered the patron of married couples.

Tuisto

According to the Roman historian Tacitus, Tuisto is the father of *Mannus*, progenitor of the three main Germanic tribes. Tuisto is therefore the grandfather of the Germans. The German version of the name is Teut, from which are derived the words *deutsch* and *Teutonic*.

Tyr (alternatively Tiwaz, Tiw)

A warrior god, renowned for his bravery and capacity for self-sacrifice, demonstrated in the story of the binding of the *Fenris Wolf*. When the fetter had been made, the gods challenged the wolf to test its strength, and he agreed to accept the challenge on the condition that one of the gods placed a hand in his jaws. Tyr did so, the fetter held, and the enraged wolf bit off Tyr's hand. The name Tyr is thought to be cognate with an Indo-European generic word for god, as in the Sanskrit *dyaus* and the Latin *deus*. Possibly the names Tyr and Tuisto are cognates and the two gods are variations of the same one.

Ull

Son of the goddess *Sif* and stepson of *Thor*, Ull is renowned as an archer, hunter, and unrivalled skier. Snorri adds that he is fair of face and a great warrior and one should ask for his help in single combat.

Urd

See *Norns*.

Vafthrúdnir

A wise giant who engages in a question-and-answer contest with *Odin*, who is in disguise, as related in the Eddic poem, *Vafþrúðnismál*. It is agreed that the loser will forfeit his life. The questions and answers go back and forth, revealing a wealth of information about the Nordic cosmogony and mythology, including the events of the end of the world when the *Fenris Wolf* will devour Odin. Finally Odin asks what message he whispered into the ear of his son *Balder* before the latter was burned on the funeral pyre. Vafthrúdnir is unable to answer and has to admit defeat and presumably surrender his life.

Valkyries

Wagner has immortalized these female warriors (the name means "choosers of the slain") in the prelude to the third act of his opera

The Valkyrie with its famous theme, the "Ride of the Valkyries." *Odin* sends the Valkyries out on to battlefields to decide which of the fighters shall die and whether they will be sent to Valhalla. In Valhalla there are other Valkyries whose task is to serve drink to the valiant heroes.

Vanadis
One of the alternative names of *Freya*.

Vanir
One of the two groups of Nordic deities. See *Aesir*.

Vár
Goddess of oaths and contracts.

Vé
Brother of *Odin* and *Vili*. The *Prose Edda* relates how the three turned an ash and an elm tree into the first human beings. In the *Poetic Edda* it is Odin, *Hoenir*, and *Lodur* who animate the trees.

Verdandi
See *Norns*.

Vidar
Son of *Odin*, Vidar is renowned for being extremely taciturn. His curious hallmark is an enormous shoe, cobbled together from bits and pieces of many different things. His main feat comes at Ragnarök when he kills the *Fenris Wolf* by thrusting his great shoe into its jaws.

Vili
Brother of *Odin* and *Vé*. See *Vé*.

Völund (English Wayland, German Wieland)

A great smith and metalworker but not one to get on the wrong side of, as the wicked King Nídud learned to his cost, as related in the Eddic text, the *Völundarkvida* (*Lay of Völund*). Nídud robs Völund and holds him captive, but Völund succeeds in murdering Nídud's sons and raping his daughter before escaping. Under the name Wayland he is deeply embedded in English folk tradition. Named after him is Wayland's Smithy, a Neolithic long barrow situated on the Ridgeway, Berkshire.

Völva (plural Völvur)

A type of female shaman, soothsayer, and magician, practicing a form of magic called *seiðr*, largely reserved for women. It is a *völva* who is the narrator in the Eddic poem the *Völuspá* (*Sayings of the Seeress*).

Ymir

The primordial giant who emerged at the beginning of the world out of the interaction of fire and ice. From his sweat came the progenitors of the giants. Ymir was fed by a cow called *Audhumla*, who then, by licking rime-covered rocks, brought forth a man called *Buri*. He in turn had a son called *Bor*, who, together with the giantess *Bestla*, had three sons who were the gods *Odin*, *Vili*, and *Vé*. These three killed Ymir and recycled his body to make the earth, his blood to make the lakes and seas, and his skull to make the heavens. From the maggots feasting on Ymir's flesh came the *dwarfs*.

NOTES

1. Snorri, 19–20.
2. Snorri, 28.
3. Snorri, 26.
4. Snorri, 29.
5. *Völuspá*, stanzas 21–23, from *The Poetic Edda*, tr. Henry Adams Bellows. Posted on http://www.sacred-texts.com/neu/poe/poe03.htm.
6. Branston, 137–41.
7. Snorri, 27.
8. Quoted by Branston, 10.
9. *Tacitus on Germany*, tr. Thomas Gordon (New York: P. F. Collier & Son, 1910). Posted on http://www.gutenberg.org/files/2995/2995-h/2995-h.htm.
1o. Snorri, 23.
11. Branston, 109.
12. Branston, 107.
13. Snorri, 3–5.
14. Branston, 122.

BIBLIOGRAPHY

Andreyev, Alexander Ivanovich. Время Шамбалы (*Vremya Shambali*), 2nd ed. Saint Petersburg: Nyeva Publishing House, 2004.

——. Оккультист Страны Советов (*Okkultist Strany Sovietov*). Moscow: Yazua, EKSMO, 2004.

Ashe, Geoffrey. *The Ancient Wisdom*. London: Macmillan, 1977.

Aswynn, Freya. *Leaves of Yggdrasil*. First edition, London: limited edition by the author, 1988.

Bellows, Henry Adams, trans. *The Poetic Edda*. Princeton, NJ: Princeton University Press, 1936.

Bennett, John G. "The Hyperborean Origin of the Indo-European Culture." *Systematics*, Vol. 1, No. 3, December 1963.

Blavatsky, Helena Petrovna. *The Secret Doctrine*. London: Theosophical Publishing Company, 1888.

Boele, Otto. *The North in Russian Romantic Literature*. Amsterdam & Atlanta, GA: Rodopi, 1996.

Branston, Brian. *Gods of the North*. London: Thames and Hudson, 1955.

Burton, Richard Francis. *Ultima Thule or a Summer in Iceland*. London: William Nimmo, 1875.

Byatt, A. S. *Ragnarok: End of the Gods*. Edinburgh: Canongate Books, 2011.

Clover, Charles. *Black Wind, White Snow: The Rise of Russia's New Nationalism*. New Haven and London: Yale University Press, 2016.

Cope, Nicholas, and Keith Critchlow. *The Knap of Howar and the Origins of Geometry*. Vienna: Kairos Publications, 2016.

Critchlow, Keith. *Time Stands Still*. Edinburgh: Floris Books, 2007.

Dasent, George Webbe, trans. *The Story of Burnt Njal*. New York: E. P. Dutton, 1900.

Dyomin, Valeriy. Тайны русского народа (*Taini Russkovo Naroda*). Moscow: Veche, 1997.

———. Гиперборея - праматерь мировой культуры (*Hypberborea—Pramater Mirovoi Kultury*). Moscow: Veche, 2003.

———. Гиперборейские тайны Руси (*Hyperborean Secrets of the Rus*). Moscow: Veche, 2011.

Eliade, Mircea. *Shamanism: Archaic Techniques of Ecstasy*. London: Arkana, 1989.

Ewing, Maurice, and William Donn. "A New Theory of Ice Ages." *Science*, June 1956 and May 1958. (A summary by Betty Friedan appeared in *Harpers Magazine* for September 1958 and in the *American Review* Vol. I, No. 4, 1961.)

Feindt, Gregor, et al., eds. *Europäische Erinnerung als verflochtene Erinnerung*. Göttingen: V & R University Press, 2014.

Goodrick-Clarke, Nicholas. *The Occult Roots of Nazism*. Wellingborough, UK: Aquarian Press, 1985.

Gould, Charles. *Mythical Monsters*. London: W. H. Allen, 1886.

Grönbech, Wilhelm. *Kultur und Religion der Germanen*. Translated from the Danish, 2 vols. Stuttgart: W. Kohlhammer, 1954.

Guénon, René. *The Lord of the World*. Translated by Carolyn Schaffer et al. Moorcote, UK: Coombe Springs Press, 1983.

Guthrie, W. K. C. *Orpheus and Greek Religion*. London: Methuen, 1935.

———. *The Greeks and Their Gods*. London: Methuen, 1950.

Helgason, Jón Karl. *Echoes of Valhalla: The Afterlife of the Eddas and the Sagas*. London: Reaktion Books, 2017.

Herman, Arthur. *The Scottish Enlightenment*. London: Fourth Estate, 2001.

Junker, Daniel. *Gott in uns! Die Germanische Glaubensgemeinschaft. Ein Beitrag zur Geschichte völkischer Religiosität in der Weimarer Republik*. Hamburg: Verlag Daniel Junker, 2002.

Karlsson, Thomas. *Götisk kabbala och runisk alkemi: Johannes Bureus och den götiska Esoterismen* (*Gothic Kabbalah and Runic Alchemy: Johannes Bureus and Gothic Esotericism*). Stockholm: Stockholms Universitet, 2009.

Kern, Hermann. *Labyrinthe*. Munich: Prestel-Verlag, 1982.

Krause, Ernst. *Tuisko-Land, der arischen Stämme und Götter Urheimat*. Glogau: Carl Flemming, 1891.

———. *Die Trojaburgen Nordeuropas*. Glogau: Carl Flemming, 1893a.

——. *Die nordische Herkunft der Trojasage*. Glogau: Carl Flemming, 1893b.

Laruelle, Marlene, ed. *Eurasianism and the European Far Right*. Lanham, MD: Lexington Books, 2015.

Marby, Friedrich Bernhard. *Runenschrift, Runenwort, Runengymnastik*. Stuttgart: Marby-Verlag, 1931.

Matthews, W. H. *Mazes and Labyrinths*. London: Longmans Green, 1922; republication, New York: Dover, 1970.

Morrow, John, ed. *The Jack Kirby Collector*, magazine series. Raleigh, NC: TwoMorrows Publishing, from 1994.

Nuttall, Mark. *Encyclopedia of the Arctic*. New York and London: Routledge, 2005.

Olsen, Scott, et al. *Mysteries of the Amazon*. Ocala, FL: published by the author, 2017.

Page, R. I. *Chronicles of the Vikings*. London: British Museum Press, 1995, paperback edition 2000.

Pálsson, Hermann, and Paul Edwards, trans. and eds. *The Orkneyinga Saga: The History of the Earls of Orkney*. London: Hogarth Press, 1978.

Pennick, Nigel. "Weaving the Web of Wyrd." *Tyr*, Vol. 3, 2007, 111–25.

Rudgley, Richard. *Pagan Resurrection*. London: Century, 2006.

——. *Barbarians*. Budapest: Arktos Media, 2014.

Sagas of the Icelanders. With preface by Jane Smiley. London: Penguin Books, 2001.

Sandbach, William R. *The Oera Linda Book*. London: Trübner & Co., 1876.

Shcherbatov, Vladimir I. Асгард город богов (*Asgard – gorod bogov*). Moscow: Molodoya Gvardia, 1991.

Snook, Jennifer. *American Heathens*. Philadelphia: Temple University Press, 2015.

Spanuth, Jürgen. *Das enträtselte Atlantis*. Stuttgart: Union deutsche Verlagsgesellschaft, 1953.

Spengler, Oswald. *Der Untergang des Abendlandes*, 2 vols. Munich: C. H. Beck, 1917, 1922.

Spiesberger, Karl. *Runenmagie*. Berlin: Schikowski, 1955.

——. *Runenexerzitien für Jedermann*. Freiburg: Bauer, 1976.

Strmiska, Michael F., and Baldur A. Sigurvinsson. "Asatru: Nordic Paganism in Iceland and America." In *Modern Paganism in World Cultures* edited by Michael F. Strmiska. Santa Barbara: ABC-CLIO, 2005, 128.

Sturluson, Snorri. *Edda*. Translated and edited by Anthony Faulkes. London: Everyman, 1997.

Tacitus. *Complete Works*. Translated by Alfred John Church, William Jackson Brodribb. New York: Random House, reprinted 1942; edited by Lisa Cerrato for Perseus online version: http://www.perseus.tufts.edu.

Thom, Alexander. *Megalithic Sites in Britain*. Oxford: Clarendon Press, 1967.

———. *Megalithic Lunar Observatories*. Oxford: Clarendon Press, 1970.

Thorsson, Edred. *The Nine Doors of Midgard*. South Burlington, VT: The Rune Gild, 2016.

Tilak, Bâl Gangâdhar. *The Arctic Home in the Vedas*. Poona: Kesari, 1903.

Turner, Frederick. *Epic: Form, Content and History*. New Brunswick, NJ: Transaction Publishers, 2012.

Vinci, Felice. *The Baltic Origins of Homer's Epic Tales: The Iliad, the Odyssey, and the Migration of Myth*. Rochester, VT: Inner Traditions/Bear & Company, 2005.

Warren, William F. *Paradise Found: The Cradle of the Human Race at the North Pole*. Boston: Houghton, Mifflin & Co., 1885.

Wawn, Andrew. *The Vikings and the Victorians*. Cambridge, UK: D. S. Brewer, 2000.

Wilkens, Iman Jacob. *Where Troy Once Stood*. Amsterdam: Gopher Publishers, revised edition, 2009.

Wirth, Herman. *Der Aufgang der Menschheit*. Jena: Eugen Diederichs, 1928.

———. *Die Ura Linda Chronik*. Leipzig: Koehler und Amelang, 1933.

Wong, Eva. *Taoism: An Essential Guide*. Boston: Shambhala Publications, 1997.

Zarifullin, Pavel. Новые скифы (*The New Scythians*). Saint Petersburg: Limbus Press, c. 2013.

ILLUSTRATION CREDITS

Figures 5–8, 12, 17, 19, provided by the author.

Figures 2 and 3, from W. H. Matthews, Mazes and Labyrinths (London: Longmans Green, 1922; republication, New York: Dover, 1970).

Figure 4, donated to the Wikimedia Foundation from the archives of Pearson Scott Foresman.

Figure 9, courtesy of artist Pierô Lalune.

Figures 13 and 14, from Halvard Hårklau.

Figures 15 and 22, courtesy of Wikimedia Commons.

Figure 16, courtesy of Axel Seiler.

Figure 18, courtesy of Landesamt für Denkmalpflege, Bremen.

Figure 20, courtesy of Alexander Uglanov.

Figure 21, courtesy of Baldrs Draumar and artist Geffrey van der Bos.

INDEX

ABOUT THE AUTHOR

Christopher McIntosh was born in England in 1943 and grew up in Edinburgh, Scotland. He studied philosophy, politics, and economics at Oxford and German at London University, later returning to Oxford to take a doctorate in history with a dissertation on the 18th-century Rosicrucian revival. After working in London in journalism and publishing, he spent four years in New York as an information officer with the United Nations Development Programme, then moved to Germany to work for UNESCO. In parallel he has pursued a career as a writer and researcher specializing in the esoteric traditions as well as nature-oriented belief systems. His books include *The Astrologers and their Creed* (1969); *Eliphas Lévi and the French Occult Revival* (latest edition 2011); *The Rosicrucians* (latest edition, Weiser, 1997); *The Rose Cross and the Age of Reason* (latest edition 2011), based on his D.Phil. dissertation; *The Swan King: Ludwig II of Bavaria* (latest edition 2012); and *Gardens of the Gods* (2005). His fictional work includes the occult novel *Return of the Tetrad* (2013), the spy thriller *The Lebensborn Spy* (2017) and the short story collections *Master of the Starlit Grove* (2014), *The Wyrde Garden* (2015) and *The Sorceress of Agartha* (2017). With his wife, scholar of religion Dr. Donate McIntosh, he produced a new translation of the Rosicrucian *Fama Fraternitatis* (2014). He has lectured widely and was on the faculty of the distance MA program in Western Esotericism at the University of Exeter, England, now discontinued. His home is in North Germany.

TO OUR READERS